T-34 IN ACTION

The Stackpole Military History Series

THE AMERICAN CIVIL WAR

Cavalry Raids of the Civil War
Ghost, Thunderbolt, and Wizard
Pickett's Charge
Witness to Gettysburg

WORLD WAR II

Armor Battles of the Waffen-SS, 1943–45
Army of the West
Australian Commandos
The B-24 in China
Backwater War
The Battle of Sicily
Beyond the Beachhead
The Brandenburger Commandos
The Brigade
Bringing the Thunder
Coast Watching in World War II
Colossal Cracks
D-Day to Berlin
Dive Bomber!
Eagles of the Third Reich
Exit Rommel
Fist from the Sky
Flying American Combat Aircraft of
*   World War II*
Forging the Thunderbolt
Fortress France
The German Defeat in the East, 1944–45
German Order of Battle, Vol. 1
German Order of Battle, Vol. 2
German Order of Battle, Vol. 3
Germany's Panzer Arm in World War II
GI Ingenuity
Grenadiers
Infantry Aces
Iron Arm
Iron Knights
Kampfgruppe Peiper at the
*   Battle of the Bulge*
Luftwaffe Aces
Massacre at Tobruk
Messerschmitts over Sicily

Michael Wittmann, Vol. 1
Michael Wittmann, Vol. 2
Mountain Warriors
The Nazi Rocketeers
On the Canal
Operation Mercury
Packs On!
Panzer Aces
Panzer Aces II
The Panzer Legions
Panzers in Winter
The Path to Blitzkrieg
Retreat to the Reich
Rommel's Desert War
The Savage Sky
A Soldier in the Cockpit
Soviet Blitzkrieg
Stalin's Keys to Victory
Surviving Bataan and Beyond
T-34 in Action
Tigers in the Mud
The 12th SS, Vol. 1
The 12th SS, Vol. 2
The War against Rommel's Supply Lines

THE COLD WAR / VIETNAM

Flying American Combat Aircraft:
*   The Cold War*
Here There Are Tigers
Land with No Sun
Street without Joy

WARS OF THE MIDDLE EAST

Never-Ending Conflict

GENERAL MILITARY HISTORY

Carriers in Combat
Desert Battles

T-34 IN ACTION

Soviet Tank Troops in World War II

Artem Drabkin and Oleg Sheremet

Translators
Dmitri Kovalevich, Vladimir Karin, Bair Irincheev,
Vladimir Krupnik, Elena Markus

English Text
Ian Heath

STACKPOLE
BOOKS

Published in paperback in 2008 by

STACKPOLE BOOKS
5067 Ritter Road
Mechanicsburg, PA 17055
www.stackpolcbooks.com

Cover design by Tracy Patterson

Printed in the United States of America

10 9 8 7 6 5 4 3 2 1

•

Cataloging-in-Publication Data is on file with the Library of Congress and the British Library.

ISBN–10: 0-8117-3483-8
ISBN–13: 978-0-8117-3483-7

Contents

	Preface	vii
Chapter 1	'Guys, let's become tankmen!' Artem Drabkin and Grigory Pernavsky	1
Chapter 2	'Against the T-34 the German tanks were crap.' Alexay Isaev	22
Chapter 3	'They couldn't penetrate my front armour.' Aleksandr Vasilievich Bodnar	45
Chapter 4	'I see that you're a real tankman.' Semen Lvovich Aria	57
Chapter 5	'My tank became just another victim.' Yuri Maksovich Polyanovski	65
Chapter 6	'The fires made it bright as day.' Aleksandr Mikhailovich Fadin	75
Chapter 7	'A shell hit the turret, and the tank filled with smoke.' Petr Ilyich Kirichenko	110
Chapter 8	'Our tanks were the best.' Aleksandr Sergeevich Burtsev	118
Chapter 9	'Only the luckier, smarter, sharper crews made it out alive.' Vasili Pavolovich Bryukhov	127
Chapter 10	'If you don't go, you'll be executed.' Arkadi Vasilievich Maryevski	149
Chapter 11	'If your unit still existed, you had to be with it!' Nikolai Yakovlevich Zheleznov	154
Chapter 12	'Once you stop, your time is up!' Georgi Nikolaevich Krivov	170
	Glossary	182
	Index	183

Preface

I started to interview Russian veterans of the Second World War in 2000. By that time almost sixty years had passed since the beginning of Operation 'Barbarossa', the German invasion of the Soviet Union. Some people said: 'It's too late. These eighty-year-old veterans won't remember anything.' Believe me, this didn't turn out to be the case at all. The horrors of the war left such deep scars in their souls that some former soldiers refused to meet me, because they couldn't bear to relive the wartime events that were etched forever in their memories. During a series of interviews, Nikolai Zheleznov, whose memories form one of the chapters of this book, requested me to stop asking him questions, because he felt so unwell after our last meeting. Naturally I obeyed. But I was nevertheless able to record many interviews with men who had fought in the celebrated T-34 tank, and a selection of these are presented here. I've tried, wherever possible, to preserve each veteran's manner of speech, and hope that the flavour of this has survived the translation process.

I should emphasise that as a source of information, an interview has a number of drawbacks, which the reader should keep in mind as he reads this book. Firstly, he should not expect the description of events to be entirely accurate. After all, it's been nearly sixty years since they took place. Sometimes several memories have merged into one, while others have simply vanished. Secondly, he should take into consideration that each narrator had his own personal view of the events he is describing. Yet the reader should not be discouraged by the contradictions between stories told by different people, and the mosaic structure that they assume. I think that the sincerity and honesty of the interviewees' accounts are more important for our understanding of these people, who lived through the hell of the war, than the number of tanks or the exact date of an operation.

An attempt to summarise the personal experiences of the many tankmen interviewed, and to distinguish features common to the war generation from those reflecting individual perceptions, is presented in the two opening chapters. Far as these are from painting a complete picture, they nevertheless represent the general attitude of the tankmen to their equipment, the relationships within a crew, and the experience of life at the front.

Artem Drabkin
September 2005

CHAPTER 1

'Guys, let's become tankmen!'

Artem Drabkin and Grigory Pernavsky

Before, I thought that 'Lieutenant'
Sounds like 'Let's party hard!'
With knowledge of topography,
He's walking on a gravel road.
A war isn't fireworks at all,
Just heavy daily labour ...

Mikhail Kulchitski

Military personnel were extremely popular in the USSR in the 1930s. There were several reasons for this. First of all, the Red Army, its men and its commanders symbolised the might of the relatively young Soviet state, a state that in just a few short years had managed to transform itself from a poor agrarian country devastated by war into an industrial giant that could seemingly defend itself. Secondly, military personnel were among the richest in the USSR. For example, an instructor in an air force academy received the extremely high salary of about 700 roubles (a loaf of white bread cost 1.7 roubles; a kilogram of top quality beef cost 12 roubles), as well as other privileges (uniforms, free catering in canteens, free public transport tickets, a room in a dorm or a subsidy to rent an apartment). Elsewhere in the country rationing persisted (it was only abolished towards the end of the decade) and it was hard to buy decent clothes. In wintertime people wore retailored clothes produced from old pre-Revolution garments, while in summertime people would stroll

1

around in old Red Army uniforms or simple canvas trousers and canvas shoes. Conditions were harsh in the cities – up to fifty families lived in a single former apartment of the pre-Revolution upper class, while the state built very little new accommodation.

Besides this, service in the army gave young peasants a chance to improve their education and learn a profession. As tank commander Lieutenant Aleksandr Sergeevich Burtsev recalled: 'Each one of us was dreaming of service in the army. I remember that men came back completely different after three years of service. They would leave as simple village boys and come back as educated, cultured, learned men in perfect uniforms and tall boots, physically strong. After service in the army a person understood equipment, and could lead people in work. When a "serving man" (that's what they were called) came back from the army, a whole village would gather to welcome him. A family would be proud that he had been in the army and of what he had become.'

Propaganda regarding the invincibility of the Red Army worked very well against this background. People sincerely believed that the Red Army would defeat its foes with 'little bloodshed, on the enemy's own soil'. The coming war – a war of machines – also created new propaganda images. If in the 1920s every schoolboy imagined himself a cavalryman with a sword in a dashing cavalry charge, in the 1930s this romantic image was completely replaced by fighter pilots in high-speed monoplanes and tankmen in impressive battle vehicles. To pilot a fighter or fire a tank's main gun was the dream of thousands of Soviet teenage boys. 'Guys, let's become tankmen! It's so prestigious!' recalled platoon leader Lieutenant Nikolai Yakovlevich Zheleznov. 'You ride, and the whole country lies before you! You're on an iron horse!'

Even the uniforms of the air force and armoured corps were different from those of other branches of service. Pilots wore blue, while tankmen wore steel grey, and men in such uniforms didn't go unnoticed even strolling down a village street. They also differed in the abundance of decorations they boasted – extremely scarce in those days – as tankmen and pilots often took part in armed conflicts in which the USSR openly or secretly participated.

Pilots and tankmen were also glorified in movies, such as *Hot Days*, *If Tomorrow Brings War*, *Fighter Pilots*, *Squadron Number Five* and others, in which romantic images of Soviet tankmen and pilots were created by superstars such as Nikolai Kryuchkov and

Nikolai Simonov. However, the war that broke out on 22 June 1941 was completely different to that which had been portrayed in the movies.

In the first months of the war the Red Army suffered heavy defeats, and tankmen were among those who felt the first blows of the Nazi war machine. Training company cadet Mikhail Fedorovich Savkin recalled his first battle, fought in a T-34 at Radzechow on 23 June 1941: 'Our tanks attacked the German artillery. The Germans opened up with heavy guns and semi-automatic flaks and mortars. Several tanks were knocked out. Rounds of all calibres smashed against the armour of our tank like hammers, but I couldn't see any guns through my observation slit. Finally I saw a muzzle flash next to a shot-down Po-2 plane, and spotted the gun concealed under a camouflage net. I fired a fragmentation round at it. The distance to the gun was very small and a fountain of mud shot into the sky where it had been.'

The Red Army high command tried to organise counter strikes with its mechanised corps and tank divisions, but these enjoyed very little tactical success. T-26 tank commander Sergeant-Major Semen Vasilievich Matveev recalled: 'They started forming mechanised corps before the war, following the pattern of German Panzer Corps. But I don't think we had a single mechanised corps that had all its equipment and personnel. My corps was less than half its regulation strength. We only had bits and pieces. My tank battalion was in fact less than a company. We didn't have any trucks or tractors at all. An army is a huge organism, and the Germans had theirs up and running (and running well, I'd say), but ours had only just started to be built up. So we shouldn't be ashamed that they were stronger than us then. They were much stronger. That's why they often defeated us in the first year of the war.'

Having lost almost all its tanks in the western military districts and most of its professional tank crews, the Red Army fell back into the heartland of Russia. Lack of tanks and the lightning speed of the German breakthroughs forced the Red Army to deploy many of its surviving tank crews as infantry. However, the confusion and chaos of the first months of retreat didn't last long. As early as late July 1941 orders came to send crews that had lost their tanks to the rear, and in August and September battle-tried personnel from mechanised corps were sent to newly formed tank brigades. The tank brigade of M. E. Katukov was formed from tank crews of the 15th Tank

Division, 16th Mechanised Corps, that had escaped encirclement at Uman; tankmen of the 32nd Tank Division, that had fought at Lvov in June 1941, paraded in Red Square on 7 November. On 9 October Stalin ordered the appointment of officers as medium and heavy tank commanders. According to this order, the post of medium tank commander was to be held by lieutenants and junior lieutenants. Platoons of medium tanks were to be led by senior lieutenants, while companies were to be commanded by captains. In order to improve the performance of tanks' crews, from 18 November 1941 they were supposed to be made up entirely of officers and NCOs. Two months later another order issued by the People's Commissar of Defence forbade the disbandment of battle-tried units that had lost their tanks in combat. Such units were ordered to be sent to the rear with all their personnel in order to be re-equipped.

If a tank unit had to be disbanded, its senior officers were sent to the Personnel office of the Red Army's motorised and armoured units for reallocation, while the crews were sent to reserve tank regiments. However, in many cases tankmen served in other units and other roles. In late December 1942 Stalin put an end to this, and ordered that all tankmen serving in other capacities were to be placed at the disposal of the Main Auto and Armour Directorate. Hospitalised tankmen were also to be sent exclusively to tank units when they became fit enough to return to duty. Stalin's order culminated in a phrase that could not be misinterpreted: 'From now on I categorically forbid anyone to employ tank crews of all above mentioned categories in other branches of service.'

By now the Red Army was slowly recovering after two lost summer campaigns. Although there was still a shortage of tanks, and the tank manufacturing plants evacuated from Kharkov and Leningrad were only just recommencing production beyond the Urals, the army was already training new crews to replace those which had fallen in action.

At the outbreak of the war the Main Auto and Armour Directorate had thirty-nine academies – thirty armour, one technical armour, one technical automobile, three auto and motorcycle, two tractor, and two motor-sled. Some were evacuated at the approach of the enemy and stopped training for a time, graduating their existing cadets as junior lieutenants. However, they soon reopened in new locations and immediately started training new personnel for tank units. Numerous reserve training regiments and training battalions were established for tank crews, while tank factories established training companies. Nevertheless, during summer 1942 the lack of tank crews became readily apparent – very few professional tankmen survived by this time, while young crews without battle experience were often killed in their first action. In October Stalin ordered privates and NCOs with battle experience, a good record, and a secondary school education to seventh grade standard, to be sent for training as tank crews: 5,000 men fitting this profile were to be provided monthly. Another 8,000 men were to have attended three or more classes of elementary school, and were to be aged under thirty-five. At least 40 per cent were to be junior sergeants and sergeants. Thereafter such orders were issued annually for the rest of the war. As Aleksandr Sergeevich Burtsev recalled: 'Some guys would come to the academy from the front, study for six months, and then go back to the front, while we were still studying. However, if a man was at the front and had battle experience, it was easier for him to complete the course – even more so when they normally sent a driver or a loader or a gun-layer. We, by contrast, were straight from school. We knew nothing.'

The tank academies were created from existing automobile and auto and motorcycle academies. The reformation of these academies played an important role in the careers of tank commanders Junior Lieutenant Yuri Maksovich Polyanovski and Aleksandr Mikhailovich Fadin: 'They read us an order of the Commander-in-Chief about the reformation of our academy into the 2nd Gorki Tank Academy ... We younger cadets shouted "Hurrah!" The older ones, who'd fought at Khalhin-Gol, in the Winter War, and liberated Western Ukraine and Belorussia, said to us: "Why are you so happy? You'll burn alive in these tin cans."'

Cadets had to learn through their own experience that service in armoured units was hard and bloody work, absolutely contrary to the rosy ideas they might have had as teenagers. The ones still alive today were mostly born in 1921–24, and trained as tankmen under the shadow of war. They ended up in tank units in many different ways. 'Why did I become a tankman? I saw myself as a warrior of the future,' recalled tank commander Lieutenant Aleksandr Vasilievich Bodnar. 'Besides that, my uncle was an officer, and in 1939 he said to me: "Sasha, you are graduating from secondary school. I would recommend you to go to a military academy. War is inevitable, so it is better to be an officer in a war – you would be able to do more, because you will know more."' Some men had set out wanting to enter other branches of service, but ended up in tank units. For example, A. S. Burtsev was sent to an air force academy, but enrolment into the academy was over so the excess recruits were sent to the 1st Saratov Armour Academy. Battalion commander Captain Vasili Pavolovich Bryukhov remembered loving military science. 'I wanted to enter a naval academy after school – it was my dream. They had such a fancy uniform!' Some future tankmen, like Semen Lvovich Aria, were already in training in other military academies, before war disrupted their plans: 'I was in Novosibirsk college of transport military engineers. After receiving a wound and shell-shock during an air raid on our train, I was sent to a battalion that was training tank drivers.' Most recruits had to enter the branch of service they were sent to.

The pre-war training programme was quite different from that utilised in wartime. A professional tank officer's course before the war was two years. He would study every type of tank used by the Red Army. He was taught to drive a tank and fire its weapons, and was taught armour tactics. In fact, a professional tank officer before the war could perform the tasks of any crew member and could even carry out the maintenance of his vehicle. According to professional tankman A. V. Bodnar, 'we had practical classes and studied the hardware in great detail. The M-17 engine is very complicated, but we knew it to the last bolt. We would also assemble and disassemble the main gun and machine-gun.'

Tankmen who arrived as replacements during the war didn't have much time for training. Units demanded replacements all the time, and the training programme was consequently minimal: 'When I graduated from the academy I'd fired three rounds from the main gun and one ammo drum from the MG,' recalled tank battalion commander Vasili Pavlovich Bryukhov. 'We had some driving classes, basic things – how to start the tank and drive it straight.' Graduates of the 1st Saratov Armour Academy A. S. Burtsev and N. Y. Zheleznov considered that their training level was higher than that – the cadets there first studied on British Matilda tanks and Canadian-built Valentines before moving on to T-34s. Tank commanders Lieutenant Nikolai Yevdokimovich Glukhov, Junior Lieutenant Arsenti Konstantinovich Rodkin, and A. V. Bodnar, who all studied at Ulianovsk Armour Academy, remembered that cadets there studied modern equipment from the outset, and training was of high quality: 'Everything we studied was useful in battle. Our knowledge of the armament and the engine were both very good.'

Living conditions within the academies also varied. According to Order of the People's Commissariat of Defence of the USSR No. 312 of 22 September 1941, all army and air force academy cadets were supposed to receive rations described as '9th catering norm', which was close to the front-line catering norm in terms of calories. However, if Lieutenant Georgi Nikolaevich Krivov, who studied at the 1st Kharkov Armour Academy (evacuated to Cherchik), considered that 'we had good catering – porridge, meat, and butter served with breakfast', V. P. Bryukhov – who studied at the same time in evacuated Stalingrad Armour Academy – recalled the catering as so bad that 'the prisoners in jails got better food'. Clearly not all academies were able to adhere to the standards set by the above-mentioned order.

Training at the academies ended with examinations. Before 1943 those who passed the exams with 'good' or 'excellent' grades were commissioned as lieutenants, and those who passed with 'satisfactory' grades were commissioned as junior lieutenants. But after the summer of 1943 all graduates were commissioned as junior lieutenants. The examination commission also carried out additional tests to select graduates for appointment as platoon leaders or line tank commanders.

Newly graduated commanders went to the tank factories, where the other members of their crews, trained by the factory's tank training battalion, awaited them. The training of these crewmen was at least three months for drivers, and up to one month for radio operators and loaders. Driver Sergeant S. L. Aria recalled: 'They taught us driving, communication with the commander, and set-up and maintenance of an engine. They made us drive across obstacles, and taught us to change a track link. [Repairing a track was an extremely hard task.] During two or three months of training we also participated in the assembly of tanks on the main conveyer of the factory.' Petr Ilyich Kirichenko, who ended up in a battalion that was training radio operators, remembered that 'after the aeroplane radio sets and aeroplane MGs that I'd studied in air force academy, learning about tank radio sets and the DT machine-gun was peanuts'. Indeed, after just one month of training he left for the front with his crew as senior sergeant. It should be mentioned that the participation of tank crews in the assembly of tanks was very common. Almost all the veterans interviewed remember assisting in this way during their stay at the factories. This is explained in part by the shortage of workers at the factories, but it was also a way for young soldiers to get a free lunch card entitling them to eat in the factory canteen.

If green lieutenants had to make do with the crews that they were given, more senior commanders with battle experience tried to pick experienced tankmen. G. N. Krivov, for instance, recalled that 'some officers who were a bit older would pick men for their crews, but we never did this'. There was actually a recognised pecking order. V. P. Bryukhov observed that 'tank commanders or platoon leaders could not pick their crew. A company commander could, while a battalion commander would invariably pick his crew from men that he knew from previous battles'. A typical example of the latter was the battalion commander's crew in which A. M. Fadin served as lieutenant, in which all the men had been decorated: 'They lived apart from the rest of the unit and didn't talk with the other thirty crews.'

Some of the time before being shipped to the front was spent bonding the crew members and units. Freshly built tanks carried out 50-kilometre marches and underwent firing practice and tactical exercises. For Fadin's crew this was done in the following manner: 'We received brand new tanks from the factory. We drove them to the firing range, where targets were set up ready for us. We quickly formed an attacking line and carried out an assault from the march, using live ammo. Then we put ourselves in order in the assembly area and drove our tanks to the railway station for shipment to the front.' V. P. Bryukhov's crew only fired three rounds from the main gun and one ammo drum from their MG. Sometimes there was no time at all for crews to familiarise themselves with their vehicle. 'They told us: here is your tank,' said G. N. Krivov. 'They assembled it before our eyes: and it didn't work at all. Before they'd even finished assembling it, the train was ready to leave for the front. We filled out the forms, received a watch, a pen, and a silk handkerchief for fuel filtration, and off we went to the front.'

Quite often crews fell apart even before they went into their first action at the front. The units that received replacements still had a core of experienced tankmen, and they replaced green commanders and drivers on the newly arrived tanks, sending them to join the battalion's reserve or despatching them to a factory to get another new tank, as happened to Y. M. Polyanovski. A. M. Fadin, who was supposed to become a tank platoon leader, didn't lose his crew, but became commander of a single tank upon arrival at the front.

All the tankmen interviewed confirmed that a 'battle vehicle's crew' wasn't a stable unit at the front. On the one hand, high losses of personnel and equipment caused fast rotation of crew members; on the other, commanders didn't care much about keeping crews together as a unit. Even rather successful V. P. Bryukhov had at least ten different crews during the war. This, apparently, is why there were no special bonds of friendship between tankmen. But there were exceptions – the crew of company commander Senior Lieutenant Arkadi Vasilievich Maryevski, for instance, went through the entire war with him. And there was always comradeship between crew-members, of course: 'We all had one goal in the tank – to survive, and to destroy the enemy,' said A. S. Burtsev. 'So the unity of a crew was very important. Such unity always brought positive results.'

Coming back to the matter of the order of the People's Commissariat of Defence about the appointment of NCOs and officers to tank crews, it is hard to say if there was any set system of ranks among different crew members. A tank commander was normally a lieutenant or a junior lieutenant. A. M. Fadin's crew's driver was a senior sergeant, while the loader and radio operators were junior sergeants. Radio operator P. I. Kirichenko was promoted to senior sergeant upon graduation from his training regiment. In reality, every crew member had a chance to get promoted to officer rank and become a tank commander, or to attain an even higher office. This happened with Kirichenko, who completed an academy course before the end of the war and became a senior technician, commander of a mobile repair team. It was quite common to retrain the most experienced tankmen, especially drivers, as tank commanders, and promote them to lieutenants and junior lieutenants. However, in the early years of the war a sergeant or a sergeant-major could be a tank commander, as in the case of A. V. Maryevski. Unlike the British Army, the US Army, or the Wehrmacht, in the Red Army a rigid rank system existed only on paper.

Upon arrival at the front, all tankmen, regardless of rank, worked together to maintain their tank. 'We refuelled it, repaired it, and loaded the ammo,' said Bryukhov. 'Even when I became battalion commander, I would still work as a regular crew member with the rest of the crew.' A. K. Rodkin echoed his words: 'We didn't care if you were a commander or not, officer or not. In battle I was a commander, but when it came to repairing a track or cleaning the gun, I was a crew member like everyone else. I considered it set a bad tone to stand and smoke a cigarette while others were working. The other commanders were of the same opinion.' Refuelling and reloading a tank with ammo rendered all crewmen equal for as long as it took. Digging their vehicle in was also everyone's responsibility. Fadin recalled: 'It took almost all night long to dig the trench for the tank, changing each other in pairs. We shifted about thirty cubic metres of soil.'

This shared labour and the feeling of interdependence upon one another in battle prevented the abuse of younger soldiers commonly encountered today. Kirichenko recalled: 'Our driver, who was older than us – older even than our tank commander – was sort of an uncle for us, and enjoyed undisputed respect. He'd served in the army since before the war and had seen it all. He looked out for us. He didn't force us to do all the dirty work, as young soldiers; on the contrary, he tried to help us as much as possible.' The role of such senior and more experienced comrades was very important at the front. They were the ones who would teach young soldiers to take the springs off hatch locks, so that they could bail out even when wounded, and would advise them to clean the jack plug of a TPU so that it would disconnect easily. And they could calm down younger men before a battle.

Interestingly enough, the veterans claimed they had no fear of death, apparently due to their young age. 'You just didn't think about it,' said Fadin. 'Of course, you felt uneasy, but it wasn't fear, it was more excitement. As soon as you got into your tank you forgot everything.' A. S. Burtsev agreed: 'I didn't suffer from fear at the front. I was scared sometimes, but there was no fear.' G. N. Krivov added: 'I didn't want to die and I didn't think about it, but on the train to the front I saw a lot of men that suffered from fear and exhausted themselves with it – and they were the first ones to get killed.' In battle, according to almost all veterans, their consciousness sort of switched off, and every survivor described it in a different way. 'You're no longer a human being and you cannot think as a human being. Probably this very thing saved us,' recalled N. Y. Zheleznov. V. P. Bryukhov remembered: 'When my tank was knocked out and I had to bail – that was a bit scary. But otherwise when I was inside the tank I had no time to be afraid, as I was very busy.' Krivov provided a very interesting description of fighting fear before combat: 'In my last battles I was in command of the company commander's tank. The guys were all his crew. One guy was extremely silent, didn't say a word, the second was very hungry. We'd found an apiary, and he was devouring bread with honey. I was just overexcited and couldn't sit still. The company commander himself was breathing heavily and sniffing.' Of course, there were fears other than the fear of death. Men were scared of getting crippled or wounded. They were afraid to go missing in action or to be taken prisoner.

Many men could not overcome their fear. Some veterans described cases of crews abandoning their vehicles before they were even hit. Anatoli Shvebig, Deputy Brigade Commander (Technical) of the 12th Guards Tank Corps, recalled: 'This became more common at the end of the war. Say there was a battle going on. A crew would bail out and let their tank roll down a hill; the tank would drive on and be knocked out. This could be seen from our command posts. Of course, measures were taken against such tricks.' Evgeni I. Bessonov mentioned the same episode, which he saw during the Orel offensive: 'The tanks were knocked out, and it was the crews' fault. They'd abandoned their vehicles beforehand and the tanks just rolled on towards the enemy empty.' However, it would be wrong to say that this was a common practice, because other veterans didn't encounter such incidents. Cases of a tank being deliberately damaged by its crew were very uncommon, but they did happen. A driver might deliberately expose the opposite side of his tank to German fire, for instance. However, if such dodgers were tracked down by *Smersh* they were punished ruthlessly. A. V. Maryevski recalled: 'Three drivers were executed in our unit between Vitebsk and Polotsk. They exposed their side armour to the Germans, but they couldn't cheat *Smersh*.'

It is quite interesting that many veterans recalled men having premonitions of their death. One recalled: 'The tank of my comrade Shulgin was blown to pieces by a heavy round that must have been fired from a naval gun. He was older than us and he knew he'd get killed soon. Normally he was a happy and humorous guy, but two days before his death he sort of retired into himself. He didn't speak to anyone. He just switched himself off.' P. I. Kirichenko and N. E. Glukhov both encountered such cases, while S. L. Aria recalled a fellow tankman who had premonitions of coming danger that saved him from death several times. Although there were no superstitious men among the interviewees, V. P. Bryukhov described how 'some men didn't shave for several days before a battle. Some thought that they had to change their underwear, some thought the opposite – they didn't change their underwear. A man survived wearing these overalls, so he'd keep them. How did all these superstitions come about? Young replacements arrived, and after a couple of battles only half of them were left. A survivor would remember 'Aha, I was dressed like this", or "I didn't shave as usual", and so would start to cultivate this superstition. And if it worked a second time he'd firmly believe in it.'

Veterans provided different answers when questioned about God. Atheism and faith in one's own strength, knowledge, and skills were all typical among young men at that time. 'I believed that I wouldn't be killed' was the most common answer. 'Nevertheless,' commented Bryukhov, 'some men had crosses, but at the time it wasn't fashionable, so even those who had them tried to hide them. We were atheists. There were some believers, but I never noticed anyone praying among the multitude of people I saw during the war.' Only A. M. Fadin confirmed that he believed in God: 'You couldn't pray openly at the front. I didn't pray, but I did have faith in God in my soul.' Yet in hopeless situations many soldiers did indeed turn to God, A. V. Bodnar among them.

In battle all fears and premonitions faded away, to be replaced by two fundamental desires: to survive and to win. The entire crew needed to do its best in battle, and every member had his own responsibilities. 'The gun-layer should always keep the gun aimed in the direction of the tank's movement, observe the battlefield through his gunsight, and report the situation to his commander,' said A. S. Burtsev. 'The loader should look to the right and to the front and keep the crew informed. The radio operator should look to the right and to the front. And the driver should watch the route ahead and warn the gun-layer about holes in the road, so that we didn't stick our gun into the ground! The commander would normally concentrate his attention to the left and to the front.'

A lot depended on the skill of two specific men: the driver and the gun commander, later the gun-layer. 'An experienced driver is a salvation for the crew,' reflected Bryukhov. 'He would put the tank into a good spot for a shot; find cover; hide and manoeuvre. Some drivers even said sometimes: "I'll never get killed. I'll place the tank in such a way that a round couldn't hit it in the place where I'm sitting!" I believed this.' G. N. Krivov considered that he survived his first battles only because of the skill of his experienced driver.

Unlike other veterans, A. V. Maryevski placed the gun-layer as the second most important crewman after the tank commander: 'The gun-layer was more important. He could replace both tank commander and platoon commander. A gun-layer was a unit in himself!' It should also be noted that Maryevski was the only veteran interviewed who preferred to be in the driver's seat even when he was a company commander: 'If a round hit the turret, both the commander and the loader would be killed. This is why I always took the driver's seat. I understood how to survive.'

Unfortunately, the average marksmanship level of tankmen was weak. 'Our tank crews were very bad gunners,' claimed Evgeni I. Bessonov, commander of tank riders of the 49th Mechanised Brigade, 6th Guards Mechanised Corps of the 4th Guards Tank Army. Marksmen like Zheleznov, Fadin and Bryukhov were more of an exception than a rule.

The function of a loader in battle was simple but physically challenging: he had to push the round into the breech of the main gun and throw the empty cartridge out through the hatch after it was extracted. According to Bryukhov, any physically strong machine-gunner could be a loader – it was easy to explain to a young man the different markings that distinguished an armour-piercing round from an HE round. However, sometimes the stress of battle was so high that loaders passed out after breathing in too much of the gun's exhaust fumes. Besides that, their hands were burnt almost continuously, as they had to throw out the red-hot cartridges right after each shot so that they didn't fill the battle compartment with smoke.

The machine-gunner/radio operator was mostly idle during battle. 'He had a very limited view, and an even more limited field of fire for his MG,' recalled Kirichenko. 'The radio operator had an MG but he couldn't see anything through its slit, and if he fired, it was only on the orders of the tank commander,' confirmed Zheleznov. Y. M. Polyanovski recalled the following episode: 'We agreed between ourselves that we'd open fire from our main gun and turret MG even before we passed the line of our own infantry. We couldn't use the frontal MG, as it would hit our own men. As soon as we opened fire, the radio operator must have forgotten our agreement in the confusion of the battle, and fired, in fact, at our men.'

He wasn't needed as a radio operator either. 'We worked on one or two frequencies, as a rule. The communications system was so simple that any crew member could work with it,' recalled Kirichenko, while Bryukhov added: 'In a T-34/76 tank the radio operator would switch from internal to external communication if a commander was poorly trained. If a commander was well trained, he'd never give away control of the radio set – he'd switch it himself when he needed to.'

But the machine-gunner/radio operator provided considerable assistance to the driver during marches, helping to change gears on the four-stage gearbox of the early T-34s. 'Besides that, since his hands were busy I'd roll cigarettes for him, light them, and put them into his mouth. That was another of my responsibilities!' said Kirichenko.

Bryukhov remembered that, because radio operators didn't have a separate hatch, 'they burnt alive the most. They were in the worst spot, with the driver on their left and the loader behind them'. This is why line T-34/85 tanks that Burtsev fought in had a crew of only four men: 'The ordinary tank commanders didn't have a radio operator in their crew. The fifth crewman was only present in the crews of platoon leaders and upwards.'

Equally important to the survival of a crew was the interchangeability of its members on the battlefield. A tank commander had normally received sufficient training from an armour academy to be able to replace any crewman who was wounded or killed. But it was harder for NCOs who'd only undergone a short training period. As S. L. Aria stated that there was no interchangeability in his crew because of inadequate training, 'but I did fire the main gun several times'. The need for interchangeable crew members was well understood by even teenage lieutenants. Zheleznov recalled: 'When bonding the crews, as a platoon leader I had to ensure that the crew members could swap with each other.' Kirichenko observed that his crew started to carry out cross-training spontaneously, as they all understood how important it was in battle.

For many tankmen the outcome of a battle was death or a wound. A tank is a fat target for infantry, artillery and aeroplanes alike, and there are mines and barricades in its way. Even a short stop can be lethal for a tank. Even the best and the luckiest tank aces were not immune from an unexpected artillery shell, mortar round or 'Faustpatron' missile. However, in most cases it was the green tankmen who were killed. 'There was an AA gun battery in the suburbs of Kamenets-Podolsk,' recalled Zheleznov. 'It burnt two of our tanks. Both crews burnt alive. Four burnt corpses were lying on the ground round one of the tanks – small, baby-sized mummy remains of fully-grown men. Their heads were very small, and their faces a reddish-brownish-bluish colour.'

The main killers were the splinters of armour that flew through the inside of a tank after it was hit by an armour-piercing round, and the fire that started if the fuel system was damaged. A hit by an armour-piercing or fragmentation round, even one that didn't penetrate the armour, could cause shell-shock or break the crewmen's arm bones. The smaller armour splinters smashed between tankmen's teeth and hit their eyes, while large splinters could cause serious wounds. Natalia Nikitichna Peshkova, *komsorg* of a motor rifle battalion of the 3rd Guards Tank Army recalled: 'I had a special sympathy towards tankmen … they suffered such awful deaths. If a tank was knocked out, and they often were, it meant almost certain death: one or two men could bail out, but not more … The most awful thing was the burns they had. In those days burns of 40 per cent of the skin area were lethal.' When a tank was knocked out and caught fire, a crewman had to depend on the speed of his reaction, his strength, and his deftness. 'Most of the guys were fast and smart. Slow and passive tankmen didn't live long at the front as a rule. You had to be fast to survive,' reflected Fadin. 'When we bailed out, without thinking about anything else, we rolled off from the turret onto a mudguard and then to the ground – and it was about 1.5 metres high – yet I never saw anyone break a leg or an arm, or get a single scratch!' Bryukhov is still puzzled by this.

Surviving tankmen were 'horseless' for only a short time. After a couple of days in reserve they would get a new tank with a strange crew and would go into battle again. Company and battalion commanders had a harder time. They fought on to the last tank in their unit, which meant that they often had to change from one destroyed or damaged tank to another several times during an offensive operation.

After disengagement the crew had to perform maintenance on their tank: they had to refuel it and reload ammo, check its machinery, clean the tank, and dig it in and camouflage it if necessary. The entire crew had to take part in this work, otherwise they would not have managed, though a tank commander would sometimes avoid doing the dirtiest and most basic work – cleaning the barrel, or washing grease off the rounds. 'I never washed the rounds, but I carried ammo boxes,' recalled Burtsev. But a trench for a tank, or a dugout under it, had to be dug by the entire crew.

During rest and preparation for upcoming battles a tank became a real home for its crew, but the comfort it provided for their accommodation was minimal. 'Care for the crew was limited to the most primitive things,' stated Aria. Indeed, a T-34 was a very bumpy vehicle to drive. Bruises were unavoidable when driving and stopping a tank. Only their *tankoshlems* (as the veterans called their helmets) saved the crewmen from serious head injuries, and tankmen were unwise to get into a tank without them. Helmets also protected the head from burns if a tank caught fire. The comfort of British and American tanks, by contrast, won the admiration of Soviet tankmen. 'I had a look at an American M4A2 Sherman. My God! It was like a hotel inside! It was all lined with leather so that you didn't smash your head! There was also a medical kit with condoms and sulphidin – they had everything!' Such were the impressions of A. V. Bodnar. 'But at the same time they weren't fit for war. Because their two diesel engines, their earth fuel cleaners, their narrow tracks – all these things didn't last in Russia.' 'And they burnt like torches,' added Aria. The only foreign tank that was praised by some of the tankmen was the Valentine. 'It was a very successful tank, low to the ground, with a powerful gun and a quiet engine,' recalled Zheleznov.

When in defensive positions, or while receiving replacements in the rear, tankmen tried not only to get their tanks in order, but also their uniforms. During offensive operations they had no time for washing or changing clothes, and even food was brought only once a day – 'they would bring breakfast and lunch and dinner all together in the evening,' recalled Bryukhov. Krivov recalled that during nine days of offensive operations he didn't see the battalion's field kitchen once.

Winter was the hardest time in the opinion of all the veterans except Maryevski, who believed that early spring or late autumn, with their changeable weather, muddy roads and sleet, were worse. Sometimes, in conversation with the veterans, it was as if there was no war in the summertime. Apparently, when veterans are recalling the hardships of life at the front their memories invariably bring up episodes related to wintertime. A major role was played by the amount of clothing that tankmen had to wear in order to protect themselves from the cold inside a tank, which turned into 'a real refrigerator' in wintertime, when they put on warm underwear, winter tunic and trousers, padded jacket and pants, and a sheepskin coat. Of course, those ubiquitous companions of all wars – lice – were also present. However, in this matter the opinions of the veterans were mixed. Some, like Fadin and Burtsev, stated that 'we didn't have lice. The crew always had to work with fuel and grease, and lice couldn't stand this'. But other veterans – in fact the vast majority – disagreed. 'We had tons of lice, especially in wintertime,' said Bryukhov, who was Burtsev's company commander. 'Anyone who says that tankmen didn't have lice because of fuel and grease is talking nonsense! Such a person was never in a tank and wasn't a tankman. There were tons of lice in a tank!' Such contradictions are common in the recollections of veterans, and could probably be explained by the different periods in which the veterans served, as well as by their personal experiences. But for most tankmen the struggle against bugs started at the very first halt in operations. Uniforms were fried in improvised lice-killers, which consisted of a barrel with a lid and a little water at the bottom, set over a fire with the uniforms hanging on bars inside. Steam bath and laundry units would also arrive at the front to wash and disinfect uniforms. Despite the hardness of the conditions in which they served, almost all the veterans recalled that few men fell sick at the front.

The appearance of tankmen was far from fancy, as their uniforms, faces, and hands were all stained with grease and the smut from exhaust pipes and explosions. Forever digging trenches for their tanks did little to help. 'By the end of every operation we were dressed in whatever we could find – German tunics, civilian suits and trousers. A Soviet tankman could only be identified by his *tankoshlem*,' recalled Captain Nikolai K. Shishkin, commander of a JSU-152 SP-gun battery. Men could get themselves more or less cleaned up only during periods of rest or when receiving replacements, but such breaks in operations were quite rare. One had to get used to dirt. 'They did issue us with padded jackets and *valenki* felt boots. But when you get all these items dirty in your tank, they don't last long, and we couldn't get replacement uniforms. For a lot of the time we felt like homeless guys in rags,' said Kirichenko.

Overall a tankman's living conditions were not so different from those of infantrymen. 'In the winter we were all filthy, covered with oil and grease, our entire bodies covered with boils as we all had flu,' explained Bryukhov. 'When we dug a trench, we drove our tank over it, covered the bottom of the trench with a tarpaulin and hung a stove from the bottom of the tank with the chimney outside – that was our accommodation.' Maryevski claimed not to have slept a single night indoors during the whole war.

A huge role in improving a crew's living conditions was played by such simple things as a piece of regular tarpaulin. Almost all the veterans interviewed claimed that it was impossible to live in a tank without tarpaulin. They used it as a blanket at night, and to protect their tank from the rain. At lunchtime it served as a table, in wintertime as the roof of an improvised dugout. When the tarpaulin was blown off Aria's tank and into the Caspian Sea, he had to steal a sail to replace it. According to Y. M. Polyanovski, the tarpaulin was especially vital in wintertime: 'We had tank stoves – a regular wood-burning stove was attached to the rear of the tank. A crew had to live somewhere in wintertime, as they wouldn't let us stay in villages. It was awfully cold inside a tank, and only two men could lie down in it. So we'd dig a good trench and roll our tank over it, cover it with the tarpaulin and nail the edges of the tarpaulin to the ground. Then we'd hang the stove under the tank and stoke it. That's how we'd heat the trench.'

'What did we do in our spare time in the war? When on earth did we have spare time?' recalled Fadin. Some men wrote letters home. Some, like Krivov, took photographs. Entertainers would visit the front with concert parties sometimes, or movies might be shown. But most tankmen were too fatigued to do much. Morale was improved by keeping in touch with events elsewhere at the front and in the country as a whole. The main source of news was the radio carried in every tank during the second half of the war. In addition, tankmen were supplied with newspapers, both national and divisional and army ones. Political information sessions were held on a regular basis. Just like many other *frontoviks*, those tankmen interviewed clearly remembered articles by Ilya Erenburg that rallied them in their fight against the Germans.

Many of the interviewed veterans stated that they hated the Germans. 'How should we treat the Germans? We treated them in a natural way: we gave them a proper beating. We hated them bitterly,' recalled Zheleznov. At the same time, respect for the enemy can be seen in many of their recollections: 'They were good soldiers,' said Fadin. 'But at the front I looked upon them simply as targets. So I just fired at those targets.' Tankmen had many opportunities to take revenge against German soldiers in battle, and tended to treat POWs with disgust; but they considered it completely improper to take revenge against civilians. However, some atrocities took place. As Krivov put it: 'The relatives of some of the guys had been killed, and they knew about it, as they were getting letters. We had one boy in our unit whose entire family had been killed by Germans. One day he was quite drunk. He had an SMG on him, and when some German POWs were marching by he fired a burst at them. We gave him a box on the ears: "What the hell are you doing?" we said. Such things happened, I wouldn't deny it.' There were also cases of rape: 'Some of our guys were desperate and went looking for hiding German women. I thought it was a disgusting thing.' There were many completely different people in the Red Army, so there were inevitably many completely different attitudes towards German civilians. Initially an all-consuming hatred towards the Germans pre-vailed, accompanied by a desire to seek revenge. This was especially visible among men who'd experienced German occupation or lost their relatives in the war. But this gradually gave way to the orders issued by the Red Army's high command, and the men eventually came to pity the German civilians. Kirichenko's observation that 'Russian people don't bear grudges' expressed a common opinion among the veterans.

One of the special features of the Red Army was its massive employment of women in a wide variety of roles, from clerks and phone operators to chiefs of staff and tank commanders. According to the veterans, everyone tried to date at the front, but in most cases this was a privilege of the top brass. 'We had a shortage of women. Our top brass got them all' stated Maryevski. Fadin confirmed his words: 'Top brass, I mean commanders, got all the girls. Company commanders that had girlfriends were an exception. A platoon leader or a tank commander was a different case. We weren't so much fun for the girls. We were always getting killed and burnt.' All the veterans confirmed that the officers of a brigade staff all had a 'PPZh' (a field wife, a play on 'PPSh'). Only a few battalion commanders had a PPZh, while company commanders and platoon leaders never had them, let alone tank commanders. Bryukhov explained the situation in the following manner: 'There were 1,200 men in the brigade, all young men, but only sixteen girls, and all the men tried to court them. A girl would find a man that she liked and they'd start dating and then living together. The rest were jealous.' Real love was often born at the front, and was later officially sealed with marriage vows. Of course, there were also 'easy' women, but Burtsev recalled that most of the women at the front were 'decent women. If they loved someone, they only loved one man, not all men at once. Women were necessary at the front. They performed tasks that were no less important than the tasks of the men. We had many women in our brigade who'd saved dozens of lives, or maybe hundreds. A man couldn't do it'.

Many tankmen only got enough to eat for the first time since the outbreak of war when they got to the front. There was a lack of food in the rear, but no major problems with catering at the front. Hot meals might be delayed, but tankmen were supplied with dry tack. A. K. Rodkin is still puzzled how the starving country managed to supply the army so well. US-made canned meat was quite popular among the men, who considered SPAM to be gourmet food. Tankmen always tried to have a supply of food in their tank, which would become their only source of catering during offensive operations. This supply could only be restocked from war booty. On one occasion Burtsev's unit captured a German supply column carrying food: 'Sausage, canned food, cheese – we stuffed our tanks with these things. We couldn't eat it all in a week! The box for the ammo belts was completely stuffed with butter. We didn't go for lunch at the field kitchen, as it didn't work well in offensive operations. Instead we ate this dry tack for a whole week.' The veterans also recalled often being given food by the local civilians, which was dubbed at the front 'catering with grandmother's rationing card'.

Officers were entitled to additional rations, which included butter, cookies, sugar and candies, but as a rule they considered it improper to eat this alone, and shared it with their crews. Fadin recalled: 'We had this officers' ration. We got it once a week or less frequently, I don't remember. It included about 300 grams of candies, a piece of American SPAM, a can of ham, and cookies. I would take all these things and put them on the common table of my crew.'

Alcohol was also present. 'The whole war ran on Narkom vodka!' claimed Bodnar. 'It was the same with us and the Wehrmacht. You can't live in a war without a vodka shot. It stimulates you before a battle and helps you relax after it.' However, some tankmen, like Fadin and Bryukhov, avoided alcohol at first, preferring to give it to their crews, but the vast majority treated themselves to one of the few luxuries of front-line life. There was no shortage of alcohol: 'There were thirty-two tanks in the battalion,' recalled Marievsky, 'but at Orel I only had four tanks left. Out of thirty crews twenty were gone, but we still had rations for thirty. After the battle, after we had captured Orel, the Sergeant-Major came around and brought us a whole thermos of pure alcohol – twenty litres.' There was a lot of war booty alcohol too. Every available container was used to hold it, even fuel tanks. The fact that the booze sometimes smelt of diesel as a result didn't bother tankmen a lot. Nikolai N. Kuzmichev recalled a typical dialogue: 'We captured a distillery plant at Lodz. The guys said: "We should stock ourselves up with alcohol. Where shall we put it? Into the water cans?" "No. We won't reach Berlin in two days. That's not enough!" [Each can could hold two litres.] "Then we need to pour it into the fuel tanks." "OK, go . . ." But we'd already filled those!' Although many tankmen said that they drank whenever they got the chance, Zheleznov, Polyanovski and Maryevski said that they always made sure their crews were sober before battle: 'God forbid if someone drank before battle! One time I almost shot my gun-layer, Vanya Pecherski – he was a Siberian hunter and had problems with discipline. To go into battle drunk meant certain death.'

Tankmen were supposed to get a regular salary, with bonuses for destroyed enemy tanks. But money was useless at the front. Lieutenant Vladimir Ivanovich Yaroshevski told how he used his pay: 'Those who had relatives transferred all their money to them. But my homeland was under occupation, so I merely transferred my money to the Defence Fund. So I never got any money, not even for the tanks that I'd destroyed. I couldn't do anything with it.'

The war fulfilled the dreams of many boys to drive a tank or pilot a fighter plane, true, but the bloody routine of the war erased all pre-war illusions. The war cost these same boys huge efforts and sacrifices. The death of comrades, wounds, dirt and fatigue became part of an everyday existence best summed up by V. P. Bryukhhov: 'Only young people could stand all this. I believe that it was young people who won the war.'

CHAPTER 2

'Against the T-34 the German tanks were crap.'

Alexay Isaev

'I destroyed five entrenched tanks. They could do nothing, as they were Panzer III and Panzer IV tanks and I was in a T-34, whose front armour their shells couldn't pierce.' Not many tank crews of the armies that participated in the Second World War might have repeated these words, spoken by T-34 commander Lieutenant Aleksandr Vasilievich Bodnar about his battle machine. The Soviet T-34 became a legend first of all because the people who sat in it, who operated its steering levers and looked through its gunsights, believed in it. An idea expressed by a well-known Russian war theorist, A. A. Svechin, is traceable in the recollections of tank crewmen: 'Whilst the significance of material in war is quite relative, belief in it has a tremendous role.' Svechin had been a combat officer in the Great War of 1914–18, had witnessed the debut of heavy artillery, aeroplanes and armoured vehicles on its battlefields, and knew very well what he was talking about. If soldiers have faith in the equipment entrusted to them they will act more courageously and resolutely on their way to victory. On the other hand, mistrust, readiness to abandon a piece of equipment genuinely or perceived to be underpowered, leads to defeat. But belief in the T-34 wasn't a matter of blind faith based on propaganda or fantasy. Its crewmen's confidence was inspired by those peculiarities of its design which made the T-34 so remarkable compared to other combat vehicles of the time, namely its sloped armour plates and its V-2 diesel engine.

The principle of enhancing a tank's protection by sloping its armour plates was clear to anybody who had studied geometry at school. 'The T-34 had thinner armour than Panthers or Tigers,' remembered tank commander Burtsev. 'Its thickness was about 45 mm. But since it was sloping its line-of-sight thickness made about 90 mm, which increased its resistance.' The application of geometrical considerations instead of a crude build-up of armour thickness gave the tank, in the eyes of its crewmen, an incontestable advantage over its adversaries. 'The arrangement of armour plates on the German tanks was poorly designed, as generally they were vertical,' recalled battalion commander Bryukhov. 'Surely that was a disadvantage? Our tanks had sloped armour.'

Such statements were based on practical as well as theoretical considerations. German anti-tank and tank guns with a calibre under 50 mm couldn't penetrate the T-34's armour in most cases. Moreover, even the tungsten-cored shells of the 50 mm PAK-38 anti-tank gun and the 50 mm Panzer III gun with a 60-calibre length of barrel, which – according to trigonometrical calculations – were supposed to pierce the T-34's front armour, would in reality ricochet off its sloping plates harmlessly. Statistical research conducted by NII-48 (Scientific Research Institute 48) in September–October 1942, regarding the combat damage incurred by T-34 tanks then being repaired in maintenance workshops No. 1 and No. 2 in Moscow, showed that out of 109 hits on the upper front part of the tanks 89 per cent had had no effect, but that destructive penetrations had been achieved by guns of 75 mm calibre or greater. Of course, the situation had become more complicated by then with the advent of German 75 mm anti-tank and tank guns. Their 75 mm shells would normalise – i.e. would maintain a straight path – when impacting with armour plates and would pierce the front armour of a T-34 from a distance of 1,200 metres. The 88 mm rounds of anti-aircraft guns and hollow-charge shells were also insensitive to the sloping of armour. But up until the Battle of Kursk in July 1943 the proportion of 50 mm guns in the Wehrmacht had been significant, and belief in the sloping armour of the T-34 had been largely justified.

As far as Soviet tankmen were concerned only British tanks enjoyed any evident advantages over the T-34's armour. 'If a shell had gone through the turret of a British tank the commander and the gunner could have stayed alive, because there were virtually no splinters,' Bryukhov observed, 'while in a T-34 the armour would spall a lot and the crew had few chances of survival.' This was because the medium hardness armour of Britain's Matilda and Valentine tanks had a very high nickel content (3.0–3.5 per cent), whereas Soviet 45 mm high hardness armour contained only 1.0–1.5 per cent nickel, resulting in much lower ductility.

At the same time, additional measures to boost the protection of the T-34 were rarely carried out by its crews. Only before the Berlin operation, according to Lieutenant-Colonel Anatoli Shvebig – formerly technical deputy brigade commander of the 12th Guards Tank Corps – were screens made of 'bed mesh' welded onto some tanks in order to protect them from Panzerfausts. In all the known cases such screening was the result of creative work by maintenance workshops and production plants. The same may be said of the painting of T-34 tanks. They were largely used just as they were delivered from the production plants, painted plain green outside and inside, though in wintertime technical deputy commanders were set the task of painting their units' tanks white (the winter of 1944–45, when the war had entered German territory, was an exception). Not a single veteran interviewed remembers seeing camouflage painted on a T-34.

The diesel engine was another obvious and confidence-building element of the T-34's construction. Most of those trained as tank drivers, radio operators, and even commanders, used to deal with fuel – at least with petrol – in the pre-war period. They knew very well from their own experience that petrol was volatile, highly flammable, and would burn very fiercely. Quite obvious experiments with petrol had been carried out by the engineers who had designed the T-34. 'In the heat of a debate, designer Nikolai Kucherenko would use not the most scientific but a vivid example of the advantages of a new kind of fuel. He'd take a burning torch and bring it to a bucket of petrol in the plant backyard – the bucket would burst into fire immediately. Then he'd dip the same torch into a bucket of diesel – the flame would extinguish as if in water . . .

This experiment illustrated the effect of a possible shell hit, capable of setting fire to fuel or even to its fumes inside a tank. Accordingly T-34 crews looked down somewhat on the enemy's tanks. 'They had petrol engines, didn't they? That was also a big disadvantage,' remembered Senior Sergeant Kirichenko. A similar attitude existed towards the tanks supplied through the Lend-Lease programme ('Many people died of bullet hits on tanks; the engine ran on petrol, and the armour was insignificant,' testified tank commander Y. M. Polyanovski) and to those Soviet-made tanks and self-propelled guns equipped with carburettor engines ('Once SU-76 self-propelled guns were brought out to our battalion. They were equipped with petrol engines – real cigarette lighters ... they burned out during the very first battles,' recalled Bryukhov). Diesel engines gave the crews a confidence that they had far fewer chances of dying in a blazing inferno than their adversaries, whose tanks were fuelled with hundreds of litres of volatile and highly inflammable petrol.

But in reality the straight application of Kucherenko's experiment with a bucket to the tanks themselves was not quite substantiated, since statistics showed that diesel-powered tanks were actually no safer in regard to fire risk than tanks fitted with carburettor engines. Data compiled in October 1942 showed that diesel-powered T-34s had burned even more often than T-70 tanks with engines driven by aviation fuel (23 per cent versus 19 per cent).

In 1943 engineers from the NIIBT (the Scientific Research Institute of Armoured Machines) in Kubinka, near Moscow, came to a conclusion regarding the possibility of fuel conflagration that was directly opposite to the customarily accepted view. 'The usage of a carburettor engine in a new tank model produced in 1942 by the Germans may be explained [...] by a significant percentage of conflagrations on diesel tanks and the lacking by the latter of any considerable advantages over the carburettor engines, especially in the case of their competent design and the presence of reliable automatic fire extinguishers.'

When bringing his torch to the bucket full of petrol, the engineer Kucherenko was setting alight the fumes of a volatile fuel. There were no inflammable fumes above the diesel bucket; but this didn't mean that diesel could not be ignited from a much more powerful means of inflammation – a shell hit. That's why the location of the fuel tanks in the T-34's battle compartment didn't enhance its fire safety at all compared to its contemporaries, which had their fuel tanks in the back of the hull and were hit far more rarely. Bryukhov confirmed the aforesaid: 'When does a tank catch fire? When a shell hits the fuel tank. And it burns when there is plenty of fuel. By the end of a battle there is no fuel and the tank doesn't burn nearly as much.'

But tank crews saw the lower noise level of German tank engines as their only advantage over the T-34's power plant. 'Looked at from one viewpoint a petrol engine is hazardous as regards fire, but looked at from another – at least it's quiet! The T-34 not only rattled but it also clattered with its tracks,' reported tank commander A. K. Rodkin. No mufflers were initially provided for the T-34's exhausts. They were led out to the tank's poop with no sound-absorbing fittings whatsoever, rattled loudly from the exhaust produced by the 12-cylinder engine. Rodkin recalled how the T-34 produced terrible amounts of dust because its exhaust jets were directed downwards.

The T-34's diesel engine and sloping armour distinguished it from all other Second World War combat vehicles. These particularities also provided the crews with confidence in their weapon. People went into combat with pride in the equipment entrusted to them. That was a lot more important than the true effect of sloping armour plates or the actual fire hazard of a diesel engine.

Tanks came about as a means of protecting the crews of machine-guns and artillery pieces against the enemy's fire. The balance between a tank's ability to withstand that fire and the capabilities of anti-tank artillery is quite shaky: as the artillery is constantly improved, even the newest tank cannot feel itself entirely safe on a battlefield. The deployment of powerful anti-aircraft and corps artillery in an anti-tank role make this balance even shakier. That's why sooner or later a situation arises where a shell succeeds in piercing a tank's armour and turns a steel box into hell.

Well-designed tanks, having received one or more hits, would continue to prove their worth even after death by providing the crew inside with the means of escape. Located in the upper front portion of the T-34's hull, the driver's hatch – unusual in tanks from other countries – turned out to be a lifesaver in critical situations. 'The hatch was smooth with rounded edges and it wasn't at all hard to climb in or out,' remembered driver S. L. Aria. 'Moreover, when you got up from your seat you could lean out practically above your waist.' Another value of the T-34's driver's hatch was that it could be fixed in several intermediate positions, not just open or closed. It was a very simple design. The heavy, cast steel hatch (60 mm thick) was supported by a hinge in the shape of a notched rack, and by shifting the bar from one notch to another it was possible to fix the hatch firmly in position so that there was no risk of it coming loose on a bumpy road or on the battlefield. Drivers preferred to have the hatch slightly open. Company commander Arkadi Vasilievich Maryevski, for instance, remembered: 'The driver always had his hatch open a palm's width: firstly, because that way you could see everything, and secondly, because the airflow – provided the commander's hatch was open – ventilated the battle compartment.'

Generally speaking, the driver was in the best possible position in the eyes of tankmen: 'The driver had the highest chance to survive,' according to platoon commander Bodnar. 'He sat low, and there was sloping armour in front of him.' Kirichenko pointed out that 'as a rule the lower part of the hull was concealed by irregularities in the ground, so it was hard to hit it. But the upper part was high above the ground and received most of the hits. So people who sat in the turret used to die more often than those who sat down below'. Statistically, in the earlier part of the war most hits were on a tank's hull. According to the aforementioned report of NII-48, 81 per cent of the hits were on the hull and 19 per cent on the turret. However, more than half of the hits were harmless (non-penetrating or only partially penetrating): 89 per cent of hits on the upper front portion, 66 per cent of hits on the lower front portion, and about 40 per cent of hits on the hull sides didn't penetrate. Of the last, 42 per cent were on the engine and transmission compartments, hits on which were harmless to the crew. The turret, by contrast, was pierced relatively easily, its softer cast armour providing poor resistance even to the 37 mm shells of automatic AA guns. The situation was worsened by the fact that T-34 turrets were often subjected to the fire of heavy artillery pieces such as 88 mm anti-aircraft guns and the long-barrelled 75 mm and 50 mm guns of German tanks. The screen of ground irregularities mentioned by Kirichenko was about a metre high in the European theatre of operations. Half of this metre constituted the vehicle's ground-clearance, the rest – one-third of a T-34's hull. Most of the front portion of the hull was not screened by ground irregularities.

While the driver's hatch was considered convenient by all the veterans interviewed, they were unanimous in their condemnation of the turret hatch of early models of the T-34, which they nicknamed the *pirozhok* (pie) because of its characteristic shape. Bryukhov described it as bad: 'It was heavy and hard to open. If it got jammed, that was it – no one could bail out.' He is echoed by tank commander Nikolai Evdokimovich Glukhov: 'A big hatch – very inconvenient, very heavy.' Combining two hatches for two crewmen sitting next to each other – the gunner and loader – into one was atypical of tank design of the period. Its appearance on the T-34 had been caused not by tactical but by technological considerations, related to the installation of the vehicle's heavy gun. The T-34's predecessor on the Kharkov plant conveyer, the BT-7 tank, had been equipped with two hatches – one for each crewman – in its turret, and was nicknamed the 'Mickey Mouse' by the Germans because of its characteristic appearance. The T-34 had inherited a lot from the BT, but received a 76 mm gun instead of the BT's 45 mm, and had its fuel tanks in the battle compartment. The need to dismantle the gun during fuel tank and gun-cradle repairs had therefore made the designers combine two hatches into one. The gun itself would be drawn out through the screwbolt-fixed lid in the back of the turret, and the cradle was removed through the turret hatch. The fuel tanks – fastened above the sponsons of the hull – would be taken out through the same hatch.

All these complications were caused by the turret sidewalls sloping towards the gun mantlet. The Germans took their tanks' guns out forwards, along with their mantlets (which were nearly as wide as the turrets). But it is noteworthy that the T-34's designers had paid a lot of attention to ensuring that tank crews could repair their tanks using their own strength. Even the gunports in the rear and sides of the turret to fire small arms through were adjusted to assist this: plugs in the gunports would be removed and a small composite crane would be installed in the holes to help in the dismantling of the engine and transmission.

One should not think that the designers gave no thought to the crewmen's needs when constructing the large hatch. In the USSR before the war it was genuinely believed that a large hatch would aid the evacuation of wounded crewmen from a tank. Nevertheless, combat experience and the complaints of crewmen urged the design group led by A. A. Morozov to switch to two turret hatches during a scheduled modernisation of the T-34, and the hexahedron turret, nicknamed the 'screw-nut', got its 'Mickey Mouse' ears back in the form of two round hatches. Such hatches were mostly installed on T-34s produced in the Ural Province – either at ChTZ (the Chelyabinsk Tractor Plant), UZTM (the Ural Plant of Heavy Machinery Production in Sverdlovsk, now Ekateringburg), or UVZ (the Ural Car Plant in Nizhniy Tagil) – after the autumn of 1942. The Krasnoye Sormovo plant in Gorky (now Nizhniy Novgorod) continued producing tanks with 'pie' turrets with one hatch till spring 1943. The task of hauling out the fuel tanks from tanks with 'screw-nuts' was carried out by removing the armour plate between the commander's and loader's hatches.

To avoid fumbling with the latch when the tank was hit, tank crews preferred not to lock the hatch but would instead fasten it with a trouser belt. 'When I was heading into attack the hatch was shut but not latched,' remembered A. V. Bodnar. 'I would hitch up one end of my belt to the hatch latch and would wind the other end around the hook which held shells on the turret, so that if something happened I'd hit it with my head to make the belt come off and could jump straight out.' Similar tricks were used by the commanders of tanks that had a commander's cupola: 'There was a double-flap hatch which had to be locked by two spring latches,' recalled Burtsev. 'Even a pretty strong man could only have opened it with a lot of effort, and a wounded one couldn't have done it at all. We used to take the springs off, leaving the latches on. On the whole we tried to keep the hatch open – it made it easier to jump out.'

Though routine servicing of a T-34 involved the entire crew in the same uncomplicated but monotonous chores, once the tank was on the move or in combat most of the responsibility was borne on the shoulders of just two men. The first of them was the tank commander, who, apart from being in charge on the battlefield was also the gunner on early models of the T-34: 'When you were the commander of a T-34/76, you fired the gun yourself, you gave commands on the intercom, you did everything yourself,' as Bryukhov put it. The second man was the driver. Tank and unit commanders valued a good driver-mechanic very highly – 'An experienced driver was half the equation for success,' said N. E. Glukhov. This rule knew no exceptions. 'Driver-mechanic Grigoriy Ivanovich Kryukov was ten years older than me,' remembered tank commander Georgi Nikolaevich Krivov. 'He used to be a car driver before the war and had already been in combat near Leningrad. Been wounded. He understood the tank well. I guess that we survived the first battles only due to him.'

The special status of the driver-mechanic in a T-34 was determined by the machine's relatively complicated handling, which required experience and physical strength. This was particularly true of the T-34s in service during the first half of the war, before the introduction of an improved transmission arrangement with permanently toothed gear-wheels. Changing gears in the earlier four-stage transmission was very complicated and required a lot of physical strength – Maryevski remembered that 'it was impossible to shift the gear lever with one hand, and I had to help myself with my knee'. In the replacement transmission changing the gear-ratio was conducted not by the movement of gear-wheels as in the past, but by the movement of small cam couplers that moved along the shafts via slots and clutched with a pair of toothed wheels. The next step in the perfection of the transmission was the introduction of synchronisers into the gearbox. These equalised the speed of the cam couplers and gear-wheels while switching gear. The Maibach-type gearbox of the German Panzer III and IV tanks may serve as an example of a gearbox with synchronisers. The so-called 'planetary' gearboxes of Czech-made tanks and the British Matilda tank were even better. No wonder, therefore, that on 6 November 1940 People's Commissar of Defence S. K. Timoshenko had sent the Defence Committee of the *Sovnarkom* (Soviet of People's Commissars) a letter in which it said: 'The plants have to design and prepare for the mass production of planetary transmission for the T-34 and KV tanks. It will facilitate an increase in the speed of the tanks and ease driving.' However, this had yet to be achieved at the outbreak of war, and during the early years of the conflict the T-34 had struggled on with the most primitive transmission of the time. It was necessary for the drivers of these early T-34s, with their four-stage transmissions, to have been very well trained. 'If a driver wasn't trained well enough he could switch to fourth gear instead of first, or third instead of second, which would have led to the gearbox breaking down,' remembered Bodnar. 'It was necessary to bring his gear-changing skills up to automatic, so that he could change gears with his eyes shut.'

Apart from the difficulties of gear-changing, the four-stage transmission was characterised as weak and unreliable, and frequently broke down. Engineers at the NIIBT testing ground in Kubinka gave the early T-34 transmission a thoroughly pejorative assessment in their report on the testing of domestic, captured, and Lend-Lease equipment: 'Transmissions of domestically-made tanks, especially the T-34 and KV, do not fully meet the requirements of modern combat vehicles, being inferior to the tanks of the Allies as well as the enemy's tanks, and are behind the level of tank-construction practices by at least several years.' A Resolution of the GKO (State's Committee of Defence) 'On the improvement of the quality of tanks', based on the results of this and other reports on the T-34's drawbacks, was issued on 5 June 1942. As a result, by the beginning of 1943 the construction department of Plant No. 183 (a Kharkov plant evacuated to the Ural region) had designed a five-speed transmission with permanent clutching gear-wheels, which the tankmen who fought in T-34s would come to regard highly. Permanent clutching gear-wheels and the introduction of an extra gear significantly simplified driving the T-34, so that it was no longer necessary for the radio operator to help the driver change gear.

Another element of the T-34's transmission that depended on the skill of the driver was its main friction clutch, which connected the transmission with the engine. Bodnar, who trained T-34 drivers following an injury, reported: 'A lot of things depended on how well the main friction had been tuned for coasting and turning-off, and how well a driver used it when taking off. The last third of the pedal stroke needed to be released slowly, with no darting off, because if one darted off the machine would skid and the friction would buckle.' The principal part of the main unlubricated friction of the T-34 was a package of eight driving and ten driven discs (later on, in the improved five-gear transmission, it would get eleven driving and eleven driven discs). These were pressed to each other by springs. Incorrect turning-off of the main friction, accompanied by the rubbing of the discs against each other, could result in overheating and buckling that could lead to a breakdown (referred to as 'burning the friction out'). By contrast, in German tanks contemporaneous with the T-34 the main friction had its discs floating in machine oil. This allowed the rubbing elements to cool down and eased up turning the friction on and off.

The servo-mechanism with which the main friction's turning-off pedal was fitted as a result of combat experience during the initial period of the war improved the situation to some extent. In spite of its 'servo' prefix (which inspired a certain amount of awe), the design of this mechanism was rather simple. The friction pedal was held by a spring, which would pass the dead point in the process of pressing on it and change the direction of strain. When the pedal started to be pressed down the spring would resist the pressure. Then, at a certain point, it would begin to help out and actually pull the pedal down. Prior to the introduction of these simple but necessary transmission improvements the strain on drivers had been very harsh. 'A driver would lose two or three kilos during a long march. He'd be exhausted. Sure, it was very difficult,' remembered Kirichenko.

Improvements in the T-34's transmission were accompanied by other developments in its design as the war progressed. The previously quoted NIIBT report included the observation: 'Due to the increasing power of anti-tank arms, manoeuvrability makes no less of a contribution to a tank's survival than heavy armour. A combination of good armour and speed of manoeuvring is the principal means of protecting a modern combat vehicle from the fire of anti-tank artillery.' The advantage in armour protection initially enjoyed by the T-34 was lost during the final stages of the war, but this was compensated for by improvements in vehicle performance. The tank began to go faster, on the road as well as on the battlefield, and to manoeuvre better. The two features that its crews had always trusted (its sloping armour and diesel engine) had been supplemented by a third one – speed. A. K. Rodkin, who fought in a T-34/85 at the end of the war, summarised it thus: 'The tankmen used to have a proverb: "The armour's crap but our tanks are faster" [paraphrased from a popular and boastful pre-war song "the armour's hard and our tanks are faster"]. The speed was our advantage. The Germans had petrol engines but their tanks weren't very fast.'

The principal purpose of the T-34's 76.2 mm main gun was 'the destruction of tanks and other mechanised means of the enemy'. The veterans interviewed unanimously considered German tanks to be their main and most formidable adversary. In the early stages of the war T-34 crews had headed into combat against any German tank with confidence, justly reckoning that the Soviet tank's powerful gun and armour would ensure success. But the arrival of the Panzer V 'Panther' and Panzer VI 'Tiger' tanks turned the tables against them. Their long guns allowed them to fight without bothering about concealment. 'Based on the fact that our 76 mm guns could only pierce their armour from 500 metres they stood out in the open,' platoon commander Nikolai Yakovlevich Zheleznov remembered. Even tungsten-cored 76 mm shells gave no advantage in such a duel, for they could only penetrate 90 mm of armour from a distance of 500 metres, whereas the frontal armour of a Tiger was 102 mm. The introduction of an 85 mm gun for the T-34 immediately changed the situation, enabling the Soviet tanks to fight the Panthers and Tigers from a distance of more than a kilometre and the old Panzer IV from a distance of 1,200–1,300 metres. An example of such a battle, on the Sandomir bridgehead in the summer of 1944, can be found in chapter 11. The first T-34s armed with 85 mm guns left the conveyors of Plant No. 112 'Krasnoye Sormovo' in January 1944, and the mass production of T-34/85s fitted with the model ZIS-S-53 gun commenced in March 1944, when tanks of this new type were produced by the leading Soviet wartime tank-production facility, Plant No. 183 in Nizhniy Tagil. Despite the speed with which the 85 mm gun went into production it was considered reliable by its crews and gave no rise to criticism.

Laying of the T-34's gun was done manually, but the turret itself had electric drive from the very start of production. Crewmen nevertheless preferred to turn the turret manually during combat. 'Your hands were crossed on the cranks for turret turning and gun laying,' recalled G. N. Krivov. 'You could turn the turret using the electric engine but tended to forget about it during combat. One would turn it with the manual lever.' This is easily explainable. On the T-34/85 that Krivov is talking about, the turret turning lever served simultaneously as the electric drive lever. In order to switch from the manual drive to the electric one, one had to set the turret turning; the lever had to be moved vertically back and forth to make the turret turn in the right direction. But in the heat of combat one would forget about it, and use the lever only for manual turret turning.

The only inconvenience caused by the introduction of the 85 mm gun was that that it proved necessary to watch the long barrel so that it didn't dig into the ground on bumpy roads or in combat. 'The T-34/85 gun barrel was four or more metres long,' A. K. Rodkin pointed out (the 1944 model was 4.645 metres, to be exact). 'The tank could have dug the ground with it in the smallest ditch. If you fired it after that the barrel would open up at the end like the petals of a flower.'

While tanks were the T-34's most dangerous adversary it was also highly effective against artillery and infantry. At best, most of the tankmen whose recollections are in this book could claim only a few armoured vehicles destroyed, whereas the number of enemy infantrymen killed by the main gun and machine-gun amounted to dozens and even hundreds. The ammunition of a T-34 consisted mostly of high explosive and antipersonnel shells. In 1942–44 the regular ammunition allowance of a T-34 with a 'screw-nut' turret comprised 100 shells, seventy-five of them antipersonnel/high explosive and twenty-five armour-piercing (including four tungsten-cored shells from 1943 on), stored in racks inside the turret and in trunks in the floor of the combat compartment. The regular ammunition allowance of a T-34/85 was thirty-six antipersonnel/high explosive, fourteen armour-piercing, and five tungsten-cored shells. The balance between armour-piercing and antipersonnel shells largely reflected the conditions under which the T-34s fought. Under a hail of artillery fire the crew in most of cases had little time for aimed firing, and shot on the move or during short halts with the goal of suppressing the enemy by the volume of their fire or hitting him with a series of shells. 'Seasoned guys who'd been in combat before told us: "Never stop. Shoot on the move. Sky or earth – no matter where the shell flies – you shoot and press on",' remembered Krivov. 'You ask how many shots I fired during my first battle? Half of the load. I kept shooting and shooting.'

As often happens, real life provided tips never anticipated by regulations or handbooks. Use of the clanking sound of the gun breech closing as an internal signalling device was a characteristic example recorded by Bryukhov: 'When a crew was well coordinated, the driver was so skilled he could hear that a shell was being loaded by the clanking of the breechblock.' T-34 guns were equipped with a semi-automatic means of opening the breechblock. The gun would recoil during a shot and the burnisher would return it to its initial position after taking up energy. Just before the recoil the breechblock lever would run onto a cam on the carriage and the wedge would come down, the pusher lugs thrusting the empty shell case from the breech. The gun-layer would then chamber another shell and it would knock away the breechblock wedge which was holding on the pusher lugs. The heavy unit, resuming its initial position under the pressure of powerful springs, would produce an acute enough sound surpassing the roaring of the engine, the clanking of the tracks and the noise of battle. Having heard the clank of the closing breechblock, the driver was ready for the command ('A short one!') and would immediately choose a flat enough patch of ground for a short stop and an aimed shot.

A target coming into the gunsight crosshairs wasn't always worth shooting at with the main gun. A T-34/76 commander or a T-34/85 gunner would use the coaxial machine-gun on infantrymen caught in the open. The machine-gun installed in the hull bow could only be used effectively in close combat, when an immobilised tank was surrounded by enemy infantry with hand grenades and Molotov cocktails. 'It was a close combat weapon,' said Bryukhov, 'for a situation when a tank was shot up and standing still. The Germans would come closer and then you could mow them down wholesale.' It was practically impossible to shoot from the bow machine gun on the move because its telescopic sight allowed only very poor observation and aiming. 'In essence I had no gunsight at all,' said Kirichenko. 'I had a kind of a hole and nothing could be seen through it.' The bow machine gun was at its most efficient when it was dismounted from its ball and socket support, removed from the tank and used from a bipod, in which capacity it provided the crew with a most effective personal weapon.

The installation of the radio next to the commander in a T-34/85 turret should have turned the machine-gunner/radio operator into the most useless crewman – a virtual passenger – not least because the ammunition allowance for the T-34/85's machine-guns had been reduced by half compared to earlier models, down to thirty-one drums. But the reality of the closing stages of the war, when German infantry were provided with Panzerfausts, increased the expediency of having a bow machine-gunner on board. 'He'd become necessary by the end of the war, to protect us from *faustniks*,' reported Rodkin, meaning infantrymen armed with Panzerfausts. 'It didn't matter that visibility was poor – sometimes he was prompted by the driver. If you want to see, you will.'

The space freed up by shifting the radio into the turret was used to store ammunition. Most of the drums (twenty-one out of thirty-one) for the DT machine-gun in the T-34/85 were placed in the driving compartment next to the bow machine-gunner, who had become the main consumer of machine-gun ammunition.

Generally speaking, the arrival of Panzerfausts had increased the role of the T-34's light arms. Even shooting with pistols out of the opened hatch became common practice. The official issue firearms of tanks' crews were TT pistols, revolvers, and one PPSh sub-machine gun. The sub-machine gun was used by crewmen after leaving the tank and during urban warfare, when the angle of gun and machine-gun elevation was insufficient for them to be used.

As German anti-tank artillery improved, fields of vision became more and more important to a tank's survival. The first T-34s had mirror periscopes for the driver and in the turret. These consisted of a box with mirrors installed above and below at an angle to each other, made not of glass (which might burst from shell shock) but of polished steel. It's not hard to imagine the quality of the image provided by such a periscope. Similar mirrors in periscopes on the turret sides were one of the main means by which a tank commander viewed the battlefield. S. K. Timoshenko's report of 6 September 1940 quoted above required that 'the sight devices for driver and radio operator are to be replaced by more up-to-date ones', but tanks were still only provided with steel mirrors during the first year of the war. Later the mirrors were replaced by prismatic observation devices, in which a glass prism was inserted into the periscope. Nevertheless, the need to improve situational awareness often forced T-34 drivers to operate with open hatches. 'The triplexes [periscopes] of the driver's hatch were completely outrageous,' recalled S. L. Aria. 'They were made of ugly yellow or green organic glass, giving a completely distorted, wavy picture. It was impossible to discern anything through such a triplex, especially in a bunny-hopping tank. That's why we fought with hatches open by a palm's width.' A. V. Maryevski agreed, adding that the driver's triplexes were easily splashed with mud.

In autumn 1942 the report by NII-48 drew the following conclusion after undertaking its analysis of damage to T-34 armour: 'A high percentage of dangerous damage to T-34 tanks from the sides and not from the front [270 out of 432 hits on the hulls of examined tanks were on their sides] may be explained by the poor familiarity of crews with the technical characteristics of the tank's armour protection or the poor visibility out of the tanks as a result of which the crews are unable to spot a gun emplacement and to turn the turret to the position least dangerous in regard to armour-piercing. It is necessary to improve the acquaintance of tank crews with the tactical characteristics of the armouring of their machines and to provide better visibility from them.'

The task of improving visibility was implemented in several stages. The polished steel 'mirrors' were removed from the commander's and loader's observation devices, and the periscopes on the turret shoulders were replaced by slots with glass blocks to provide protection from splinters. This took place during the transition to the 'screw-nut' turret in the autumn of 1942. The new devices enabled crews to organise all-round observation: 'The driver looked from left to right. You, the commander, tried to look around. And the radioman and loader mostly looked right,' recalled Bryukhov. This enabled the crew to spot danger coming from any direction and to fire or manoeuvre accordingly.

It took longest to provide a good means of observation for the tank commander. The task of introducing a commander's cupola on T-34s wasn't accomplished until almost two years after the outbreak of war, commencing only in the summer of 1943 after lengthy experiments to find room for the freed-up tank commander in the 'screw-nut' turret. The commander still functioned as a gunner, but now he could raise his head and have a good look around. The opportunity it provided for all-round observation was the main advantage of the cupola. As A. V. Bodnar recalled: 'The commander's cupola could rotate around, and the commander, while not occupied with firing the gun himself, could see everything, direct fire, and maintain communication with the rest of the crew.' To be more accurate, it wasn't the cupola itself that rotated but its top, fitted with a periscope. Before that, in 1941–42, other than a 'mirror' on the turret shoulder the tank commander had only a fixed periscope, formally called a periscopic gunsight. By turning its vernier this had provided him with a quite limited view of the battlefield. The commander of a ZIS-S-53-armed T-34/85 was exempted from gunner's duties. Apart from his commander's cupola with perimetric slots he also received his own prismatic periscope, which rotated in the hatch and even allowed him to look backward. But Zheleznov remembered not using the commander's cupola: 'I always kept my hatch open, because those who kept it closed burned. They had no time to bail out.'

All the tankmen interviewed admired the gunsights of German tanks. V. P. Bryukhov's recollections are typical: 'We always noted the high quality of the Zeiss gunsight optics. They maintained that high quality till the end of the war. We had nothing like that. The gunsights themselves were more convenient than ours. We had a triangle in the crosshair and hairlines left and right of it. They had corrections for wind, distance, and so on.' In reality there were no major differences in the information provided by German and Soviet telescopic gunsights. The gunlayer saw the crosshair and 'fences' of corrections for angular speed, and both Soviet and German gunsights had corrections for distance, though these were introduced in different ways. The German gunner would turn a pointer on a radially situated scale of distances; every type of shell had its own sector. Soviet tank manufacturers had gone through this stage in the 1930s – the gunsight of the three-turret T-28 tank was of a similar design – but in T-34s the distance was set out by a gunsight wire moving along a vertical scale of distances. Thus there was no functional difference between Soviet and German gunsights – the difference was in the quality of the optics, which deteriorated badly in Soviet gunsights in 1942 due to the evacuation of the Izyum optical glass plant. The slaving of the gunsight to the gun barrel may be placed among the real shortcomings of telescopic gunsights on early models of the T-34. A tankman training his gun vertically had to move up and down to keep his eyes on the gunsight ocular, which moved along with the gun. Later an articulated gunsight typical of the German tanks was introduced.

The deficiencies of the T-34's observation devices required the driver to keep his hatch open, which in turn forced him to sit right behind the levers in the full blast of the icy wind sucked in by the engine fan. Such Spartan conditions were a typical grudge held against Soviet-made combat vehicles. 'The lack of comfort for the crews may be pointed out as a deficiency,' remarked S. L. Aria. 'I crawled into American and British tanks. Their crews operated in more comfortable conditions: the tanks were painted in light colours inside, the seats were semi-rigid with elbow-rests. There was nothing like that in a T-34.' There were no elbow-rests at all on crew seats in T-34 turrets, only on the driver's and radio-operator's seats. But in fairness elbow-rests were characteristic only of American vehicles: turret seats had no elbow-rests in either British or German tanks (except for the Tiger).

But there were real design deficiencies. One of the problems encountered by tank designers in the 1940s was the accumulation of fumes from the guns in the fighting compartment. The breech-block would open after each shot to eject the empty shell, and gases from the gun and the ejected shell flooded into the crew compartment. 'You'd yell: "Load anti-armour, load anti-personnel",' recalled Bryukhov. 'Then you'd turn around and see the loader lying lights-out on the ammo boxes. He'd been poisoned by fumes and lost consciousness. Few could last out a heavy fight to the end.'

Electrically-driven suction fans were used to remove gunpowder fumes and ventilate the battle compartment. The first T-34s inherited one fan in the frontal part of the turret from the BT tank. It was appropriate for a turret with a 45 mm gun, for it was placed just above the gun breechblock, but in the T-34 turret it wasn't above the smoking breechblock but above the gun barrel. In this respect it was of dubious utility. But in 1942, at the peak of shortages of component parts, it lost even this fan, and T-34s left the plants with empty cowls on their turrets. In the course of tank modernisation accompanying the introduction of the 'screw-nut' turret the fan shifted to the rear of the turret, closer to the area where the fumes concentrated. The

T-34/85 model received two fans in the turret rear because its large gun called for intense ventilation of the battle compartment. But the ventilators didn't help during a heavy fight. The problem of protecting crewmen was partially resolved by expelling gunpowder fumes from the barrel by means of compressed air (as in the Panther tank), but this didn't solve the problem of the empty shell, emanating its own poisonous fumes, being ejected into the fighting compartment. Experienced tankmen therefore advised throwing empty shells through the loader's hatch immediately. The problem was only eliminated after the war, when bore evacuators were introduced that sucked the fumes out of the barrel after each shot even before the breechblock opened.

The T-34 tank had, in many respects, a revolutionary design, and like any transitional model it combined innovations with out-dated technology. The introduction of a machine-gunner/radio-operator into the crew was one such compromise. The main task of the crew-man sitting near the bow machine-gun was working on the tank's wireless. On early models of the T-34 the radio was installed on the right-hand side of the driver's section, next to the radio-operator. The need to keep a crewman engaged in tuning and maintenance of the radio was a result of the deficiency of communication systems in the first half of the war. It wasn't due to the need to work a radio key, as the Soviet-made wireless sets installed on T-34s didn't have a telegraph mode and couldn't transmit Morse. The radio-operator had been introduced because tank commanders were simply unable to perform maintenance of the radio on top of their other responsibilities. 'The radio was unreliable,' reported Bryukhov. 'The signaller was a specialist, but the commander wasn't that good at it. Moreover, after hits on the armour the tuning would go off and bulbs would shatter.' The allocation of a specialist crewman to operate the two-way was typical in other armies which fought in the Second World War. For example, the commander of a French Somua S-35 tank combined commanding, loading and gunlaying functions, but had a wireless operator who was exempted even from the duties of a machine-gunner.

In the early stage of the war T-34s were equipped with two-way 71-TK-3 radios, but not all machines had them. This was also true of German tanks, in which usually only the tanks of platoon commanders and higher were provided with radios. According to regulations of February 1941, a company of German light tanks was

supposed to have Fu.5 two-way sets installed in three Panzer II and
five Panzer III tanks, while two Panzer IIs and twelve Panzer IIIs had
only Fu.2 receivers. In a company of medium tanks, five Panzer IVs
and three Panzer IIs had two-way sets whilst two Panzer IIs and nine
Panzer IVs had only receivers. Panzer I tanks had no Fu.5 two-way
sets at all except in special command vehicles. The Red Army had
essentially an analogous concept of 'radio' and 'linear' tanks. The
crews of 'linear' tanks had to operate by watching the manoeuvres of
the unit commander or by responding to orders transmitted via flag
signals. In 'linear' tanks the space intended for the radio was filled
instead by ammunition drums for their DT machine-guns – 77 drums
with 63 rounds each instead of 46 as in 'radio' tanks. As of 1 June
1941 there were 671 'linear' T-34 tanks and 221 'radio' ones.

But the main problem of the T-34 signalling system in 1941–42
was not the quantity of the radios but the quality, the 71-TK-3's
capabilities being quite limited. 'It worked for about 6 kilometre
distance on a march,' reported Kirichenko, and similar opinions were
expressed by other tankmen. 'The 71-TK-3 set was a complicated,
unstable two-way,' said Bodnar. 'It frequently broke down and it was
very hard to fix.' It nevertheless to some extent compensated for
its shortcomings by enabling crewmen to listen to broadcasts from
Moscow.

The radio situation deteriorated seriously during the evacuation of
Soviet radio manufacturing plants between August 1941 and the
middle of 1942, when the production of tank wireless sets practically
ceased. However, when the evacuated plants returned to production
it became normal practice to fit radios in all tanks. The T-34 received
a new set based on the RSI-4 aircraft radio – the 9R set and its
later upgrades, the 9RS and 9RM. The 9R was much more reliable
because of its quartz frequency generators. It was British in origin
and for a long time it was produced using components supplied via
the Lend-Lease scheme. The T-34's radio station was now moved
from the driver's area into the battle compartment, being fitted to the
left side of the turret on T-34/85 tanks, where it could be operated by
the commander, now released from gunlaying duties. Nevertheless,
the concept of 'linear' and 'radio' tanks remained.

Each tank also had an intercom system, but its reliability in early
T-34s was low and the main means of communication between the
commander and his driver were by means of the former placing
his boots on the driver's shoulders. 'The intercom system worked

poorly,' confirmed S. L. Aria. 'That's why signals were sent using the feet, in other words the commander's jackboots on my shoulders. He'd press on my left or right shoulder and I would turn left or right accordingly.' The commander and the loader were able to talk to each other, although more often they communicated with gestures: 'If I poked my fist under the loader's nose he knew he had to load an armour-piercing one,' remembered one commander, 'if an open palm with fingers spread apart, a fragmentation one.'

The TPU-3bis intercom installed in later T-34s worked much better. 'The intercommunication system was mediocre on the T-34/76, and we had to command with jackboots and hands, but on the T-34/85 it was superb,' agreed Zheleznov. The commander therefore began to communicate with the driver via the intercom, not least because he could no longer put his feet on the driver's shoulders as the gunner was positioned between him and the driver's compartment.

Unlike the transmission, the T-34's engine aroused practically no criticism amongst its crews. Burtsev considered it extremely reliable, though conceding that it was best to give it a thorough inspection before setting out on a march. The massive fan installed into the same block as the main friction required caution when driving, since a mistake by the driver might lead to the fan's destruction and a breakdown. The initial period of service of each newly received tank called for adaptation to its own unique specifics: 'Each tank, each tank gun, each engine had its unique peculiarities,' remembered Zheleznov. 'It was impossible to know them in advance and they could only be uncovered in the course of daily service. In the end we turned up at the front in unfamiliar vehicles. The commander didn't know the accuracy of his gun. The driver didn't know what his diesel could do and what it couldn't do. Sure, they'd adjust the guns at the production plants and make 50-kilometre test-runs, but that wasn't enough at all. Obviously, we tried hard to learn more about our machines before combat and took every opportunity to do so.'

Of the entire power plant, only the air-filter had design deficiencies requiring serious revision. The old-type filter installed on T-34s in 1941–42 didn't work very well and impeded the normal functioning of the engine, which led to rapid wear of the V-2 diesel. 'The old air-filters were inefficient, occupied a lot of space in the engine compartment, and had a large turbine,' recalled Bodnar. 'They needed frequent cleaning even when the road hadn't been dusty.' 'If the air-filter was cleaned according to the manufacturer's instructions the engine would work well,' said Rodkin, 'but it was hard to do everything properly during fighting. If the filter didn't clean the air well enough, the oil wasn't replaced on time, the mesh wasn't cleansed, and it let dust through so that the engine got worn out quickly.' These early filters were subsequently replaced by the 'Cyclone', which Bodnar considered 'very good'. These 'Cyclones' enabled a tank to get through a whole operation without an engine breakdown, even when there was no time for maintenance.

The tankmen invariably praised the T-34's duplicated ignition system highly. Apart from a traditional electric starter there were also two ten-litre containers of compressed air, which could be used to start the engine even if the electric starter had become disabled, as used to happen frequently in combat due to shell hits.

The caterpillar tracks were the most frequently repaired part of a T-34, and spare tracks were even taken into combat. 'The caterpillars used to break apart even without bullet or shell hits. When earth stuck between the road wheels, the caterpillar – especially during a turn – strained to such an extent that the pins and tracks themselves couldn't hold out,' A. V. Maryevski remembered. The caterpillars were also a serious give-away, as Rodkin explained: 'A T-34 didn't only roar with its engine, it also clanged with its caterpillars. If a T-34 was approaching you'd hear its pillars clanging first and then the engine. The point is, the jags of the tracks were supposed to fit exactly in between the rollers on the driving-wheel, which clutched them in rotation. But when a pillar had stretched out, and got worn, and the distance between the teeth had increased, the teeth beat on the roller and produced a characteristic sound.' The lack of rubber tyres on the road wheels because of wartime shortages increased the tanks' noisiness. 'Unfortunately we received T-34s from Stalingrad tank producing plant that had no tyres on the road wheels,' said Bodnar. 'They rumbled terribly.'

The road wheels of Stalingrad-produced tanks had internal shock-absorbers instead of tyres. The first road wheels of this type, sometimes called 'steam-engine' wheels, had been produced by the Stalingrad Plant (STZ) well before the really serious stoppages in rubber supply took place, when early frosts in the autumn of 1941 froze the rivers and prevented the arrival of barges loaded with road wheels coming from the Yaroslavl Tyre Plant. The STZ engineers had therefore produced a solid cast road wheel with a small shock-absorbing ring inside it close to the centre. When stoppages in rubber supply began other plants adopted this practice, and from the winter of 1941–42 till the autumn of 1943 most T-34s were produced with running gear consisting of road wheels with internal shock-absorbers. After the autumn of 1943 rubber shortages ended and T-34 production switched back to rubber-tyred road wheels. All T-34/85 tanks were produced with rubber-tyred road wheels. These reduced the tanks' noisiness and provided the crews with a modicum of comfort.

As the war went on the role of the T-34 gradually changed. At the beginning of the conflict the well-armoured T-34 with its imperfect transmission, unable to sustain long marches, proved a good infantry-support tank. But it steadily lost the advantage in armour it had enjoyed at the beginning of hostilities. By the end of 1943 or beginning of 1944 the T-34 had become a relatively easy target for 75 mm tank and anti-tank guns, while hits from the 88 mm guns of Tigers, anti-aircraft guns, and PAK-43 anti-tank guns were invariably lethal. But those elements of its design which hadn't received proper attention before the war, or which there had been no time to correct to an acceptable level, were gradually improved and sometimes even replaced. The power plant and transmission in particular were up-graded until they could perform almost faultlessly, while remaining easy to maintain and simple to operate. All this allowed later T-34s to do things that were unthinkable in the early war period. 'For example,' said Rodkin, 'when we moved from Elgava across eastern Prussia we covered more than 500 kilometres in three days. The T-34 sustained marches like this pretty well.' But in 1941 a 500-kilometre march would have been a practically lethal exercise for a T-34 tank: marching towards Dubno in June 1941, the 8th Mechanised Corps under D. I. Ryabyshev had lost nearly half of its vehicles. A. V. Bodnar, who was in combat in 1941–42, assessed the T-34 in comparison to German tanks in the following words: 'From the point of view of operating them, the German armoured machines were more perfect, they broke down less often. For the Germans, covering 200 kilometres was nothing, but with T-34s something would have been lost, something would have broken down. The technological equipment of their machines was better, the combat gear was worse.'

By the autumn of 1943 the T-34 had become an ideal vehicle for independent tank units assigned to deep breakthroughs and outflanking. It had become the main combat vehicle of Soviet tank armies – the main instrument of offensive operations on a colossal scale. Long advances, with open driver's hatches and often with headlights on, became the typical type of T-34 operation. They would cover hundreds of kilometres, intercepting the lines of retreat of surrounded German armies.

Operations in 1944–45 were essentially a mirror image of the 1941 Blitzkrieg, when the Wehrmacht had reached Moscow and Leningrad, using the tanks inferior to Russian T-34 and KV in terms of armour protection and gun power, but extremely reliable. In the closing stages of the war the T-34/85s in turn carried out outflanking movements and encirclements, while the Tigers and Panthers trying to stop them were disabled by breakdowns and abandoned through lack of fuel. The T-34s now had the means to deal with the German tanks' superior armour – the 85 mm gun – plus reliable two-way radios that enabled them to play a team-game against the German 'cats'.

The T-34s that went into combat during the first days of the war and the T-34s that burst into the streets of Berlin in April 1945 differed significantly, not only externally but also internally. But at the end of the war as well as at its beginning, Soviet tankmen saw in the T-34 a machine they could believe in. Initially their confidence came from its sloping armour that could deflect the enemy's shells, its diesel engine resistant to inflammation, and its all-defeating gun; and as the war drew to a victorious close it was its high speed, reliability, stable communications, and powerful gun which enabled them to stand up for themselves.

CHAPTER 3

'They couldn't penetrate my front armour.'

Aleksandr Vasilievich Bodnar

The war found me in Ulyanovsk Armour Academy, where I had already studied for eighteen months. The commander of the Academy, Hero of the Soviet Union Vladimir Nesterovich Koshuba, former commander of the 35th Light Tank Brigade in the Winter War against Finland, in which he'd lost a leg, climbed onto the rostrum and said, 'My boys, the war has begun. It is going to be very hard and long. Study hard and don't make me send you out prematurely. Study as much as possible. When it's necessary, we'll send for you. There will be enough war for everyone'.

However, for the first couple of weeks we were waiting for the Red Army to stop the invaders and then throw them out of the country. They told us before the war: 'We will destroy the enemy with little bloodshed on his own native soil.' Although this didn't happen and the Germans reached the gates of Moscow, none of us cadets had any doubt that even if Moscow was surrendered the war would go on. We had the Urals, with Siberia behind them, and a huge population!

Why did I go to an armour academy? I should explain that when I was still in secondary school, even we schoolchildren could see that war with Nazi Germany was inevitable. This is why I thought that my future was in the Red Army. Besides that, my uncle was a military man, and in 1939 he told me, 'Sasha, you will finish high school.

I advise you to go to a military college. We cannot avoid war, so it's much better to be a commander in the war – you can do more because you will be better educated'. These words played a part in the making of my decision, and I enrolled in one of the best schools – the Ulyanovsk Armour Academy.

First they trained us to be T-26 or BT platoon leaders, but after KV tanks were adopted and went into production the academy changed the course slightly and started to train us as heavy tank commanders. There were two courses, each of three companies of 100 cadets; in each company were four classes with twenty-five people. Thus 600 people studied simultaneously in the two courses and every year the school had 300 graduates.

The school was provided with a special battalion; it had all the machines that we studied. This battalion was located in camps twenty kilometres from the Volga. We went there in the winter and summer. We drove and fired from the tanks, serviced and repaired them, and so on. They trained us well, and there were a lot of practical classes. The main emphasis was on driving and firing tank weapons. We had both stationary and moving practice targets at our firing range. There was a special narrow-track railway built for them, and a small engine was installed in a dugout to move the targets. We practised firing training in defence, when a tank was in a trench, the distance to the targets was known, and there was a good grid of reference points. In an offensive, the firing was conducted both during short stops and on the move. When we fired from a 'short', the commander shouted at the driver, 'Short!' The driver stopped the tank, and the commander counted to himself, 'twenty-one, twenty-two, twenty-three'. In that time he had to aim the gun and make the shot. Firing on the move was not very effective and was usually aimed in the general vicinity of the target.

We studied the material in great detail. The M-17 engine was very complicated, but we knew it down to the last screw. The gun and machine-gun – we took them all apart and put them back together. The tank was fully understood by the crew.

Radio sets in tanks were rather rare in those days, and radio connections often failed, so they taught us to maintain communications with signal flags. There were a total of twenty commands and one had to know them by heart, but at the front I never saw anyone using this system – tankmen would just run from tank to tank or yell to each other at the top of their lungs. Some tanks even lacked an intercom for communication between crew members! All commands were supposed to be given by voice: 'Driver – forward! Driver – short!', or 'Loader – armour-piercing!' At the front I would more often give orders with gestures: if I shook a fist in front of the loader's nose he knew that I meant an armour-piercing round, an open palm meant a fragmentation round. In general, I was trained well enough to use a BT tank, but the only time I practised in a KV heavy tank took place when they let us drive one in Lenin Square in Ulyanovsk. We drove up to the Lenin monument, put the tank in reverse gear, and drove back again, twice, once in first gear and once in second.

In October 1941, after studying for eighteen months in the Academy instead of two years, I was commissioned as a lieutenant and ended up in Vladimir, where the 20th Tank Brigade was in process of formation. It took us a week to put the brigade together: formation started on 1 October and on 9 October we were already loading onto trains. We were sent to the vicinity of Moscow. Tanks were waiting for us there – in Golitsyno, in Dorokhovo. The brigade went into the Moscow battle with a mixture of very different tanks: I think there were no more than seven KV tanks, no more than twenty T-34s, and the rest were T-60s, BTs and T-26s. So the brigade was fairly weak. I received a KV tank and on 11 October we were already on the Borodino field.

The enemy broke through in the sector of the 32nd Division, and our brigade that was in reserve was deployed and dug in. My tank had only its turret and 76 mm gun sticking out of the ground. In my first battle I burnt two German half-tracks at 500-600 metres distance without any fear, and when the crews bailed out I mowed them down with my MG. My tank received two glancing hits from a Panzer IV's main gun, but of course they didn't penetrate the armour. During the six weeks that followed we were in retreat, fighting back and taking casualties. I managed to survive those battles, but I don't remember much about them.

In December our counter-offensive started and on 21 January 1941 the brigade reached the outskirts of Ruza. The city itself was on a hill on the western bank of the river of the same name, and our bank was gently sloping. The infantry was pinned down by enemy fire and wouldn't advance. In all, we had four KV tanks in the brigade, and the rest were T-26s and BTs. That is to say, I was like a grenadier. Those little tanks didn't play a role, they burned like candles, but the

Germans still didn't have the means to burn KV tanks from the front. So the commander of the division to which the 20th Tank Brigade had been attached said: 'Send a KV tank out onto the ice to cover the infantry.' And the battalion commander said to me: 'Son, you're going to drive on ice.' 'Well,' I said, 'you do know that the tank weighs forty-eight tons and it's 21 January, which means that the ice isn't forty centimetres thick yet and it won't hold?' 'Son, you have to drive on the ice, otherwise the infantry won't stand up. Make sure you don't drive far, so that when you start to sink you'll still have time to jump out.'

My driver was Miroshnikov, a former actor from the Voroshilovo-grad theatre, who was four years older than me (he never called me 'Comrade Lieutenant', but always just said 'well, Lieutenant, come on, Lieutenant'. I considered this normal because I had only just arrived, and he had fought from the western borders and already had the Order of the Red Banner). So I told him: 'Miroshnikov, you just make sure you put the transmission in neutral if we go to the bottom; that way when they pull the tank out it won't drag, it'll roll on its tracks.' 'We know this, Lieutenant, we know.' Then I told the rest of the crew: 'Don't close the upper hatch.'

We drove seven to eight metres and then the tank sank to the bottom. Thank God that we all had enough strength to swim to the shore in our tank overalls, padded jackets, and felt boots. The infantry had already seized the enemy shore, so there was no machine-gun fire from that side. We stripped naked right there on the bank and they wrapped us each in a sheepskin coat and sent us to the grove, gave us a glass of vodka each, and said, 'Sleep!' We slept through the night, and in the morning the commander of the repair brigade woke me up and said, 'Bodnar, let's go to Moscow for some cable to pull out the tank'. By evening we'd returned to Ruza. The sappers hooked up our tank, pulled it out, dried it, replaced the batteries, and three days later I was on the offensive again.

What does this episode prove? Tanks were attached to infantry units. For example, it would be decided that 'this tank company will support the attack of this rifle regiment'. When we came to see a rifle regiment commander, he'd say: 'Oh, tankmen! Great! Now we'll have better times! We won't stand up until you pass us!' This meant that we'd be attacking at the speed of advancing infantry! This would, in turn, cause unnecessary losses. Infantry thought that tanks were their armoured shield. Later in the course of war we learnt how to use tank units for independent missions. Of course, there were still direct infantry support tanks, but there were no longer situations when all the tanks were just supporting infantry.

In April 1942 we approached Gzhatsk, which is today called Gagarin. We took over the defences there and replacements of hardware arrived. We received a lot of T-34 tanks, and the battalion consisted mostly of these. Unfortunately, those that we received were all produced at the Stalingrad tractor plant and their road wheels lacked rubber rims, so that when they moved they rumbled like hell. A lot of T-60s produced by the Gorki plant also came. But KVs were still very scarce because the Leningrad Kirovski Plant stopped supplying them and the Chelyabinsk Plant hadn't yet started producing them. So we could only assemble our KVs from knocked out and damaged tanks. I was appointed the leadership platoon commander in Captain Medvedev's tank battalion. The leadership platoon consisted of the T-34 of the battalion commander and two T-60 tanks. I turned in my KV and moved to a T-34 with my driver Miroshnikov. My former KV drove over a mine during the battles that followed. I know nothing about the fate of its crew.

There were only slight differences between a KV and T-34, so it would take a well-trained tankman a week at most to retrain from one tank to the other. When it was quiet at the front, I'd try out the panoramic sight, work with the main gun, and try my best to drive the new vehicle. It's easy and exciting to learn new equipment when you're young!

In early August our brigade was transferred to the Kalinin front and took part in the offensive from Shakhovskaya station towards Pogoreloe Gorodishe-Rzhev. This was the first attempt to cut off the so-called 'Rzhev balcony'. I remember that the battalion commander, Aleksandr Mikhalovich Medvedev, gathered us company commanders and platoon leaders together and told us: 'The Germans are to be driven all the way to Smolensk, so act decisively. Go forward and complete your missions.' But we didn't advance far. Although the offensive was successful for the first five or six days and we managed to advance by about seventy kilometres, we couldn't defeat a 'summer German' yet.

I participated in the offensive. I was one or one-and-a-half kilometres behind our combat formation and suddenly saw a field dotted with our dead and wounded soldiers. Young guys, with Guards badges, in brand new uniforms. A German machine-gunner in a pillbox had wiped out our soldiers. This was such an inept way of crossing no-man's-land. Our soldiers were ready for anything, but their commanders didn't know how to attack properly. They needed to bring up the mortars, some artillery, to suppress this machine-gun, but no, the commanders urged, 'Onward! Onward!' It was a hot day. I remember that a nurse ran across the field and cried, 'Oh, kind people! Help me! Help me get them into the shade!' I helped her drag the wounded over. The majority were in a state of shock, that is to say unconscious, so it was hard to tell who was wounded and who was already dead. It was a very depressing sight. After that I never saw such inept command again, that let one German machine-gun wipe out an entire field full of people. Such things only happened during the first, defensive period of the war, when we still didn't know how to fight properly. But we learned to fight. Like Peter the Great learned from the Swedes, so we learned to fight from the Germans, right up until Stalingrad. And after Stalingrad we didn't need to learn from them any more: we could fight for ourselves.

I remember how much equipment the Germans abandoned as we advanced: supporting vehicles, repair shops. We stopped at this vehicle and there was a white towel for servicing it. I'd have been happy to use such a towel to wipe my nose, but they had boxes of them, just to clean and repair things. I thought, 'Yeah, you sure live well, guys!' Then I came across a BMW motorcycle. I'd never seen one like that and I didn't know how to ride a motorcycle at all. When I sat down on it, I didn't know how to shift the gears because I didn't know where the clutch was. And when I grabbed the handle of the clutch it lurched away. I thought, 'OK, so long as it goes. I'll simply adjust the speed using the gas'. My tank commander was driving in the T-60 tank, and I rode the motorcycle behind him. I rode like that until the evening, before I wound up back with the brigade and the counter-intelligence officer said: 'You need to fight, so I'm taking the motorcycle from you.'

On 7 August we reached Klivcy village. By that time we had three tanks left in the battalion: the *tridtsatchetverkas* [T-34s] of the battalion commander and Lieutenant Dolgushin, my friend and classmate from Ulyanovsk Academy, and one T-60. The rest were destroyed or damaged. Our losses were very heavy, and we mostly suffered them from German AT artillery, as the Germans didn't deploy their tanks en masse. However, when I was catching up with the battalion in a T-60, I saw eight Panzer II and Panzer III

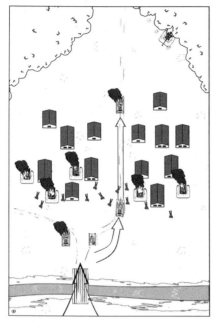

Battle near Klivcy village.

tanks knocked out by our AT-rifle teams. It wasn't really a typical experience for the Germans, who could rarely be ambushed so efficiently: but on this occasion the tanks were standing in line in an open field with intervals of fifty metres.

There was a law during the war: a brigade received a battle mission and tried to complete it until its last tank was knocked out, and only when its last tank burnt would the brigade disengage and be sent to the rear to get new tanks. The battalion commander called for me and told me: 'Son, I have no battalion to command, I will not go into this battle. This is your destiny. You have two *tridtsatchetverkas* – my tank and Dolgushin's – and a T-60. Try to break into the village at night and hold out. Infantry should arrive in the morning.' That was the mission. There was a small river in front of us and a bridge across it. The Germans would normally booby-trap bridges, but there was such a swamp on the banks of the river that I knew we'd definitely get stuck if we went that way and fail in our mission. So I decided to take a risk and let the T-60 drive across the bridge, possibly sending the tank and its crew to their deaths. A miracle happened – the bridge wasn't booby-trapped, and we made it to the other bank.

We approached the village. The Germans opened up from guns and MGs, and we responded with MG fire. It was growing dark and I had to peep out of the hatch – I couldn't see a damn thing (during an assault I wouldn't lock the hatch but instead tied it up with my belt, one end attached to the hatch's lock and the other to a hook that held the ammo in the turret, just in case my arms were wounded, so that I could still open my hatch by hitting it with my head).

I saw Dolgushin's tank catch fire, and thought, 'Why aren't you bailing out? Why aren't you bailing out?' Then I saw them bail out and I thought 'Thank God!' I wasn't even thinking about myself.

I was left with one T-60 and one T-34 in the outskirts of the village. The night was quiet. In the morning – early morning, because it was still chilly, six o'clock or something – the Germans mounted a counter-attack. For the first and last time I saw how the dense line of German infantry advanced, clothed for the night in overcoats, with automatic weapons and carbines. I saw their faces – hairy and, as I thought, drunk. I kept mowing them down with my machine-gun and shreds of their overcoats flew out from their backs, and then they just fell. It seemed a lot like a firing squad execution ...

I did it. I held out. I destroyed five dug-in German light tanks. They could do nothing against me, as I was in a *tridtsatchetverka*, and they couldn't penetrate my front armour.

The battle was over. Our infantry pulled up on the scene. After midday there was an echoing knock at the bottom of the tank and a soldier said, 'Lieutenant Bodnar. A note for you from the battalion commander'. I said, 'Pass it through the bottom hatch'. The message read: 'Son, at five o'clock in the evening Katyushas [rocket launchers] will fire. As soon as they fire, try to break through with the infantry to the opposite end of Klivcy.' That was the whole order. Everything was clear: there were no separation lines from neighbouring detachments, no reference points, just: 'Son, try to break through to the other end.' And so I gave orders to get ready.

And off we dashed. I saw a clearing bathed in sunlight at the other end of the village and had only one wish – to get to that clearing. If it was not defended, that would mean the village was mine, and I wouldn't advance further – I would have carried out my mission and stayed alive. As soon as I thought that, I saw through the periscope a German anti-tank gun! A round hit the side of my tank! The driver cried, 'Commander! They killed radio operator Tarasov!' I bent down to see Tarasov – he was all black, the round had gone right through him. There was another bang. The tank stalled and caught fire! We had to save ourselves, because the tank was burning. I threw back the hatch, yelled 'Bail out!' to the other two crewmen, and jumped out into a potato field. Bullets whistled around.

I had been wounded, and blood gushed from my left leg. The driver crawled over and said, 'Lieutenant, give me your revolver and I will protect both you and me'. 'And where is yours?' 'Well, it got accidentally unhooked and remained in the tank.' But I knew he always took it off and laid it on the seat because it impeded his work with the levers, and so this time fate punished him. 'No,' I said,

'I can't do that because I'm wounded, and if anything happened I wouldn't have anything to kill myself with, because I'm not going to give myself up as a prisoner, to be tortured. And why did the tank stall?' The driver told me that before the second hit the batteries, which send the current to the starter, were damaged. 'So why didn't you try to start it with compressed air?' 'I forgot,' he said. While we lay there, the tank stopped burning. I lay there and kept saying, 'Why aren't you burning, why aren't you burning?' After all, if it didn't burn I was facing a penal battalion, because I only had the right to leave the tank under two circumstances: if it caught fire or if its armament was out of order. But now the gun was fine and the tank had stopped burning. It turned out that the tank itself wasn't burning, but the vapours inside it were. And once the vapours all burned out, and the oil burned out on the bottom as well, the tank had stopped burning.

I lay there, thinking about my responsibility for the abandoned tank, and what would become of me if I survived. So I told the driver, 'Crawl over there. You alone can crawl over there. The Germans think that we're all gone, so crawl over there and try to start the tank'. I wanted to live so badly! 'Then,' I said, 'drive over us and try to get us in through the bottom hatch.' Then I'd thought that it was possible, because I really wanted to live, but now I understand that it was impossible. What kind of a driver, under enemy fire, would drive over us, open the bottom hatch, and pick up me, wounded, as well as Slepov, the loader? It's impossible.

The driver jumped into the tank. The tank let out a roar, turned like a dog chasing its tail, and drove back to our lines. Now I can see that he did the right thing. Otherwise, if he'd tried to pick us up we'd all have been killed. And so he went back to our lines and saved the tank. But back then ... Incidentally, I later read an article about this battle in *Komsomolskaya Pravda* newspaper. It said there: 'Seven times the Germans set fire to the tank and seven times the driver put it out.' Well, this, of course, was all a lie, written by some battalion *Komsomol* secretary who'd never seen action.

Slepov and I remained among the potatoes. Towards evening the shooting died down, and we began to crawl. We found one of our dugouts from 1941 – no Germans were there. We crawled into it and snuggled up next to the back wall. I said to Slepov, 'Bandage me above the knee,' he took his belt off and tied it on my leg, but the blood had really stopped by that time. Then we heard Germans. They'd followed our tracks – we'd trampled some potatoes, after all.

One of them gave orders to another to go into the dugout, but the latter refused. Instead they began to spray the bunker's breastwork with automatic weapons. The ground came down on my head, but the bullets didn't come through. Thank God they didn't throw a hand grenade in. Slepov gestured for me to move aside, but I waved my hand – it's okay, they weren't penetrating. I wanted to sleep very badly because I had lost a lot of blood. I had seven cartridges in my revolver, a '38 issue. Every second one would be a misfire, so I figured to fire three bullets at the Germans who would crawl inside, and save the fourth one for myself. But the important thing was to stay awake long enough to shoot myself, because if I fell asleep the Germans would wake me up by cutting stars into my back. So I picked up cold soil and pressed it against my forehead and my cheeks so I didn't fall asleep.

And so I lay there unscrewing the insignia from my collar tabs, so that if I did get taken prisoner they would take me for a private and torture me less, and I thought, 'Lord, save me! If you do, I'll always believe in you'. And that is how it happened. And even to this day, I believe . . .

At that very moment I heard a salvo of Katyushas. The Germans were hit. They yelled 'Vai, Vai, Vai' and ran – they now had other things to worry about besides us. I could hear them dragging one of their wounded away, and another German crept backwards into our dugout and . . . fell asleep! It was like a fantasy. The eighth day of the offensive was on, and the Germans were already drunk and exhausted. I gestured to Slepov to go and stab him with a knife. And he gestured back that he didn't know how to do it with a knife. Then I pointed at Slepov's temple, meaning that I'd execute him if he didn't follow my orders. He understood, crawled away, took the knife. I only heard the German wheeze once, but Slepov kept cutting him for a while.

When it got dark, we crept out and decided to try and make it to our lines. Night, stars, dew. Slepov wasn't wounded, I was, but we had to crawl towards our men and again I gave an impossible order: 'Crawl,' I said, 'alone, because you can run if our guys open fire on you, and you can crawl up, and tell them to send an infantryman to follow your tracks to get me.' Who'd really have believed that some lieutenant was lying there? And I couldn't even be sure that Slepov would get there . . . But I really wanted to live. He went, and I crawled towards a house in the hopes that by the time the night passed I might reach our lines. I reached the house and heard German speech, a drunken German uproar. A woman was sitting near the house and crying. I pointed my revolver at her and said, 'Crawl to me'. 'Why are you here?' she said. 'The Germans are in my house; my children are hiding in the forest. What am I to do with you?' 'Crawl,' I said, 'or I'll kill you.' She was somewhere around my mother's age – thirty-seven or thirty-eight. She crawled and I embraced her. 'Crawl, I say, to our army.' She knew where to crawl and by morning we reached our forward positions and heard Russian speech.

'Well, are you going to stay or crawl back?' I asked the woman. 'I'm going back, my kids are there.' And I still regret that I didn't tell her thank you that day. She crawled away, and I said, 'Guys, I'm a wounded lieutenant, and I was in the tank that fought alongside you this morning'. I heard an old voice: 'Sure, you're all wounded crawling about. German spies . . .' 'I'm a lieutenant, I was with you in the tank.' Then I heard a young voice, 'Guys, come on. He is that lieutenant, he was there . . .' I heard someone say, 'Get up and raise your hands!' 'I can't stand up, my leg is wounded.' Then I heard them saying to the young guy, 'Crawl to him. If anything happens, fire a burst'. He crawled over to me and pulled me back, and I said, 'Are there any tanks left?' 'Yes, there's one small one there.' 'Get me their commander.' The commander came running. 'Comrade Lieutenant, Comrade Lieutenant.' 'Take me to our jumping off position,' I said. Well, that made him happy because he could go to the rear, away from the war, and rescue a lieutenant on top of that. In general it was good for both him and me. They took me to the jumping off position, from where I'd started out yesterday, and the battalion commander said to me, 'Son, I knew that it would turn out this way, but it turned out better than I thought. And now you're through with fighting, thank God'.

They took me into a dugout. Brigade commander Konstantinov's wife said, 'Cut open his boot and overalls'. They did. She said, 'Oh, you're all messed up. A glass of vodka!' They gave me a glass of vodka and they operated, put on a bandage, and the next day carried me to the Shakhovskaia station. They carried me on a stretcher: a small soldier in front, and an old, tall one behind. I said, 'At least switch places if anything happens'. 'That's OK, Lieutenant, we'll get you there.' But when the Junkers dive-bombers started strafing Pogoreloe Gorodishe and Shakhovskaia they dropped me in the middle of the road, and dived into a roadside ditch. Afterwards I asked them, 'Why didn't you get me into the ditch as well? Wasn't it necessary?' 'Well, it just happened . . .' That's life. They took me and laid me in the grass. I remember they gave me such great, rich borsch soup. And then strong, hearty girls started to carry us wounded soldiers on stretchers into a train going towards Moscow. They shouted, 'Hurry, before the German bombers get to Moscow', because at night they flew over the city. When they had loaded us up, we started off and I heard them start to sing songs in the next car. I asked an old soldier, 'What is that?' 'Oh, it's the girls that loaded us up.' 'And why are they going to Moscow?' 'To give birth.' 'What do you mean, to give birth?' 'Well, in October, when they took them into the Army, their mothers said, "Go and get pregnant quickly and return home".' And so that's how it worked out. That's the law of life, and I don't condemn them.

For this battle I received the Order of the Red Star. I was put in the hospital at Bobylskaia station. A friend said, 'Sashka! They wrote about you in *Komsomolskaya Pravda*!' I read: 'The tank under the command of Lieutenant Bodnar burst into the village first . . .' It must have been fate that it was in that very issue when I was in hospital, and that my friend saw it. But I don't know what happened to my driver and loader. I spent nine months in different hospitals. The wound was bad and didn't heal easily.

In mid-1943 I was finally discharged from hospital, with a walking stick, as unfit for front-line service. So they sent me to a tank training regiment located in the town of Upper Ufalei. I was commissioned as a training company commander and for the rest of the war I trained T-34 drivers for the front, because I knew what a driver had to be, and how to train them.

Being over eighty years old, I now feel sorry that we treated each other in such a barbaric manner in the war. They dragged our dead from the roads into swamps with prime movers, and we did the same. We have very few German war cemeteries – a few in Moscow and a few in Stalingrad. When I was in Germany at the end of the war, in Lipeschenzdorf, I saw a cemetery of Russian POWs from the First World War. I thought: 'Back then the Germans were more civilised. They understood that dead POWs should be buried properly.' But the Germans we fought in the Second World War, intoxicated by Nazi ideals, were quite different. We weren't so civilised either – we would come to their field cemeteries, destroy the grave crosses and move on.

CHAPTER 4

'I see that you're a real tankman.'

Semen Lvovich Aria

When the war broke out I was training in the Novosibirsk Military Transport Engineers. During the autumn of 1941 our entire course was sent to the front at Moscow. I didn't reach the front, however, as our train was destroyed in an air raid and I ended up in a hospital with severe shell-shock.

After recovery I was sent to 19th Training Tank Regiment in Nizhniy Tagil. The regiment consisted of battalions that each trained men for specific roles in a tank crew: one battalion trained tank commanders, another trained turret men [loaders], and so on. I ended up in the battalion that was training drivers. They taught us to drive, how to maintain communication with the tank commander, and about the design and maintenance of tank engines. It was very hard to start a tank's engine in wintertime. You had to warm the engine up two hours before departure – you had to put a tray sized a bit less than a tank under the vehicle, pour diesel fuel on it, and set it on fire. After an hour-and-a-half the tank – which would be completely covered with smut, just like the crew – could be started. They took us to a firing range where they made us negotiate obstacles and change damaged track links. Repairing a track was an extremely challenging operation.

A crew was supposed to be interchangeable, but it wasn't so in reality – our training was too short. For example, I only fired a few rounds from the main gun. During our two or three months of training we also took part in the assembly of tanks on the main conveyer of the factory.

What can I say about the *tridtsatchetverka*? In principle, it was a successful design, a rather reliable vehicle. But thinking about flaws, I should mention that the intercom worked in the worst manner. This is why communication was carried out by means of the commander's feet: his boots were on my shoulders, and he pressed my left or right shoulder depending on where he wanted me to drive the tank; a tap on my head meant to stop. When I worked as a lawyer after the war, the director of our consultancy was retired Colonel Krapivin, Hero of the Soviet Union, a tank regiment commander during the war. When I told him how we fought the enemy with commanders' boots, he said: 'Oh! Now I see that you're a real tankman.'

Besides that, the triplex on the driver's hatch was beyond complaint! These were made from a poor quality yellow or greenish glass that produced a twisted and wavy image. It was impossible to see anything through this triplex, especially when driving cross-country. This is why drivers fought the war with half-open hatches. In general, crew comfort in a T-34 was minimal. I saw the insides of American and British tanks, where the crew was in far more comfortable conditions. Their tanks were painted light colours inside, and had soft seats with arms. However, these Western tanks had petrol engines and burnt like torches. Besides that, they had a narrow wheelbase and would easily capsize on the slopes of hills.

After training the crews were formed, loaded onto a train together with T-34 tanks, and sent to the front through Central Asia. They ferried us across the Caspian Sea from Krasnovodsk to the Caucasus. The tarpaulin got blown off our tank in the process. I should add that it was very hard to live in a tank without a tarpaulin. It was essential: we used it as a blanket when we went to sleep and as a table when we ate, and we had to cover the tank with it during transportation by railway, otherwise it would get filled with water. The tanks we had were produced in wartime: the upper hatch didn't have any rubber inserts, while the driver's hatch had some rubber inserts but they could not hold water. So that's why it was bad not to have a tarpaulin. So I stole a sail from a warehouse to replace it.

We reached the Northern Caucasus, where we took part in the battles for Mozdok as part of the 2nd Tank Brigade. Then we were transferred to the 225th Tank Regiment, which was fighting in the Mineralnye Vody and Kuban areas. This was where I had an incident that cost me a posting to a penal company. During the winter of 1942–43 our brigade suffered heavy casualties in the battles for Mozdok. On a gloomy winter's day our column entered Levokumskayya Cossack settlement after a long march. The retreating Germans blew up the bridge over the Kuma River behind them, and in its place there was a temporary log crossing constructed by our engineers out of whatever they could find. After inspecting it with great suspicion, our battalion commander asked the engineers' commander: 'Will a tank be able to cross it? A 25-ton tank?' 'Have no doubt!' the engineer replied. 'It's Guards' unit work! But do it one tank at a time.'

The first tank crept slowly and carefully over the unstable structure. The second one set out just as carefully but deviated slightly from the central axis, made it only to the middle of the crossing, and crashed into the rushing waters together with the bridge, leaving only its driving wheel above the surface. Its crew was fished out of the ice-cold water, but not without some difficulties.

After an energetic back-and-forth cursing match with the engineers, and threats of execution, the battalion commander found an old local man who promised to show us a ford. After putting the Grandpa into his Willys jeep, and having explained to me about my responsibilities as the lead driver, the battalion commander ordered us to follow him. 'Don't drive too fast, but don't fall behind either,' he said. 'If anything is wrong, I'll signal with my flashlight.'

And so we set out on the unpaved roads along the river. Meanwhile, complete darkness came down. We didn't have headlights after the very first battle, and even if we'd had them we still couldn't use them because of the enemy's air force. That's why I simply followed the bouncing blue light of the commander's jeep in the darkness, slightly diluted by the treacherous moonlight from behind the clouds, without being able to see the road. The column followed me. We drove for about ten kilometres in this way.

As we found out later, the battalion commander simply didn't notice an insignificant little bridge over a ravine and drove across it without stopping or signalling. But when our tank attempted to cross it at high speed it collapsed at once. The tank hit the ravine's opposite slope with its front armour, turned onto its back, and slid to the bottom.

When I regained my senses after the initial shock, I found myself buried under a pile of 76 mm rounds that had fallen out of their cases, mixed with machine-gun magazines, tools, and all sorts of belongings that we had in our tank. Acid from capsized batteries was pouring down in thin trickles. Everything was illuminated by the ominous green signal lamps of their discharge. I was OK, apart from some bruises. My first thought was that I'd killed my crew, because the crew usually didn't stay inside the tank during marches, but sat on top of the gearbox – a warm spot behind the turret – covered with the tarpaulin. However, it turned out that all of them were alive – they'd been thrown forward to the ground when the tank turned over. I heard my commander, Lieutenant Kuts, yelling from outside: 'Aria! Are you alive?' Then I crawled out through the bottom hatch. The battalion commander appeared immediately, like a devil out of a box. He expressed his opinion of me in the worst Russian obscenities and said: 'I'm leaving one vehicle to pull you out. You are to haul your tank up, put everything in order, and follow us by morning. If you don't manage it, I'll execute you!'

We dug a way out of the ravine overnight, and used the tow tank to turn ours first onto its side, and then onto its tracks, with its inner parts rumbling threateningly every time it turned over. Then we unloaded all the metal debris from inside and I started the engine with an emergency starter, using compressed air.

We had one hour left before dawn for sleep and snacks. Moving on at dawn, we reached the ford, crossed the river, caught up with our column by midday, and reported in to the battalion commander. All four of us were exhausted to the limit, but I was worst of all. I kept falling asleep in my driver's seat and in my dreams I saw a tank in front of me in the column. That was dangerous. The lieutenant, seeing my condition, had remained inside with me, cheering me and kicking me in the back from his seat in the turret from time to time. There was no one to replace me. The commander excused himself from driving, citing minimal driving practice in training, while the gunner, Kolia Rylin, and the radio operator, Vereschagin, had not been taught driving at all. So I went on suffering alone at the control levers.

During the very first break, after eating porridge with Lend-Lease canned meat, we found an oil leak in the engine – a consequence of the fall into the ravine. We decided that the leak was insignificant and moved on after tightly wrapping the crack with several layers of insulating tape and putting wire on top of that.

After another five kilometres' march we halted for a short break, and after that our engine wouldn't start. We called for the company's technical officer. He crawled inside for a short while, tried to turn the turbine with a crowbar, and pronounced: 'Only a moron could expect that such a tourniquet would hold the oil leak! It all leaked out! Your engine is dead, it's seized.' 'What are we going to do?' our lieutenant asked. 'The brigade commander will decide what you're going to do. Your tank cannot be repaired in the field, the engine needs to be replaced. We need a repair facility for that. Wait here for now, I'll report it. We'll send something to tow you tomorrow.' The column left and we remained alone. A blizzard was whirling across the empty, snow-covered steppe. There wasn't a tree, nor a bush, only a couple of low sheds far from the road.

It was impossible to sit inside the ice-cold tank. We tried to construct something like a cabin by throwing our tarpaulin over the gun. We lit a bucket with diesel fuel inside to provide the illusion of warmth. Somehow we managed to eat. A couple of hours later we couldn't be recognised from soot and smut.

'So,' the lieutenant summarised, 'we can just freeze to death here, or go spend the night there.' He waved his hand towards the sheds in the distance. 'They have a chimney there, so there's a stove too. There's probably also some straw too. We'll leave a guard at the tank. You need to get some sleep,' he nodded at me, 'that's why you'll be on watch first for an hour-and-a-half. Then I'll send someone to replace you, and you'll be able to rest all night long.'

So I remained with the tank with a light machine-gun on the shoulder. The time dragged by agonisingly in the dark. I walked back and forth. Back and forth. I couldn't lean against the tank – my eyes would just close. But the replacement didn't arrive after an hour-and-a-half; no one was to be seen after two hours. Completely exhausted, apparently, they slept like logs. I fired a burst from the machine-gun – no effect. I had to do something, otherwise I would simply freeze to death. I could no longer stand on my feet.

I locked the tank and started stumbling across the snow-covered steppe towards the sheds. I woke up the lieutenant, who was sleeping on the straw, with difficulty, and told him about how wrong it was to do things like that. Rylin, still half asleep and unable to understand what was going on, was raised from his warm bed and sent outside with the machine-gun. I collapsed into his place without undressing and fell asleep immediately.

Rylin stood in the cold wind for a while – and broke his oath of service . . .

We came out of the shed at dawn, cursing Vereschagin, who'd slept through his turn. We looked at the road – and our tank was gone. It wasn't there. It had been stolen. Rylin was nowhere to be seen either. We found him in the neighbouring shed, sleeping peacefully while hugging the machine-gun. When we explained the situation to him he ran outside as if bitten to check it out. After seeing it for himself, he informed us that, as it turned out, after he'd got to the road in the night he'd found the tank was missing and had returned and gone to sleep. In response to the natural question of why he hadn't woken us and why he had gone to sleep in a different shed, he explained that he hadn't wanted to disturb us ...

This version of events, despite its utter absurdity, completely relieved him of guilt. That's why he stood his ground firmly and lied unabashedly, looking all three of us in the eye. Since we had nothing except logic to refute this nonsense I, as a sentry that had abandoned his post, was the next scapegoat. Of course, Lieutenant Kuts as the commander was also made responsible for everything.

So we started ambling along the wide Kuban road, over the frozen wheel ruts, with a feeling of doom and without our belongings. After walking for about ten kilometres in complete silence, we reached the outskirts of a large Cossack village, where we found the tracks of our ill-fated tank. It turned out that the fast repair team arrived at night and found the tank unguarded. They unlocked it with their own key and then towed it away. Of course, they saw the field camp and realised where the crew was, but decided to have a little joke ...

This joke, combined with the stubborn lies of our comrade-in-arms Rylin, cost us dearly. The brigade commander ordered Lieutenant Kuts and me to be court-martialled, and this was done after a short investigation.

That's how I ended up in a penal company. However, before that I had to spend time in a cell full of doomed men, and then a long period wandering in Kuban. Lieutenant Kuts, another sentenced man and I had one set of documents for the three of us, but the Lieutenant and the other man ditched me and escaped, and I was left alone and without any papers. All the events that followed were like a wild adventure, with an extremely disturbing end in sight. After long wanderings I finally found this penal company somewhere at Taganrog. There were about 150 losers like me in the company. We were armed only with rifles. We didn't have machine-guns or SMGs. All the officers were regular line officers, not *shtrafniks*, while all the rank and file and NCOs were *shtrafniks*. You could escape from there alive only if you were wounded or if you were recommended by your commanding officer for cancellation of your sentence.

I took part in a reconnaissance in force. An assault is the hardest of all tests. You know that you can get hit, but you have to go forward towards the enemy firing at you. You are lying on the ground and see that a tracer burst from an MG is getting lower and closer to you, knowing it might reach the level of your body and cut you in half. To be short, war is war, there is nothing more I can say. It was an 'all or nothing' situation, so I diligently tried to fulfil battle missions. After that battle I was recommended for cancellation of my sentence and sent to a regular army unit, and they sent me to the 2nd Reserve Army Regiment in Azov. There they put me into a team of cadets to be sent to an armour academy for tank commander training. But I'd already seen what it was like to be a tank commander, so I deserted from there. I just ran away. What does it mean to be a tank commander? It's the worst of all! It means that you're a regular soldier but at the same time you're held responsible for everything and everyone. I didn't want to become a commissioned officer at all! So when 'merchants' came to the Reserve Army Regiment to pick up replacements for some artillery unit, I just threw my bag into the truck and drove away. In those days they could simply execute me for such a trick, but somehow it didn't happen. When we reached the front line, it turned out that the artillery unit was a Katyusha rocket regiment. It was a real stroke of luck! We received good food, excellent uniforms, and losses were much lower. I was very happy to end up in such a privileged unit. For some time I served as a motorcycle driver, and a runner at the regiment HQ. Because they had a motorcycle but didn't have anyone to ride it the officers didn't start any investigation about me. A couple of months later the motorcycle was destroyed by the Germans on the move, but it wasn't me riding it. After that I was sent to a Katyusha battalion as a forward observer.

What did we fear the most at the front? Death. Every minute and every hour death was near. You could be sitting drinking tea in peace and quiet and be killed by a random artillery round. It's impossible to get used to this. It doesn't mean that everyone was scared all the time, waiting for death. Death just came flying or it didn't come. It was scary to be hit by a massive air raid. The feeling was that every bomb was coming straight at your head. It was awful! I remember we had a soldier called Nekrasov – he almost became a mental case. When one air raid was over, we couldn't find him anywhere. We finally found him in some trench, but he refused to get out! He had such a fear in his eyes!

Some men wore talismans, crosses that were supposed to help them survive. There were men who had a gift of foresight of deadly danger. For example, we had a big Georgian guy in our unit, Kondrat Khubulava. He saved me from death two times, and of course he saved himself too. The first case was when we were sent to establish communications with a rifle regiment. We were going through a trench with him, and all of a sudden he told me: 'We're not going any further.' I asked: 'Why?' 'We won't go further, just stand here for a while!' We stopped and several seconds later an artillery round hit the trench in front of us! I mean, it would have killed us! The second time we were standing in a ruined house during an air raid. He told me: 'Let's get out of here and move to another corner.' We moved to another corner and the place that we had just left took a direct hit from a bomb. Such were the weird incidents. That sixth sense – I didn't have it.

Many years after the war I tried to discover the fate of the other members of my crew, but the Central Archive of the Ministry of Defence didn't have any information about them.

CHAPTER 5

'My tank became just another victim.'

Yuri Maksovich Polyanovski

I was in the eighth grade when a school for young motorists was opened at the Pioneer Palace. I'd studied there in the evenings after school for two years, learning to become a driver. On 21 June 1941 I received a temporary driver's license, since I was only seventeen at the time. The war began the next day.

My father, who was a rather well-known writer, left for the front as a volunteer. I remained behind, with the task of evacuating the children of our friends to Ioshkar-Ola, or 'Horrible Hole', as it was called (it rhymes in Russian) – although I did put forward the condition that if I took care of that, he'd take me to the front as well. Soon after we evacuated I received a notice to present myself in the 52nd Army of the Volkhov Front. When I arrived I showed my driver school certificate of completion and was accepted as a 1.5-ton truck driver. Soon afterwards my father was transferred to the political department of the 1st Guards Division, which was near Voronezh at that time.

They wouldn't let me stay in the 52nd Army without my father and ended up sending me to the Pushkino Automotive School. By coincidence, just as I arrived there it was being reformed into a tank school. I stayed for a year, and when a threatening situation developed at Stalingrad we were all allowed to graduate. That was how, at just $17\frac{1}{2}$ years of age, I became a junior lieutenant and a T-34 tank commander. I received my first tank at the Nizhniy Tagil factory, but when I arrived with it at a tank regiment at the front it was taken away from me, and I was sent back to the factory. The second time I was sent out with a tank it was to Cheliabinsk.

Every tank factory had reserve tank regiments attached to it, where all sorts of people were sent – from tank schools, from hospitals, from the front. Crews were formed out of this common melting pot. In my second crew the loader was two years older than my father. He was an old worker from Leningrad, who was very good at stealing chickens. The newly formed crews practised combat as part of a platoon or a company by walking about without tanks. Afterwards they practised driving the tanks and firing at the range.

We received our tanks, embarked on a train, and set out for the front. We unloaded near Kharkov in August 1943, received ammo and fuel, and went into battle as a part of the 2nd Battalion, 24th Brigade, 5th Mechanised Corps, 5th Guards Tank Army.

After capturing Kharkov, we were transferred to the Poltava sector. There, near the village of Korotych, I found myself in trouble for the first time. Our mission was to cut the Kharkov-Poltava road. There was a railway we had to cross on our way there. This ran along a high embankment parallel to the road, but about ten kilometres to the north of it. That embankment could not be bypassed, and our entire battalion was concentrated in front of the only crossing. As soon as a tank tried to drive through the crossing – bang, it was finished. My tank became just another victim. I had been warned not to drive on the road beyond the crossing since it had been mined, so after rushing through the crossing I went to the left. We'd managed to go only a short distance when the Germans put a round into my tank's engine. Smoke filled the crew compartment, the tank halted, and we had to bail out – otherwise we'd all have been killed. I gave the order: 'Abandon vehicle through the top hatch.' We jumped out and crawled back to our lines. The radio operator decided not to go through the top hatch. Instead, he decided to get out from the bottom. Later, when we got the tank back, it turned out that he was killed.

We reached our battalion, where a counter-intelligence officer approached me: 'Did the tank burn or not?' 'Why do you care?' 'We have to send an evacuation vehicle during the night to pull it out. If it burned, then we don't need to get it back. If it didn't, then you have to be court-martialled for abandoning your vehicle. What are we going to do?' I said, 'Tonight I'll go myself to see what happened to it'. That night we went, praying to God that the tank was burned, that the Germans had finished it. They had.

There was one Gorky native in our unit, Sasha Beredin. A young, pretty wife with an infant had seen him off to the front. He got lucky – he was assigned to a command tank with two radios, which became the tank of our brigade commander, and the brigade commander's position was a little behind the lines, from where he'd conduct the battle by using his tank as a command post. But so many tanks were destroyed at that railway crossing that there was practically no one else to send. So the brigade commander sent his own tank. I told Sasha: 'Look, don't even think about driving on the road, you'll get blown up even if it looks empty. Better try going right at first – I already tried going to the left and got destroyed.' He went, but apparently as soon as he saw an open road in front of him, he just floored it ... but he didn't get far. The tank ran over a mine and exploded. We went searching for his body after the battle – it was lying there all mangled.

I ended up in the battalion reserve without a tank: only a platoon remained of the entire battalion, and this was deployed in an ambush, apparently waiting for a German counter-attack. At that time the commander of one of the remaining tanks went out to relieve himself, and the fragments of a mortar shell that exploded nearby wounded him in the backside. He was sent to the hospital and I was ordered to take his place as tank commander. I got onto the tank, knocked, and they opened the hatch: 'I'm your new commander,' I said.

Soon all our tanks still fit for combat were transferred to the 29th Brigade, which was deployed about five kilometres away. I'll remember the little village of Barminvody for the rest of my life. We passed it on our way to the brigade. There was a medical battalion there – its girls were playing the piano, dancing ... We stopped, got out, danced a little. You know, as the song goes: 'Even though we haven't been introduced ...'

While we were still on our way to the 29th Brigade it was routed. Near the town of Valki some infantry stopped us – they had powerful artillery, but no tanks. We weren't obligated to work with them, but they said: 'Please stay, we'll even get some alcohol for you.' Basically, they outwitted us. After all, three tanks wouldn't have made a difference: the Germans had both Tiger tanks, camouflaged in groves, and artillery.

At dawn on 2 September our three tanks were sent out to conduct a reconnaissance in force – that's the military term for it, but in reality to get killed. It was a good thing that before that I forbade my men to drink, even though the infantrymen came through on their bargain and supplied us with alcohol (there was one occasion in our battalion when a crew, while inebriated, had suffocated inside their tank after it was knocked out and started burning). So we went. The Germans opened fire, and we fired back, no one knew at what. I had to look into the periscope and bend towards the gunsight, and it was when I was looking through the sight that we got hit. The round pierced the turret above my head. It didn't hit me, but slivers of armour struck my head, tore my helmet, and damaged my skull. I fell on the tarpaulin covering the ammo. After that a fire started, since the next thing to get hit was the engine compartment. Much later I found out that the loader's head was smashed, and he also fell. The driver and radio operator saw us both lying there with blood on our heads but didn't realise that I was only wounded, so they decided to run for it. They got lucky: the Germans, after seeing that the tank was on fire, stopped observing it, so they managed to jump out unseen. The tarpaulin on which I landed started to smoulder, and when the fire reached me the pain woke me up. My first thought was: 'The fire might reach the ammo, then it's the end of me.' I got out of the driver's hatch, crawled back a little, and then lost consciousness. When our infantry advanced to the attack they found me and took me back.

I recovered quite quickly. One day I was standing on a porch and saw a tank drive out of the gate of the nearby tank repair brigade. It had the markings of a neighbouring battalion. I ran towards it: 'Guys, where're you going?' 'We're taking the tank back to the battalion.' 'Take me with you.' 'All right.' I climbed onto the tank and left without any papers. I reported back to the brigade, where a letter from my father was waiting for me: 'We are in Kupiansk, 100 kilometres from Kharkov.' I went to the commander: 'I haven't completely recovered after being wounded, I need leave.' The counter-intelligence officer supported me: 'He's an OK guy, let him have five days.' 'You'll be back, right?' 'Of course!' It took me a day to get to Kupiansk, where I was told: 'Yes, they were here, but they moved on to the village of Studenok.' I spent another day getting there. When I reached it – they'd moved on to the Donbass. I went there – and they were already in the Dnepropetrovsk region. I found them on the fifth day, but my father wasn't there: he'd been called back to the Political Directorate in Moscow. What was I to do? I could've been court-martialled for that. They took me to General Russiianov: 'You can remain here,' he said, 'I'll send a coded telegram about it. You can be an adjutant for the technical chief at the corps HQ until your father returns.' 'No thanks,' I said, 'please send me to a tank brigade.'

So on 9 October 1943 I ended up in the 2nd Battalion of the 3rd Zaporozh'ye Tank Brigade, 1st Guards Mechanised Corps. They gave me a tank, and on the 13th I participated in the liberation of Zaporozh'ye. They promised us that if we managed to capture the Dnieper Hydroelectric Plant intact, we'd all be awarded the title of the Hero of the Soviet Union. So the motivation was there all right! We attacked during the night by the light of our headlamps. There was a moat filled with water in front of the city. We drove armoured evacuation vehicles (tanks without a turret) into that moat, and used them as bridges to cross to the other side. We broke into the city. The Germans used the dam to evacuate to Khortitsa Island, blowing up a part of it along with their troops that hadn't managed to cross. We drove right over those that remained on our side, and our Zaporozh'ye campaign ended there.

After that the 1st Guards Mechanised Corps was pulled back to Poltava for rest. But our 9th Brigade, the 20th Tank Regiment, and a motor rifle battalion of the 3rd Mechanised Brigade were sent up the Dnieper to Novomoskovsk. We marched about 100 kilometres, forced the Dnieper, and set out towards the west. We didn't know where we were going, and there was no resistance from the Germans. I was relieved of my duties as tank commander and appointed a communications officer at the brigade HQ. The brigade was led by Lieutenant-Colonel Murashko, a brave man.

We reached the Kherson-Znamenka railway, which was about 100 kilometres from the Dnieper. We cut it near Chabanovka Station and established defensive positions several kilometres from it. The brigade HQ deployed in the Sharovskii State Farm, while one battalion advanced to Pavlovka village and another to Kirovograd. They didn't capture the city, of course, but they fired some shots at it. Soon I got a mission to take two newly arrived officers (a junior and a senior lieutenant) to the 2nd Battalion, which was deployed two to three kilometres from Pavlovka. While on the way, we saw an abandoned tank of the 1st Battalion in a swampy area. We could see that it had been covered with reeds, which had burned.

Its crew wasn't around. An old man was sitting nearby near his makeshift shelter. We asked him: 'Whose tank is this?' 'Some soldiers camouflaged it, but when the Germans started shooting incendiary bullets they ran away.' 'Did the Germans approach it?' 'No.' Then I said to the two officers: 'Why do we have to walk? Let's ride.' Kuzmenko, the senior lieutenant, said: 'No!' I replied: 'Come on, let's do it!' We got into the tank. The battery was dead but I started it with compressed air. We drove to the village and found the deputy battalion commander, Captain Kozin. 'Here, we brought you a tank.' 'Good. Because we lost one tank in a swamp, and we don't have to report it now! Drive to Kardaev's company. He has two tanks in an ambush position. Join them.' 'I don't have a crew!' 'Take the junior lieutenant. You'll be the gunner, and he'll be the loader.'

We got to Kardaev's company and dug a shelter for the tank. Suddenly an armada of German tanks set out from the village of Mitrofanovka right at us. There were up to fifty tanks there! And we had three tanks, and no fuel! We'd refuelled at Novomoskovsk, but that was it. We started shooting and knocked out something. The HQ wrote later that we knocked out eight tanks. I don't know for sure, but something was certainly burning. The rest quickly surrounded us. We abandoned the tanks, only managing to pull out the gun locks, and ran. I was firing my handgun, but after I ran out of ammo I threw it away, leaving myself with only a single hand grenade. I decided: 'I'll blow myself up rather than be captured.' A German APC drove at me firing, but missed. The bullets passed right next to me and I instinctively fell to the ground. Apparently they thought that I was killed and they drove past me. That's how I ended up in an enemy encirclement, but my men managed to get away. When the battle quietened down I got up and started walking east. In the evening I reached Chabanovka Station, saw a small fire not far away, and started walking towards it.

There was a Russian guy with his wife near the fire, cooking food. He was Ivan Pakhomov, a railway worker. He said: 'Why are you walking around in your uniform? Let's go change.' He took me to a cellar: 'Take everything off. Here are some work clothes. You will tell everyone that you're a worker.' As soon as I changed, some Germans rode in on a motorcycle. They didn't give us any trouble. Ivan said to me: 'We're going to the railway junction, my wife's sister lives there. You'll come with us.' He had an *ausweiss* (German passport) and the blue armband of a worker, which he gave to me. We reached the junction, where his sister-in-law's husband, Sasha Chaporev, told me: 'You'll have to say that you're my brother who used to live in Krivoy Rog, but now the Russians are advancing and you had to run.' In the morning all of us went to work. Mel'nechuk, the chief of the work crew, suspected that I wasn't who I claimed to be, but he still covered for me. That's how I spent six weeks working on the railway. The Germans were mopping up, looking for encircled soldiers, and I saw them drag in Sergeant Osipov, the brigade commander's adjutant. I managed to exchange a few words with him. He told me that Brigade Commander Murashko had perished.

Gradually our front was advancing. One day the Germans ordered all the railway workers to evacuate. They brought in a cart of TNT and blew up every rail from two sides, splitting each tie in two. Seeing that the Germans were fleeing, six of us decided to take cover in a dugout near the junction, used to store tools. We hid, but kept talking loudly like idiots, so the Germans heard us and pulled us out. Everyone except me had German papers, which they presented, but I had nothing. The crew chief Mel'nechuk, who knew German well, saved me – he said that my papers were being processed for renewal.

They led us along the railway to the junction, where they put us inside the crossing keeper's hut, which had windows on three sides. There was a bench near the wall, where our guards sat down, and a deep trench had been dug nearby in case of bombing. The guards sat down and started talking in German. Mel'nechuk translated for us: 'They're thinking about what to do with us. It's too far to take us to the HQ – twelve kilometres. What if the Russians catch them? If they let us go, then the Russians will draft us into the army. They want to shoot us.' At that moment a ground attack aircraft flying above us saw the Germans and fired at them. They dived into the trench, and we jumped out the window and started running. The Germans were probably glad that we ran away – fewer problems for them! Some time later we heard choice Russian cursing – our troops! I immediately realised that the guys would be drafted into the army in several days, and I'd never be able to prove that I didn't have any dealings with the Germans. I went to the counter-intelligence department of one of the units of the 5th Guards Army, explained everything, and they immediately locked me up in a cellar. Then they kept taking me from one village to another: 'Fine, you haven't been in German hands – sign here. But still, what mission did the Germans give you?' They kept doing it for three weeks.

It was winter outside – the month of December – but I was lightly dressed. One of the other prisoners there was a man with a huge black beard. He had a splendid coat. I would've frozen to death, but he put me under his arm, shared his coat with me. The Germans had appointed him a village elder, so when our troops came, those who were unhappy with him immediately turned him in. He told me: 'Of course, I couldn't avoid carrying out the orders from German command, but I tried to sabotage them as much as I could. I was even in touch with the partisans, but now they're far away. What am I to do?' And then he was taken away and never brought back. I asked a guard – he said he was taken to a different place. Then when they took me for another interrogation I came out and saw him hanging . . .

When my father found out that I'd turned up he came to Novaia Praga with a letter from Russiianov, about sending me to the 1st Guards Mechanised Corps to be checked. I went to Poltava, where the corps was located. They released me immediately and appointed me to a mechanised brigade as a deputy rifle company commander. Gradually everything settled down, though the wounds I'd received in the summer became infected, and I had to keep going to the medical battalion for treatment.

One time that I returned from the medical battalion an officer approached me: 'Comrade Junior Lieutenant, you're called by the court-martial chairman Lieutenant-Colonel Dedov.' So they dragged me in there. The Chairman said to me: 'You'll be a people's juror in the trial.' 'But I just got out from under investigation myself!' 'That's not a problem.' They collared another officer too, and we had to act as people's jurors. There were two men on trial – really for nothing. After the adjournment I said that I wouldn't sign the court papers. In the first case two sentries had been guarding some stores, and one of them was killed. Someone had fired a shot. The survivor was accused of shooting his comrade, but there was no proof of his guilt. They told me: 'Sign the papers, we'll send him to a penal company.' 'No, I'm not going to sign this.' The other case involved a guy from Western Ukraine. When the Germans were there they assembled the peasants and said: 'Take your horse, carry stones, do this and that.' When we liberated the area, this guy was drafted into the army, and he told someone that the Germans made him carry something. He was accused of serving the Germans and sentenced to be shot, which was commuted to service in a penal company. But the entire population had been forced to work for the Germans! He didn't leave with them, after all, so what was he on trial for? Even I could've been tried on that basis, since I'd worked for the Germans on a railway! Basically, it was difficult. I went through such things as well, but I didn't blame the counter-intelligence people themselves even for a minute.

Soon I was arrested again. Here's how it turned out. Apparently, before our corps – which had spent a year in Poltava – was sent to the front, an encoded message came to the division telling them to send all unreliable men to be checked. Our chief of counter-intelligence and my father, the chief of the political department, had been called to Moscow, and deputy chief of the political department Kiselev had been left in his stead. He and I fell out over a woman, Vera Smirnova, who Kiselev had his eyes on. I can't say she was beautiful, but back then they were all beauties in our eyes! We'd become friends, but there were no intimate relations between us. One evening I came to her place and stayed for the night, and that's when Kiselev showed up. In order to get rid of him, she told him: 'My fiancé is here.' 'Show him!' I came out. So in order to get rid of me, he included me on the list of the unreliable men. On the night of 12 November 1944 I was lying in a house – not alone, but with a nurse. They knocked, and the owner of the house opened the door: 'Where's such and such?' They arrested me, and I told her: 'Run, don't tell anyone anything.'

They took me with other prisoners to Kharkov. There they put us up at the tractor factory, where the Germans used to have a POW camp. We didn't spend much time there, but were soon transferred to Scherbinka, near Moscow, to the 174th Special Camp that had been set up to check officers who'd been POWs or encircled by the enemy. There were two ways out of there: either prison, or as a private in a penal battalion. But they treated us well. They didn't try to scare us, but the counter-intelligence people kept trying to catch us contradicting ourselves. There were sixty-four of us in a small cell. You could only lie on the floor sideways. Even though it was winter, it wasn't heated – it was hot there anyway. Everyone farted, since they only fed us rotten cabbage! One day I was called to the investigator: 'Your papers came. Everything is in order, you should be released. But you've lost so much time while you were here that you'll have to go to a penal battalion. Are you a tankman? Do you know the DT machine-gun?' 'Yes.' 'The infantry version is the same, only with legs. You'll be a machine-gunner with the rank of private. If you do well, your officer rank will be restored.'

I kept trying to inform my family about my situation. By a miracle I was able to get someone to deliver a note to my aunt, and she took it to General Markov, the Chief of Armoured Forces, whom I knew in person through my father. Naturally, he took measures, and on 31 December 1944 I was released. General Markov said: 'You'll spend a month-and-a-half studying to be a technician, get some rest from the camp, and then go to your corps.' Then in the early spring of 1945 I was sent to the 382nd Guards Self-Propelled Artillery Regiment as the deputy commander for maintenance of an SU-100 self-propelled gun battery. We fought our way to the Alps and finished the war beyond Baden-Baden.

When the war ended my 9th Brigade was in Linz, where we captured a large number of German motor vehicles: trucks, cars, you name it. As the maintenance officer, I was ordered to go and pick out cars for our regiment. When I got there on 9 May I was met by my friend Maks Ivanov, a battalion maintenance officer. 'Forget these cars,' he said, 'let's go drink a cup with our allies. Then you can drive your cars.' There were already Americans there, with a barrel of looted alcohol – everything was prepared to celebrate our victory. I said: 'If I drink I'll get tipsy and won't be able to pick out anything. Let me go pick our cars, then we'll come back and drink.' So we went. Suddenly we heard screams and loud noises, and ran back. They were all lying there with foam coming from their mouths. Some were already gone, some went completely blind. It turned out that the barrel contained antifreeze based on methyl alcohol. Eighteen Americans died and twenty-two of our men. On victory day!

CHAPTER 6

'The fires made it bright as day.'

Aleksandr Mikhailovich Fadin

I was born in Knyazevka village, in the Arzamas district of the Nizhniy Novgorod area, on 10 October 1924.

On Sunday, 22 June 1941, I woke up quite late, around ten o'clock in the morning. I washed, had breakfast, and then decided to visit my aunt. When I arrived I saw her in tears. I asked her what was wrong, and she told me that war had started and that her husband Pavel had gone to the local military commissariat to volunteer for the Red Army. I hastily said goodbye and went to the dormitory of Gorki River Ship Academy, where I was studying at that time. On my way to the academy, everybody in the tram I took thought the war would not last long. 'A dog has attacked an elephant,' someone said.

On Tuesday, 24 June I went to the military commissariat. The square in front was full of men. Everyone wanted to talk to the military commissar. I don't know how, but I managed to sneak into the building and met a *politruk* in the corridor. He asked me why I'd come and I replied that I wanted to go to the front. After he learnt about my age, he said: 'You know, boy, just carry on with your studies. That's enough of a war for you to fight! So far, you see, we have enough volunteers to recruit.' One month later I went to the military commissariat again. On the good advice of a friend, I added two years to my age. I received a medical card and I was accepted into the 2nd Gorki Automobile and Motorcycle Academy.

They took us to Ilyino, where we had dinner, after which we were told that we were part of the 9th Company, 3rd Motorcycle

Battalion. Our studies started the very next day. We studied military manuals, drill, singing marches and marching as a company. Each one of us made his own dummy rifle from wood. On 7 August we were sworn in, went to the steam-bath for the first time, and were issued summer military uniforms. Soon after that we received real weapons.

We started our studies of motorcycles with the AM-600 model with sidecar, and then the IZh-9; then we switched to the new M-72 that had just entered service in the Red Army. We had several classes of theory, and then we were taken to a driving range for lessons. In those days even a bicycle was a luxury that wasn't available to every boy, so many cadets didn't know how to ride one. So first they were trained to ride bicycles before they were given motorcycles.

The winter of 1941 was very tough. In December temperatures went down to minus 42–45°C. It was awfully cold. The temperature in our classrooms wasn't much higher than outdoors; but if during tactical training in the field we could at least move around to keep ourselves warm, in classes we had to sit still and listen to the instructors. In addition we were dressed rather lightly, in *budyonnovka* winter hat, cotton uniform, long *kirsa* boots with warm foot wrappings, summer underwear, and mittens with one finger.

By that time the road from the railway station was completely blocked by snow, which meant that during December the academy didn't get any supplies of food. For the entire month we received just two pieces of dry bread instead of our regular allowance of 700 grams per day. In addition to that we received five pieces of sugar per day, while our lunch and dinner were a bowl of red beet soup. Nevertheless, we didn't lose heart and believed that these were just temporary hardships.

In late November 1941, when the Germans were standing at the gates of Moscow, the entire 2nd Gorki Automobile and Motorcycle Academy wrote a letter to Stalin with a request to send us to the front. Just two days later we received a telegram from Stalin, in which he thanked us for our readiness, but noted that the Motherland would need us later, and also demanded that we studied harder and prepared for the coming battles better. The main message that we read between the lines in this telegram was that Moscow would not be surrendered to the Germans, and that was the main thing. Indeed, just several days later our counter-offensive started.

In March 1942, after completing an eight-month course as motor-cycle platoon leaders, the academy sent about 400 men to the front. We cadets of the 3rd Motorcycle Battalion were ordered to continue our studies, but to take the course for truck platoon leaders. We completed this course in June, and in late July we were taken for internship to the Mars-3 plant in Moscow. After completing this internship, we came back to the academy and prepared for our graduation exams.

In late August an assembly was announced in the middle of the night, and every cadet was sent to the medical department for yet another inspection. They selected 100 cadets, including me, and we listened to an order from Commander-in-Chief Stalin that renamed the academy the 2nd Gorki Armour Academy. (Those who didn't pass the medical examination graduated as truck platoon leaders.) We younger cadets shouted 'Hurrah!' at the news, but the older ones, who'd fought at Khalhin-Gol, in the Winter War, and had liberated Western Ukraine and Belorussia, said: 'Why are you so happy? You will burn in these tin cans.' We were very well trained as truck platoon leaders, so it was easy for us to switch to a tank course.

In early April 1943 a state commission arrived at the academy in order to inspect its first graduation batch. Exams for hardware and weapons firing were the most important ones: if one passed them with 'good' grade, he'd be commissioned as a junior lieutenant. If one passed them with an 'excellent' grade, he'd be commissioned as a lieutenant. I passed the hardware exam with 'excellent'.

I had a firing exam looming. According to the programme, we were supposed to fire on short stops. 'Excellent' was given if a cadet fired a shot in less than eight seconds, 'good' in nine seconds, 'satisfactory' in ten seconds, and if you lingered for more than ten seconds you failed the exam. However, I guess I was the first cadet in the academy who started to fire on the move.

In our training we used a primitive machine to learn aiming the gun – it was a swing that the cadets moved by themselves. After that we were taken to a firing range that was set up on a *kolkhoz* field. The target was pulled by a tractor using a rope about 300 metres long. Our firing distance was about 1,200–1,500 metres. All the cadets were afraid of hitting a tractor by mistake! Our battalion commander was a *frontovik* who'd lost his right hand in action. He'd always tell us: 'Your stops have to be as short as possible, and it's better not to stop at all.' When I told the guys I was going to try firing on the move, my company commander, Senior Lieutenant Glazkov, told me not to fool around, but I decided to try anyway. I did it! I knocked out a dummy tank with the very first shot! Glazkov came running up, shouting: 'I warned you, you lousy cadet! What if you've missed?' So he started scolding me. Then the battalion commander drove up in his car: 'Who fired?' 'Cadet Fadin, a hollow-headed guy!' 'What? He did a great job! You should teach them all to fire like him, to fire on the move!'

So at the firing exam they allowed me to fire on the move, but the examiner, a colonel, warned me: 'Keep in mind that if you miss with all three rounds you won't graduate even as a junior lieutenant, you'll only be a senior sergeant.' I got into my tank. My driver was an experienced instructor. When I received the 'Prepare for battle!' order, I immediately placed myself at the sight. Just when we were about to reach the firing range, the driver said: 'Wait a bit. We'll come to a level patch of ground soon.' I took the target in the cross-sight, fired – and the rear of the dummy tank went missing! I also destroyed the second target, an infantry concentration. It was my finest hour! We drove back to the starting position, and the Colonel came running up, shook my hand, and took off his wristwatch and gave it to me as a gift. However, none of the other cadets dared to fire like me – there was too high a risk of missing.

On 25 April 1943 I was commissioned as a lieutenant, and in early May I was sent to the 3rd Reserve Tank Regiment at Factory No. 112. The crew of which I was appointed commander included as its driver-mechanic Senior Sergeant Vasili Dubovisky, born in 1906, who'd been the personal driver of President of the USSR M. I. Kalinin in 1936. My gunner was Junior Sergeant Golubenko, born in 1925, and the radio operator was Junior Sergeant Vasili Voznyuk from Odessa, born in 1919.

By late May 1943 preparation of our replacement company was about over. On 30 May we received brand new tanks from the factory and drove them to the firing range, where targets were set ready for us. We quickly formed an attacking line and carried out an assault with live ammo. Then we put ourselves in order in the assembly area and drove to a railway station for shipment to the front. We unloaded from the train at Maryino station, Kursk region, in early June, and were incorporated into the 207th Tank Battalion of the 22nd Guards Tank Brigade, 5th Guards Stalingrad Tank Corps. The battalion had been quite worn down in the fighting. After breakfast and inspection of our vehicles at noon on 11 July we received an order to fall in by companies. Then they read out a list, and our ranks were reinforced with battle-tried officers and men, while newly arrived tankmen without battle experience were excluded from the companies and sent into reserve. As a result of this I was demoted from tank platoon leader to tank commander. The next day we started our offensive.

Three red signal flares shot into the sky. After driving several hundred metres we saw advancing German tanks. Both sides opened fire, Katyusha missiles flew over our heads, and the German defences were enveloped in clouds of dust. At that point a tank battle commenced. I never imagined that I'd end up in such a slaughter-house! The worst thing would be to get lost in the confusion and ram into one of the nearest tanks. After my first two shots I got into frenzy: I wanted to get a German tank into my sights and destroy it, but I didn't manage to do it until the afternoon – it was a Panzer IV, that immediately caught fire after my hit. A bit later I managed to catch an APC with a pennant on its right mudguard and hit it with two HE rounds. Fiery debris flew in all directions. It was a beautiful hit! After that I moved on, trying to hold the attacking line of our company. By dusk the Germans had started an organised withdrawal and we captured Chapaev town. By dawn next day we only had eighteen tanks left out of our original sixty-five. We washed ourselves and had a snack, although we were not especially hungry, and then we went into battle again.

The offensive ended for me on 16 July, when our tank took two hits and caught fire. By that time our brigade had just four or five tanks left in running condition. We were driving on the edge of a sunflower field. Imagine yourself – the fourth day of the offensive, having had almost no sleep, we were completely exhausted. The first round hit our road wheel and knocked it out, the next one hit the engine. We bailed out and hid in the sunflower field. On the way back to our lines, I saw four T-34 tanks some 300 metres from us. Just when I was about to walk over to them, my driver grabbed my hand: 'Stop, Lieutenant, wait! Don't you see they have German crosses on them? These are Germans in Russian tanks!' 'God damn it, you're right. I guess these are the guys that knocked us out.' We lay down and waited for the tanks to pass by. Then we walked for about one-and-a-half hours. By chance we ran into the battalion's chief of staff (he was later killed during the liberation of Kiev): 'You did a great job, Lieutenant, I've already recommended you for a Guardsman title.' (What did you think? That if you're in a Guards Corps you're a Guardsman right away? No! They only gave you this title after your first battle, when you'd proved that you could fight.)

After four days of the offensive only seven out of sixty-two academy graduates survived; by autumn 1944 there were only two of us left.

We were sent to the battalion reserve, where we had a good rest for several days and had quite good catering. Although the academy had fed us quite well in 1943, lack of nutrition had still been noticeable in 1941 and 1942. Now I ate more than I'd ever be able to eat in peacetime: but in wartime I just wanted to get as much as I could. I could eat it all. Then we started preparing for the Belgorod-Khmelnitsk offensive operation. I didn't get a new tank, but was appointed liaison officer of the brigade staff. I served in this capacity till 14 October, when I was ordered to take over the tank of fallen Lieutenant Nikolai A. Polyanski. I must thank brigade chief of staff Major Mikhail P. Voshinski, who made me a real officer in two months: I could read maps, and understood the functioning of a tank company, a battalion, and even a brigade. These things were not comprehensible to a mere tank commander, platoon leader, or even a company commander, unless he worked on the staff.

I found Polyanski's tank and walked up to the crew. The driver-mechanic, Vasili Semiletov, was working on the transmission, while the other three crewmen were lying on the ground nearby, and, as I noticed, intently studying me. They were all much older than me, except for loader Golubenko, who was a member of my first crew and was the same age as me. I immediately felt that they didn't like me. It was clear that I had to become their leader and commander immediately, or it would never happen. If it didn't, then either the tank and its crew would wind up dead in the very first battle, or, more likely, the crew would fake illness and avoid action as much as possible.

The self-confidence I'd learned during my work on the brigade staff helped me out. I said sternly: 'What sort of tank is this? Why is the crew lying on the ground?' The youngest crew member, Sergeant Golubenko, stood up, and reported: 'Comrade Lieutenant! The crew has just completed repairs and is waiting for a new commander.' 'At ease, Comrades. I request everyone to assemble round me.' They followed the order, although quite slowly. They walked up to me, unshaven, untidy, with cigarettes in their hands. I saluted to them, introduced myself, and told them that though I'd heard many good things about their late commander his crew didn't seem to live up to that reputation. Then I walked to the front of the tank and suddenly gave the order: 'Fall in!' They all fell in, but didn't drop the cigarettes. I said 'Stop smoking!' and they reluctantly threw their cigarettes on the ground. I told them that it was unpleasant for me to go into battle in such an untidy, dirty tank with a strange crew: 'I see that you don't like me either, but if the Motherland says so, I'll defend my country the way I was taught, and will do my best.' I saw the older men of the crew stop grinning. I asked the crew: 'Is the vehicle in running order?' The driver replied: 'Yes, but the electric motor for traversing the turret is out of order and we don't have spare blank track links. All three have spikes.' 'So we'll fight the war on this one. Mount the tank!' They followed my order more or less well. I mounted the tank and said that we were going to Avetisyan's company.

I took a map, found our position, and directed the tank to Valki village. On the way we were caught by German artillery fire at the edge of Novye Petrivtsy village. We had to hide the tank behind the wall of a half-destroyed building and wait for darkness. When the tank was parked and the engine turned off, I explained to the crew where we needed to get to and the purpose of my manoeuvres. Loader Golubenko said: 'You can work with the map very well, Lieutenant!' 'It looks like you know tactics just as well,' added radio operator Voznyuk. Only driver Semiletov was silent, but I saw that the crew's cold reception was already a thing of the past. Now they believed in me. When it started to grow dark we moved out, and reached the company escorted by German artillery and mortar fire. We dug a trench for our tank and thoroughly camouflaged it.

Our preparation for the assault on Kiev, in which our brigade was supposed to take part, started with a briefing for all tank commanders, platoon leaders and company commanders in the battalion commander's dugout on 2 November 1943. It was rather dark and it was raining a bit. We were thirteen officers and three commanders of self-propelled guns. Lieutenant-Colonel Molokanov, chief of the brigade political department, very briefly described our mission to Dmitri Chumachenko, the battalion commander. From his words I understood that the assault was to begin at eight in the morning the next day.

During that night all of us, except for the sentries, slept like logs. At 6.30 am on 3 November we received our breakfast and decided to eat it in the open, not in the dugout. We sat down alongside the dugout, with the battalion's steaming and smoking field kitchen next to us. As soon as we sat down, the enemy artillery opened fire. The only thing I managed to shout was: 'Everybody down!' One round landed some seven to ten metres behind us, but the splinters didn't hit anyone. The next one hit the ground ten metres away, didn't detonate, and started spinning through the air. It threw an idle soldier from its path, tore a wheel from the field kitchen, capsized it and the cook, who was still serving food, flew into the corner of a house, and only stopped on the other side of the street in a garden. The enemy fired two or three more rounds and then quietened down. We forgot about any breakfast after this. We picked up our few belongings and got into our tank, waiting for the beginning of the assault. Our nerves were stretched to the limit.

Soon our own artillery barrage started and I ordered: 'Start the engine!' When I saw three green flares in the sky, I ordered 'Forward!' In front of us was a thick wall of smoke and dust, in which I could see the flashes of explosions. From time to time I could see the individual explosions of rounds falling short. The tank jerked – we had just crossed our front-line trench. I gradually calmed down. All of a sudden I realised that our infantrymen were there, charging forward and shooting on the move. Tanks on my left and right were also firing. I looked into the sight, and could see nothing except for fallen trees. I said to the loader: 'Fragmentation round!' 'Roger, fragmentation round' replied Golubenko. I fired the first round at the trees, as I thought it was the enemy's first trench. When I saw the explosion of my round I completely calmed down, and felt as if I were on a firing range in regular training. I fired the main gun at the fleeing Germans in their mouse grey uniforms. I got excited by firing at the panicking enemy and ordered: 'Increase speed!' Then we arrived in a forest. Semiletov sharply reduced speed. 'Don't stop!' 'But where should I drive?' 'Forward, just forward!' The old engine of the tank was roaring as we felled several trees. To the right was the tank of Vanya Abashin (my platoon leader). It too felled a tree and continued moving. Peeping out from the turret hatch I saw a small cutting leading into the forest and directed my tank there. In front of me, to the left, I could hear the shots of our tanks' main guns and the barking sounds of shots from Nazi AT guns. To the right I could only hear tank engines, but I could not see the tanks themselves.

My tank continued advancing along the cutting into the forest. I thought that I should be on my guard and periodically fired the main gun and MG along the cutting. Then the forest grew thinner, and all of a sudden we arrived in a large clearing. I saw Germans running in all directions across the clearing and fired my main gun. At the same moment I saw strong automatic smallarms fire coming from small hillocks on the other side of the clearing. A group of Germans flashed between the hillocks and all of a sudden I saw the muzzle flash of an AT gun. I fired a long burst from the MG and shouted: 'Fragmentation!' to the loader. Then I sensed a hit, as if our tank had struck a strong obstacle, stopped for a second, and then moved forward again, turning to the left. Again, just like on the firing range, I found the group of Germans at the AT gun and fired at them. I heard a yell from Fedor Voznyuk: 'The gun and crew are blown to pieces!' The driver shouted: 'Commander, our right track is torn!' 'Leave the tank through the bottom hatch and repair the track! I'll provide covering fire.' By that time our tanks and infantry were in the clearing. It took us about an hour to repair the track with a spiked link (we didn't have any plain ones). Not only that, but when our tank was slewing on its left track it had got sucked into a bog, and some ten metres from us there was a minefield that the Germans had sown across the dry part of the clearing. So we had to pull our tank out backwards, not forwards. That took us a further two hours.

We only caught up with the battalion at nightfall, when the Germans managed to stop us at their second defensive line. During the night of 3–4 November we refuelled our tanks and reloaded ammunition. We also managed to rest a bit. At dawn on 4 November Chumachenko gathered his surviving tank commanders and took us to the front line for reconnaissance. Nine commanders were left of the thirteen who'd been briefed the day before. Three SP guns were still with us. We reached the trenches of the infantry and Chumachenko said: 'Do you see those solid barricades of logs 300 metres away?' 'Yes, we do.' 'The enemy is behind those barricades, so our infantry can't even lift their heads. Drive up to this clearing immediately, form a line, and attack the enemy.' Why on earth the Germans didn't fire at us, a group of officers standing out in the open right in front of their defences, I can't imagine ...

We drove to the clearing and began the assault. We managed to
break the barricades and the Germans fled. We chased them along
cuttings into the depths of the forest, and by the evening we'd reached
the edge of the forest at Vinogradar Sovkhoz. A battalion of German
tanks, including Tigers, greeted us with a counter-attack there, and
we had to withdraw into the forest and set up defences. The Germans
drove up to the forest with three medium tanks on point, while their
main force formed two columns and entered the forest. It was already
growing dark, but the Germans decided to start a night battle, which
they normally avoided.

I was ordered to block the main cutting with my tank. To the right
and a bit behind me Vanya Abashin's tank was covering me, and to
the left was a JSU-152. The enemy's point was going deeper into the
forest, as we let them pass through, but their main force was now
approaching us. From the noise of its engines I could hear that they
were led by a Tiger.

I said to my driver, Semiletov: 'Vasya, move forward a bit, slowly –
that tree in front of us is cramping my shooting range.' After forty-
eight hours of fighting I'd become very good friends with the crew
and they understood me almost without the need for words. Having
improved my position I saw the enemy. I didn't wait for Semiletov to
stop, but fired a round at the leading German tank, which was about
fifty metres from me. There was a flash against the front of the
Nazi tank, and all of a sudden it caught fire, illuminating the entire
German column. Driver-mechanic Semiletov shouted: 'God damn
you, Lieutenant! Why did you fire? I didn't get to close my hatch!
Now the gases have blinded me.' But at that moment I forgot
everything except the enemy's tanks.

Golubenko reported to me without any command: 'Loaded!' My
next shot killed the second German tank as it emerged from behind
the burning one. This one also caught fire. The forest became bright
as day. I heard Ivan Abashin firing his main gun and the long sound
of a shot from the 152 mm SP gun on the left. I could now see several
burning German tanks through the gunsight. I shouted to my driver:
'Vasya, drive closer to the burning tanks, otherwise the Fritzes will
escape.' I approached the first burning tank almost to point-blank
range, and at its right side I found my next target – a German assault
gun. It blew up after my shot struck it. We continued to pursue the
enemy all the way to Vinogradar Sovkhoz, where we made a stop to

get ourselves in order. There we had a snack and prepared for the decisive assault on the city.

Brigade commander Colonel Koshelev and chief of the political department Lieutenant-Colonel Molokanov came to our position in the morning of 5 November. The surviving crews of seven tanks and three SP guns lined up in front of their vehicles. The commanders spoke to us and informed us that the first crews to enter Kiev would be awarded with the Golden Stars of Heroes of the Soviet Union.

Thirty minutes later we formed a battle line and started our assault. Quickly capturing the southern outskirts of Pusha-Voditsa, we crossed Svyatoshino and then cut the Kiev-Zhitomir road. An anti-tank ditch dug back in 1941 was in our way, but we had to cross it in order to enter the city. My tank drove into the ditch and got stuck – the engine was roaring at full throttle, half-metre long flames shooting from the exhaust pipes (this meant that the engine was completely worn out), but we couldn't get out of the ditch. In order to increase our tractive force, I shouted to the driver: 'Reverse and drive out backside first!' And so we reached the first street. Then another technical problem! The spiked track link that we'd had to use for repairs in the forest lifted the right side of the tank by ten centimetres, which meant I couldn't aim properly. So we stopped, borrowed a track link from another tank and started repairs.

The battalion received orders to advance into the city centre. The leading tank reached the T-junction and all of a sudden went up in flames, turned to the right, and rammed into a house at the corner. The scouts who were riding the tank were thrown off. Lieutenant Abashin and I opened fire at a German SP gun as it tried to escape, and my second round hit its rear and immobilised it. After a short delay Chumachenko arrived on the scene and ordered Lieutenant Abashin to take the point. We drove on after the 'Forward!' signal, and soon we reached Kreshatik. The city was liberated.

In the evening we received orders to leave the city and advance towards Vasilkov. However, as we were crossing a small river our tank got stuck, and due to the poor condition of its engine it couldn't get out. We had to bring in a tractor and tow it to the repair work-shop. The repair workers tried to fix it but after seven days of vain efforts they announced to me that my tank wasn't repairable under field conditions and added that I wouldn't get it back until 1944.

That was the end of the battles round Kiev for me. Chumachenko recommended me and six other tank commanders for the Golden Star of Hero of the Soviet Union.

During our preparations for the upcoming battles I had permission to pick the best men to crew my next tank, as I had to part company with the old crew. Without bragging, I can say that men specially requested to be selected for my crew. However, I didn't change anyone from the tank's appointed crew, except for the driver. My radio operator was a young guy, Kleshevoi (I don't remember his first name), and the loader was a Sergeant-Major whose name I've completely forgotten. Several experienced drivers of the battalion talked me into taking Petr Tyurin as my driver. On 27 December 1943 the brigade received orders to start an offensive in the direction of Chekovichi, Guta-Dobrynskaya, Kamenny Brod, and Andreev. I was ordered to take the point for the first time.

We drove to the front at night. The weather was cold, the soil was frozen solid. Morning snowfall softened the sound of our clashing tracks. The engine of the new tank worked very well, and we advanced at high speed. I was nervous, as it was completely unknown where and how the enemy would engage us. We drove through the fields, bypassing villages in order to make shortcuts, and this calmed me down a bit. After some twenty kilometres we entered a small village and stopped. The brigade column caught up with us quite soon. The rest was very short, and we received orders to continue our advance: but I had a problem. My driver-mechanic Petr Tyurin said that he couldn't drive the tank, as he couldn't see in the dark. But we didn't have anyone to replace him. The crew members couldn't replace each other. Other than the driver only I could drive the tank. Tyurin kept this up for some twenty minutes, but at the end of that I realised that he was lying; if he were really suffering from night-blindness he would have behaved differently. He'd just lost his nerves – it was indeed very hard to drive forward not knowing what would happen to you the next second. I lost my temper and shouted at him: 'Why the hell did you volunteer for my crew then?' and added, addressing deputy battalion commander Arseniev: 'Comrade Guards Senior Lieutenant! Please find a new driver to replace Tyurin at the very first stop.' Then I turned back to Tyurin and loudly shouted at him: 'Now you take your place and drive the tank!' I ordered 'Forward', and, straining my eyesight as much as I could, started to direct my driver through the tank intercom. I had to often peep into the tank, which was weakly illuminated, to check my map, and soon forgot about Tyurin, who drove the tank quite confidently.

At dawn we could see Kamenny Brod village in the distance, and in front of it, some 500 metres ahead, I saw a dark object that I mistook for a tank in the semi-darkness of dawn. I fired two armour-piercing rounds at it and saw sparks and pieces flying off the object. I realised that I'd made a mistake, and when we drove up to it I saw it was a large boulder. All of a sudden two German Panzer IV tanks emerged from the village and drove at top speed to the right away from us, escaping towards Chernyahov town. I shouted: 'Tyurin, catch up with them, catch up!' But he got afraid and stopped. The German tanks were already about 1.5–2 kilometres from us, but I fired a couple of rounds at them and missed. To hell with them, we had to capture the village.

Some 300 metres from the nearest buildings we met a small old man who showed us a passage through the minefields and told us that there were no Germans in the village, but the next village was full of German tanks. We thanked him, entered the village, and moved through it to the other end. The buildings were all in one row along the main street and behind them to the left and right I could see wide fields. Two other tanks caught up with me, one of them being Ivan Abashin's tank. When we reached the end of the village I saw the next village 1.5 kilometres ahead. It was on the same road. Before I could look at the map to discover its name, I saw German Panzer IV tanks, painted white, rolling back and forth in the field. Behind them I saw Tigers and Panthers emerging from their shelters behind the huts of the next village and starting to form a battle line – I counted seven of them. The Panzer IVs were forming a second line behind them: there were about fifteen of them. I didn't hesitate for long and ordered: 'Armour-piercing round, load!' 'Armour-piercing – ready!' I fired at the Tiger on the right flank – and missed! What the hell? I looked at the gunsight, and it was misadjusted five grades to the right. That's why those tanks had escaped from me at the approach to the village. I adjusted the sight and heard over the radio that our two companies were also forming a battle line. I peeped out from the tank's turret and saw our entire battalion forming a battle line in the open to the right from the village, in order to meet the enemy head-on. This was an ignorant decision of the battalion's commander that cost us dearly, but I will tell that story later.

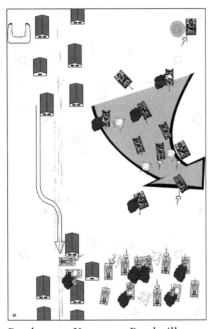

Battle near Kamenny Brod village.

I don't know what happened to me, but I decided to attack the Germans alone – against twenty German tanks! I completely lost my mind! 'Drive forward, to that village!' I ordered Tyurin. The second tank of our platoon under Ivan Abashin followed me. To the left of the road I saw a slope going down to a river. This meant that we could turn off the road, hide in the river valley and approach the enemy unnoticed. Just as I had this thought a Tiger on the left fired at me from one kilometre away. He would have killed me, but the solid armour-piercing round hit the handle of a plough left standing in that field, changed its trajectory, and flew by several centimetres from my turret. It was a real stroke of luck! If all the German tanks had opened up on me, I'd have been blown to pieces, but for some reason they didn't. I shouted to Tyurin: 'Turn to the left and follow the river valley to the first hut of that village!' Ivan Abashin duplicated this manoeuvre.

I drove to the last hut of the village, as I thought it hid me from the deploying German tanks. I decided to see what the Germans were doing and report to my company commander over the radio. Just as I ran up to the corner of the building it got hit. A German tank, camouflaged by a haystack about 1.5 kilometres from the village to support the deployment of the main German force, had targeted the hut, and I was thrown backwards. I could hardly stand up, as my legs became heavy and I could barely control them. I walked back to my tank very slowly, my hands shaking. At that moment a Panzer VI Tiger, painted yellow, emerged from a trench some 300–400 metres in front of us. We were right out in the open. Why didn't he shoot? I don't know. Before I jumped into the tank, I shouted to Ivan Abashin: 'Shoot, you fucking loser, shoot! Shoot him, goddam it!' But he was just standing and looking at the Tiger. I guess it was shock. To be honest, I had better training than him, especially after service as a liaison officer on the staff.

With some effort I got into my tank and aimed at this approaching Tiger. However, due to my shell-shock and excitement I couldn't estimate the distance to the Tiger precisely, and I decided to withdraw. I ordered Tyurin to turn around and drive back to Kamenny Brod the same way we'd come. The German tanks had already completed their deployment and assailed our battalion, and our tanks were burning. I drove parallel to them some 200 metres distant at 50–60 kilometres per hour, passed them, went behind the last hut and made a sharp turn. I stopped between the hut and a barn with a haystack next to it, thinking: 'I'll kill you all from the side.'

The German tanks passed the village and drove past me. I looked into my sight, but a pile of manure was blocking my view. I drove forward a bit, turned the turret, and I saw a German Tiger on the right flank with his right side towards me. It was ready to fire at one of our tanks that was standing in its way. I didn't see my hit, but the Tiger jerked, stopped and started smoking. The tank of 2nd Platoon commander Konstantin Grozdev drove up to me. He should have hidden behind a hut and shot at the German tanks, but he just stuck close to my tank. The German tank covering the deployment of their main force from a distance must have fired at me then, but it hit Konstantin's tank. The turret blew off and flew through the roof of the nearest house. Konstantin bailed out ... more accurately, the upper part of his body bailed out: the lower part remained in the tank. He was still alive. He looked at me and his hands scratched the ground. Can you imagine such a sight? I shouted to Tyurin: 'Get back!' We managed to turn and then we were hit. The tank started spinning but made it all the way to the other side of the street. A solid armour-piercing round had hit our right-side gear, tearing off a large chunk of armour and exposing the gears but failing to inflict any other damage. Then the German tanks turned away to the left and disengaged.

We'd burnt four German tanks, including one Tiger, but had lost eight tanks ourselves. We'd met them head-on, but we should have hidden behind the huts, let them enter the village, and then hit them from the sides. We'd have destroyed them all that way. But instead, we lost an entire company! Mostly we lost the tanks crewed by replacements, the young men without battle experience, but many managed to bail out. Later we found out that with our arrival in

Kamenny Brod this German force was surrounded and so they'd
bluffed us in order to break out through our lines.

We quickly regrouped and started in pursuit. It was growing
dark. Our mood was at its worst, having just lost so many men, but
the main thing was to deprive the Germans of the chance to set up
defences. At around nine o'clock darkness, rain and sleet completely
blinded me. We slowed down and other tanks caught up with me.
We formed a battle line and continued our advance. It started to get
light little by little and we saw a mud road. I heard a radio message:
'Fadin, take your position.' I sped up and took the point of the
battalion. Two more tanks followed me. With the arrival of daylight
we felt a bit less depressed, but not for long. Standing in the turret of
my tank, I could see the outline of a large village through the morning
mist. I thought it was Chernyahov town. But as this thought flashed
through my mind we came under heavy German artillery fire.

We deployed and began our assault immediately. Two hundred
metres to my left a battery of new SU-85 SP guns opened fire from a
stationary position, while the brigade's AT battery deployed to their
front. We attacked with our three tanks, firing at the huts on the edge
of the village.

I looked into my sight and saw a column of tanks moving into
town parallel to us some two kilometres away. Artillery was firing at
them and at us from somewhere on the right. I was just thinking that
we'd done a good job coordinating the assault when I noticed a man
in a white sheepskin coat run towards us from the houses on the edge
of the town. He ran up to the AT battery commander and hit him in
the face. It turned out that the 21st Guards Tank Brigade had already
entered the town and we were firing at friendly troops! We quickly
changed our plans and drove to the centre of the town.

Another message came over the radio: 'Fadin and Abashin, drive
to the railway station.' I turned to the right and saw the two-
storey stone station building. I turned my turret in order to fire along
the street, and all of a sudden the tank shook from the powerful
explosion of a large-calibre German shell that had hit our right rear.
The tank continued to move, slowly turning to the right. Tyurin
shouted: 'Commander, they finished off our side gear.' 'Can we
move?' 'Barely.' We drove to the building next to the station and I
jumped off in order to inspect the damage. The remaining part of the
armour covering the right gear was completely gone, as if cut off by a
knife. Two gears were broken and the other ones had cracks. I had no

idea how we could continue to move. At that moment battalion commander D. A. Chumachenko drove up in his tank and ordered us to take up defensive positions and wait for a repair team.

We placed our tank in the middle of an apple orchard adjacent to the house. Soon we saw the repair truck that the battalion commander had sent to us. I spoke to the repair team and ordered my gun-layer and radio operator to stay inside the tank and continue to observe the battlefield, while I went to the station building to observe the town from there. All of a sudden I heard shouts, SMG bursts, and a shot from the main gun of my tank. I turned around and ran back as fast as my feet could carry me. It turned out that the Germans cut off to our rear had attacked the tank. The repair team and my crew took up a defensive position, and my loader fired a fragmentation grenade at point-blank range at the assaulting infantry. The Germans lost about ten men, and the surviving thirteen surrendered.

The repairs took about twenty-four hours and then we had to catch up with the brigade, which was advancing and fighting day and night. I don't know how anyone got any sleep. We could only take short naps here and there, a total of one or two hours per day. Exhaustion led to indifference, which resulted in losses. We entered Skriva town in darkness. Everyone was so exhausted that no one noticed the arrival of New Year 1944. We managed to rest for three or four hours. Then we were woken up by someone hitting our turret with a stick – field kitchen workers were inviting us for breakfast. During breakfast we were summoned to the battalion commander. Eleven officers gathered at Chumachenko's staff car with its special cabin. The battalion had eight tanks left, three SP guns, and two squads of scouts. Chumachenko introduced us to a new company commander, Technical-Lieutenant Karabuta, and then briefed us. Our mission was to march to Tarascha town, capture it, and hold it till the rest of the brigade arrived.

We moved out before dawn. My tank with five scout tank riders was again ordered to take the point, about 1.5 kilometres ahead of the main column. Soon a 'Frame' – a FW-189 reconnaissance plane – appeared overhead, which meant we could expect the arrival of the Luftwaffe any time. That was a good guess! Eighteen Ju-87 dive-bombers appeared in the sky. We formed a battle line, maintaining 100–150 metre intervals between the tanks, and drove forward at high speed. The air raid was intensive but didn't do any damage – none of our tanks were hit. A small village could be seen in front of us, from which came SMG bursts and the fire of field guns. We opened fire on the move, forcing a small German delaying force to flee.

We continued to advance in battle formation, as if we knew that the enemy was very near and we were about to engage. Two more waves of eighteen aircraft materialised in the distance, made a wide turn, and started bombing us. This confirmed my guess that the enemy was very near. Soon we saw a large village, Berezanka, and a huge German column with no end in sight going through it. The column looked black against the background of white snow.

The head of the column, with cars and horse-drawn carriages, had already passed through the village and sped up in order to escape. As it turned out, these were rear units of the enemy's freshly-arrived 88th Infantry Division. When we saw this practically helpless enemy in front of us, we dispersed from battle formation along the column, in order not to let a single carriage slip away. As ill luck would have it, the local population came out of their houses and rushed towards us, begging us to enter the village faster. This prevented us from firing directly at the Germans, as we had to fire over their heads. The Germans fled into the fields, abandoning their carriages and vehicles.

As I drove along the column machine-gunning the fleeing Germans, I saw a group of Fritzes who were doing something round the carriages at the edge of the village. They were unhitching horses and taking them away. I fired a fragmentation round at them. After the bodies had been thrown aside in all directions by the explosion, I noticed a field gun that they'd been trying to set up right on the road. I peeped out from the turret and saw three other such groups trying to unhitch the horses towing their guns. I managed to fire three or four rounds and they all hit this artillery battery. Then we rushed to the first gun and I ordered Tyurin to pass it while I killed the crew with our machine-gun. After I'd regained my senses following this rapid-paced battle, I peeped out from the turret, inspecting the battlefield. It was a terrible sight. Abandoned German vehicles and carriages were standing on the road, both destroyed and intact, and there were dead Germans and horses all around.

We took about 200 prisoners and we didn't know what to do with them, as we only had a scout platoon riding our tanks with us. We had to order several scouts to escort the prisoners to the rear. We stopped in the village and picked up some war booty. Tyurin and Kleshevoi brought two pig carcasses and put them on top of the transmission compartment: 'We'll share them with the families of the houses where we stay.' Then Tyurin gave me a pair of officers' long boots and told me that one couldn't go around in *valenki* boots all the time, and a lieutenant would never be issued such good boots. The long boots fitted, and I still remember how strong and waterproof they were.

Senior Lieutenant Vladimir Karabuta walked up soon after this and ordered me to advance to Tarascha town, which lay some ten kilometres to the west of Berezanka. The frozen mud of the road enabled us to drive at high speed. We passed through Lesovichi village, where there were no Germans, and reached Tarasha, into which we drove at high speed. Civilians were nowhere to be seen. That was a bad sign – the Germans must have an ambush somewhere. I saw a road crossing in front of me, but at that moment a woman ran out of the nearest house waving her hand. I stopped the tank, peeped out of the hatch and shouted to her, but I couldn't hear her reply because of the roar of the engine. So I got off the tank and went towards her: 'What's the problem?' She shouted back that there were German tanks some 300 metres in front of me at the road crossing. I thanked her and walked back to my tank. At that moment Vladimir Karabuta, who'd also jumped out of his tank and heard about the enemy ambush, said: 'Fadin, you're already a Hero of the Soviet Union so I'll go first.' And with that he started to pass my tank. I jumped into my own tank and shouted to Tyurin: 'Follow him, and as soon as he's knocked out pass him and drive forward!' Tyurin followed him. Everything happened just like I thought. After driving some 100 metres Karabuta's tank took a hit on its hull front and caught fire. I passed him, fired a shot into nowhere, and rushed forward. Only at that moment did I see a heavy assault gun which we called Ferdinand about 100 metres from me. It was standing with its rear against a small stone building, controlling the road crossing. When I saw the Ferdinand, I hit it with an armour-piercing shell and ordered Tyurin to ram it. Tyurin ran into the Ferdinand and started to squash it. The crew tried to bail out but were hit by my loader's SMG fire. Four Germans lay dead on the roof of their assault gun, but the fifth managed to escape. I ordered Tyurin to reverse. Other tanks and SP guns were now driving along the road and firing.

I calmed myself down, picked up my scout tank riders and drove along the street heading into the centre of town. The firing had stopped and an ominous silence hung in the air. The company commander and his crew seemed to have been killed (it later turned out that the company commander survived), so I had no one to give me orders to move forward. But someone had to lead by example. As I'd been in the point and had dealt with that Ferdinand so easily, I saw it as God's will that I should move on. At a road crossing I turned to the left and drove along a street going down to a river. I drove up to a bridge, and just as I was wondering if the bridge could hold us a heavy German truck came over the bridge from the other side. The Germans didn't notice our tank in the darkness and drove right into us. Its driver, realising what had happened, jumped out right onto the ice of the frozen river. I only had to press the trigger. My HE round went through the driver's cabin and exploded inside the truck, which was full of infantry. It was a firework! Pieces of bodies littered the bridge and the ice of the river. I said: 'Pete, drive forward.' We pushed the remnants of the truck off the bridge, drove over the dead bodies, and moved up the street. Our scouts jumped off the tank at the bridge, apparently to search the bodies of the Germans for wristwatches and handguns. We didn't have any wristwatches then.

We slowly moved forward, turned, fired a round along the street, and drove on at top speed. When we came to a T-junction I hid my tank in the shadow of a house. The Germans were nowhere to be seen. Our tanks were out of sight too. We shut down our engine and observed the surroundings. It was a rather scary prospect to drive on at night without scouts or tank riders, through streets that were brightly illuminated by moonlight, but I felt uncomfortable just sitting there doing nothing. There was a dead silence. All of a sudden I heard several tank engines start running, and three of our tanks drove past me at high speed. Immediately I heard explosions and gunshots in the direction that they went. A battle flared up simultaneously in the eastern suburbs of the town, where the main forces of the brigade were. I waited. The battle in the direction that the three had just rushed was quickly dying away – apparently, all our tanks got burnt.

Some 15–20 minutes later I heard a German tank coming from that direction. I decided to let it drive up close and destroy it from a distance of 100 metres. I had a crazy thought. I decided that I should destroy it in a beautiful way, so that I could write on its charred armour: 'Lieutenant Fadin destroyed this tank'. What stupidity! In order to do so, I had to let him drive right up to the junction, i.e. just 15–20 metres from me, and hit his side with an armour-piercing round as he started turning to the left (for some reason I was sure that he'd turn left). So I held the tank in my sights as it approached. It was a small tank, a Panzer III or Panzer IV. It entered the junction, turned to the left, I went to turn my turret – and it didn't turn! The enemy tank rushed away along the street. I shouted to Tyurin: 'Start the engine, we'll catch up with it and kill it during the chase!' But the tank didn't start right away. We'd let him get away! I jumped out from the turret to the rear of the tank. A tarpaulin attached to the rear of the turret had been spread out by the scouts riding our tank, to cover the cold armour they had to sit on, and its edge had got stuck between the gears of the turret traversing mechanism and jammed it.

I pulled the tarpaulin out, jumped back into the tank and ordered Tyurin to drive up the street where the German tank had just escaped, hoping we could still catch up with it. At that moment I heard over the radio: 'Fadin, Fadin, come back urgently.' I turned my tank around and drove back to the bridge. The battle was obviously ending, and the Germans had started to withdraw. That is how we liberated Tarascha during the night of 4–5 January 1944.

During the morning of 5 January we were putting ourselves in order and managed to get some sleep. At 1400 hours we started our march westwards towards Lysaya Gora town. Just as before, they gave me four scout tank riders and ordered me to take the point.

We entered the suburbs of Lysaya Gora. I could see the white walls of Ukrainian peasant huts on the left and a small dark forest on the right. I ordered Tyurin to speed up. Driving at high speed through the streets of Lysaya Gora, we took three or four hits from a semi-automatic gun in our left side. The tank veered to the right into a hole, so that we could only fire into the air. We stopped. I opened the hatch and got out, and saw that my left gear was destroyed: the tank could neither move nor turn in order to fire at the enemy. The battalion commander drove up and ordered us to wait for a repair team, leaving a rifle squad to protect my tank.

We set up outposts, took the pig carcass still on our tank from the destruction of the German column, and woke up the owner of the nearest house and his wife and got them to fry us some pork. It was a nice dinner, but rest was the last thing on our minds. We started to prepare for defence of our knocked-out tank. We took the MG out of the turret and the radio operator's MG, and prepared hand grenades and an SMG. With the seven riflemen and their squad leader we had enough firepower to repel an infantry attack. At around nine o'clock in the morning four locals came running to tell us that there were at least twenty Germans heading in our direction. We sent the locals away in order to avoid civilian losses and prepared for battle.

Three or four minutes later Germans in white snow camouflage carrying SMGs emerged into the street and walked in our direction in a disorganised group, almost in a crowd. We opened a hurricane of fire at them at my command, and apparently killed ten of them. They were pinned down, and then they evacuated their dead and didn't disturb us any more. At around 1400 hours the main forces of the brigade arrived, having defeated the Germans that opposed them. They left a repair team with us, picked up our infantry, and moved on towards Medvin town to catch up with our battalion.

The repair team worked on our tank from 6 January to 9 January to get it back into fighting condition. We spent our time in the company of some beautiful local girls. In the evenings we'd gather together round a table, telling stories of our childhood or playing cards. Our battalion commander Dmitri Chumachenko arrived on the morning of 9 January. He praised me for my actions in Tarascha town and ordered me to take over a half-company of tanks that had arrived following repairs. With these we liberated the small village of Vinograd.

Some time around 17 January we were ordered to turn in our remaining tanks to the 20th Guards Tank Brigade and transfer to the Corps reserve to receive replacement crews that were supposed to arrive from the rear. It took us several days to receive the replacements, in the vicinity of Medvin town. For the first time all the surviving officers of the brigade were gathered together since the previous batch of replacements had arrived in November. I didn't see many guys I knew. This was because the first ones to be killed were always the replacement crews that had just arrived from the rear and had the lowest level of training. The brigade always suffered its worst losses in the first battles after receiving replacements. The ones who survived their initial battles quickly learnt the ropes and became the core of the brigade.

During this short period I was appointed commander of Chumachenko's tank. The crew was very experienced: they'd been at the front for a year or more. The driver was Guards Sergeant-Major Petr Doroshenko, awarded with the Order of the Great Patriotic War 1st and 2nd Class and the Order of the Red Star. The gun-loader was Guards Sergeant Fetisov, awarded with two Medals for Bravery, and the radio operator was Guards Sergeant Elsukov, awarded with the Order of the Great Patriotic War 2nd Class and the Order of the Red Star. Besides that they all had campaign medals 'For the defence of Stalingrad'. Even for 1944, by which time decorations were being issued on a more regular basis, these were extremely prestigious awards, and this crew was the only one of its kind in the whole brigade. They lived apart from the other thirty crews and didn't talk to them, so when I arrived in the house where they lived and told them I was their new commander their reception was quite cold. It was quite natural that it was hard for them to accept the leadership of the youngest lieutenant in the brigade, who got this promotion after just three or four months at the front, especially given the fact that Doroshenko and Elsukov were both much older than me. I also understood that I had to prove my right to command them.

On 24 January the brigade entered the gap in the German defences made by the 5th Mechanised Corps and advanced towards Vinograd town. We went into action at dawn, almost immediately after the infantry assault of the V Mechanised Corps. The entire field in front of the German defences was littered with the corpses of our men. How was that? It was no longer 1941 or 1942, when we lacked the ammunition and artillery to destroy the enemy's weapon emplacements. Instead of dashing to the attack we drove slowly over the ploughed field, passing between the bodies of our fallen men or letting them pass between our tracks, in order not to squash them. After we'd passed the first line of our infantry, we increased speed and quickly captured Vinograd.

On the morning of 26 January the battalion commander was ordered to send his tank and crew to brigade commander Guards Colonel Fedor Andreevich Zhilin, who'd lost his tank in battle. Thus I became commander of the 22nd Brigade commander's tank.

It was a nightmare fighting the war in Ukraine in the spring of 1944. An early thaw and sleet turned the roads into quagmires. All logistics tasks had to be carried out by horses, as wheeled vehicles got stuck in the mud. Our tanks could move, but the motorised rifle battalion fell behind. We had to ask the local population to assist us, and local women and teenagers carried ammo rounds over their shoulders, or carried ammo boxes in pairs, sinking knee-deep in the mud.

In late January we were carrying out an encirclement of the German forces in Korsun-Shevchenko and ended up getting encircled ourselves. We barely made it out, losing eight of our tanks sunk in the Gorny Tikich River in the process. After that we had to repel the assaults of Nazi troops that tried to break out of the encirclement. To cut a long story short, by 18 February, when we were ordered to concentrate at Dashukovka village, the brigade had only the brigade commander's tank (i.e. mine) and the motorised rifle battalion left. However, the motorised rifle battalion comprised just sixty-eight men and two 76 mm guns and was stuck somewhere in the mud on its way to the village. The Brigade HQ was in a village about a kilometre from Dashukovka, where the motorised rifle troops were supposed to arrive in five or six hours. The enemy had just thrown our troops out of Dashukovka, breaking our encirclement ring. Colonel Zhilin, the political officer and I drove up to a deep ravine that separated us from Dashukovka. The latter was on a hill, extending from north to south, forming a street about two kilometres long. It was surrounded by deep ravines on three sides, while on the far northern edge there was a slope towards the mud road from Lysyanka village. There was a weak firefight going on. It was obvious that both sides were exhausted and had no more reserves left. A six-barrelled German mortar occasionally fired at our infantry from the northern edge of Dashukovka. We came back to our own.

I parked the tank at the hut chosen by our brigade commander and went in in order to get some warmth and dry my wet boots. When I entered the hut I overheard a radio conversation between Colonel Zhilin and the corps commander, Hero of the Soviet Union General Alekseev: 'Zhilin, close the gap.' 'But I only have one tank left.' 'So you close the gap with that tank.' The brigade commander turned to me and said: 'Did you hear that, son?' The mission was clear. I was to support the infantry of the 242nd Rifle Regiment that had retreated from Dashukovka just thirty minutes before and thus opened a three kilometre wide gap for the Germans. I was to capture Dashukovka, reach its northern outskirts, and deprive the enemy of the possibility of withdrawing or breaking through to the surrounded units by means of the only road, some 500–600 metres north of Dashukovka. I had to hold this road until the arrival of the Corps reserves.

I left the hut. I didn't know what forces the Germans had in Dashukovka or how I would drive them out of the village. My crew was calmly eating bread with canned meat. I yelled at them: 'Prepare for battle!' At first the crew looked at me puzzled, and made a couple of jokes about my haste, but when they realised I wasn't kidding they threw away their food and ran to the tank. I ordered them to throw off the tarpaulin so that the incident that happened in Tarascha wouldn't be repeated, and told them to throw out everything unnecessary from inside the tank and to load more ammo. Thus I was able to go into battle with double the usual amount of ammunition, 150 rounds instead of seventy-five.

We prepared the tank for battle in a matter of minutes. The brigade's entire top brass came out of the hut to see us off. I waved my hand to everyone, stood up on my seat, held on to the lid of the commander's hatch and ordered: 'Forward!' I remember that this was the first time when I wasn't anxious or nervous, as I'd normally be before an assault or the first shot of a battle. The farewell words of our political officer Nikolai Vasilievich Molokanov – 'It has to be done, Aleks!' – cheered and inspired me.

We went to a turn of the ravine at the closest point to Dashukovka village and slowly drove down the slope. We had only one choice: to negotiate the ravine and start our assault at the southern edge of the village. We quickly rolled down the slope, but we could not get up the other side of the ravine: when we were halfway up the tank rolled back to the bottom at high speed. We made several attempts, but it was all in vain. Temperatures dropped in the evening and covered the slope with ice, which is what was making our task more complicated. After a while I recalled how I'd negotiated the anti-tank ditch near Kiev in reverse gear. We also found twelve spikes in the spare parts box and attached six of them to each track. It took us about thirty minutes to do all this. After that we turned the tank around, and the loader, radio operator and I started pushing it uphill. We were so exhausted that we didn't realise that the efforts of three men meant nothing to a vehicle that weighed twenty-eight tons, and if the tank had rolled back down the slope we'd have been squashed. However, our anger and willpower and Doroshenko's skill as a driver, as well as the spikes, did their job. The engine roared but we slowly crawled up the slope. After reaching the edge of the ravine the tank stopped for a second, but finally it rolled onto to the even surface and Doroshenko started to turn it around. The Germans heard the loud roar of our engine and started to shoot illumination flares into the sky. Their smallarms fire intensified. I looked around, ordered the crew to

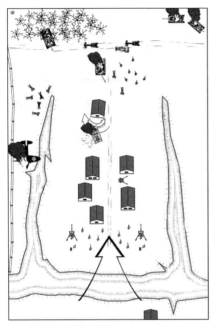

Battle near Dashukovka village.

get into the tank, and we rested for half an hour. I closed the hatch and immediately fell asleep. Apparently, the same happened to my crew.

I was woken up by a loud bang on the turret. It was the commander of the 242nd Rifle Regiment. I opened the hatch and introduced myself. He praised me for negotiating such a deep ravine. 'See those moving lights in the distance?' he said. 'Those are German trucks. I think that several German units have already travelled along the road out of the encirclement. I have the remains of my regiment here – about a company strong. You should use the cover of darkness to support an attack by my infantry. Reach the northern edge of the village and stop German traffic on the road by your fire. The motorised rifle battalion from your brigade is about to arrive, so help is near.'

I could see the small lights of cigarettes twinkling some 200 metres in front of me, where the infantrymen were lying in wet snow. I ordered the driver forward and shouted: 'Prepare for battle!' I showed my open palm to the loader: 'Fragmentation round!' I stopped the tank some ten metres from the infantry and inspected the line of men lying in the snow. They were mostly armed with rifles and only a few had SMGs. Apparently they'd been scratched together from all the units of the regiment. The line was about 300–400 metres long and I estimated there were about fifty men. I peeped out of the hatch and spoke to the infantrymen: 'Guys, we will now throw the Germans out of the village and reach its opposite edge, where we'll take up defensive positions. So don't lose your entrenching tools in the process! Advance in short rushes ahead of the tank, firing at the enemy on the move. Don't be afraid of my fire, as I'll be firing over your heads.' One infantryman shouted to me: 'Since when do tanks advance behind infantry?' I answered that this was a good question but that in this assault we had to act like I said. 'I'll be destroying the enemy's MGs, and when we're some 200 metres from the village I'll rush forward and you follow me. Now, look at me and go forward at my order!' The engine roared. The Germans shot several illumination flares and seven MGs immediately opened fire on us. I set the sight at night-shooting and started destroying them from right to left. My rounds suppressed three or four MGs in the first minute or two. I peeped out of the tank and ordered: 'Forward!' The infantry stood up reluctantly, but still started the assault. The enemy again opened fire from four or five MGs. I destroyed three of them and ordered my driver to advance 20–30 metres. I fired two rounds at the edge of the village, and then, firing on the move, destroyed another German MG. I could see that my infantry was advancing in short rushes.

The enemy could only return rifle fire. Apparently the Germans had left just a small delaying party of about one rifle platoon in the captured village, without a single AT gun. They must have thrown the rest of their forces into breaking through to the encircled units. A decisive moment came – the infantry now believed in me after seeing how I'd dealt with the MGs, and they continued to advance in short rushes, firing at the enemy. I couldn't miss this favourable opportunity: I peeped out of the tank and shouted: 'Great job, guys, now assault!' I passed the infantry and rushed into the village, firing on the move. I stopped for a second, fired two rounds along the street at the fleeing Germans, and fired a long burst from the MG. I noticed some monster vehicle trying to turn from around the corner into the street. I immediately shouted to Doroshenko: 'Squash it!' He threw the tank forward and hit this monster with the right side. It turned out that it was a German six-barrelled mortar.

We continued to drive along the street, killing the Germans who were running out of the huts and milling around their vehicles. Many managed to escape into the ravine, but those that were afraid of the darkness of the ravine and ran along the main street were all killed. Soon we reached the northern edge of the village and started choosing a good defensive position. A hut stood alone some 200 metres away. I drove to this and parked my tank with its left side towards the wall. I could see lone German vehicles driving along the road some 800 metres from me. The mission was complete – the road was in my gunsight.

My infantrymen started to arrive little by little. Only twenty of them were left. I ordered them to take up an all-round defence and dig in, as the enemy could outflank us through the ravines. But just as I'd feared, the infantrymen didn't have entrenching tools with them and they all flocked to my tank, seeking protection from it. When I saw this, I told them to spread out and find a good defensive position and be ready to repel the enemy's counter-attack at dawn. Several minutes later a whole host of lights appeared on the road in front, from behind a grove that was to the left of us. This was a German truck column carrying infantry (the Germans drove with their head-lights on during night marches for the entire war). Through my gunsight I estimated their speed at about forty kilometres per hour and waited for them to enter my field of fire. I didn't expect the Nazis to give me such a gift! I fired at the first truck and turned it into a huge fireball. Then I fired at the last truck (it was the eleventh in the column), and it jumped into the air and fell in pieces. Chaos ensued on the road. A half-track that was the second vehicle in the column tried to pass the burning truck and immediately got stuck in the mud. Other trucks also tried to drive off the road to left and right and also got stuck. The half-track caught fire from my third round, and I continued to fire at intervals of six to eight seconds. Doroshenko shouted to me: 'Lieutenant, don't destroy all the trucks, we should get some war booty too!' 'All right, got you.' The fires made it bright as day. I could see the silhouettes of Germans running in panic against the flames of the burning column. I fired several fragmentation rounds at them and emptied a DT MG disc, firing short bursts.

Night gradually gave way to dawn. It was misty and light sleet was falling. The enemy didn't counter-attack, but instead tried to evacuate their wounded from the battlefield. My infantrymen were frozen to their bones and tried to warm themselves the best they could. Some of them went to seek warmth in the huts at the edge of the village.

My crew didn't lose their concentration. As experienced troopers, they knew that the Germans would soon try to drive us out of the village. Indeed, a bit later a young soldier walked up to my tank and shouted to me: 'Comrade Lieutenant, enemy tanks!' I started to open the hatch in order to look around, but before I could lift my head I felt a bullet hit the hatch lid. A tiny splinter of armour scratched my neck. I closed the hatch and looked in the direction indicated by the young soldier. Two Panzer IV tanks were trying to sneak past our position through a ploughed field on the right, some 1.5 kilometres away. 'Here they come again.'

I told the infantry and crew to prepare for battle and ordered a fragmentation round to be loaded, as the two tanks were far away and I had to find their range first. The round exploded some five to ten metres from the first tank. It stopped, and I hit its side with the second armour piercing round. The second tank tried to drive away, but I immobilised it with two rounds. One crew member bailed out from the turret and ran away into the field. The 19th of February was beginning well.

I relaxed and was almost punished for this – a bullet hit the edge of my hatch when I lifted it in order to look around. The young soldier who'd pointed out the German tanks came and shouted that some German officers were looking at our position through binoculars from the other side of the ditch. After saying this he turned to walk away but suddenly swayed and dropped to the ground. I looked through the triplex and saw a small stream of blood flowing from the back of his head. I said to my driver: 'Pete, reverse and drive around the house. Be ready to come back to this spot.' The tank slowly reversed and emerged from behind the hut. I turned the turret and through the sight saw four men with binoculars lying in the snow some 400 metres from me, right behind the ravine. The group of officers, led by a General whose collar was adorned with fox fur, were inspecting the terrain and my position. Fetisov set the fuse and reported: 'Fragmentation round, ready!' I aimed, and the round exploded right in the middle of this group. Immediately I saw at least fifty Germans in snow camouflage running from all sides to rescue the wounded. I then took my revenge for my young infantryman, firing fifteen fragmentation rounds at them. Having calmed the Germans down in this way, we came back to our previous position on the right side of the hut and awaited their next move.

No one replied to my messages over the radio, and I only had fourteen rounds left, consisting of one armour-piercing, one shaped-charge, and twelve fragmentation rounds. In addition to that, both Elsukov and I had a half-full ammo disc for our DT MGs.

All of a sudden an aircraft emerged from behind the grove that was to the left of us. We dubbed such aircraft 'Caproni' at the front. This was an Italian-made aircraft and it could dive very well. It turned around and flew at 50–70 metres' altitude along the ravine to the left from the village, at the spot where I'd destroyed the group of German officers. Doroshenko again drove the tank into its firing position and I started to observe the aircraft. It turned around again and flew towards us. The Germans fired green signal flares and the aircraft responded with a green flare. It turned around again, dropped a large box and flew on.

There was a road perpendicular to the road that we'd closed, with a telegraph line along it. The aircraft was flying back and forth along this line of poles, and as I knew the approximate distance between the poles, I could roughly estimate its speed. It flew quite slowly, 50–60 kilometres per hour. After the aircraft dropped its cargo and flew past us, I decided to try and shoot it down if it turned back again. I ordered Fetisov to set the fuse and load a fragmentation round. The aircraft turned around, I aimed and fired. My round hit its engine, and the aircraft broke in two. It was quite a show! Next instant the field was literally swarming with German soldiers who'd been hiding in the snow and now ran to the remains of the aircraft. I forgot that I was short on ammo and shot about ten fragmentation rounds at this mass of Fritzes.

I set the tank back in its previous spot and I remained excited for a long time. I'd seen a lot of things, but shooting down an aircraft ...! The radio was still silent, I had enough ammo to destroy two armoured targets and MG ammo enough to repel one platoon-sized infantry attack. The time was ticking. There was complete silence all around us, a silence that promised a quick end of play. I heard one of the infantrymen shouting to me from the ground: 'Comrade Lieutenant, an assault gun has appeared on the left behind the ravine.' I ordered Doroshenko: 'Drive around the hut as you did before.'

We emerged from behind the hut and I saw a German assault gun with its main weapon aimed right at us, but apparently it didn't have time to get a better aim, as we quickly hid behind the hut. However, that route of retreat was shut. It was clear that the Germans would start their breakout attempt in a matter of a few minutes.

The German assault started head-on, from the road. About 100 infantrymen in white overalls with SMGs advanced openly along the road, firing long bursts. They were just 300–400 metres from me. At first I didn't understand why they acted so boldly. If I'd had ten fragmentation rounds and four or five MG ammo drums I could have calmed them down in a matter of minutes. Then I heard the roar of a heavy German tank engine, a Tiger or a Panther, amid the cacophony of SMG bursts. That's why they were so bold. They had a heavy tank with them. I shouted to the three or four infantrymen that remained to peep from behind the hut and see what was on the left on the road. None of them responded.

I made the decision immediately: let the Tiger approach me and kill it head-on with my last armour-piercing round as I suddenly emerged from behind the hut. I said to Doroshenko: 'Pete, start the engine and don't shut it. We let the Tiger come closer, jump out from behind the house and when you count four, without my command, you hide behind the hut again.' The radio operator and I fired a couple of short bursts from the MGs, killing several of the attacking Fritzes.

The noise of the engine was very near. I shouted: 'Forward!' We rushed into position and saw the Tiger with tank riders some 150 metres from us. The Tiger had just started moving after a short halt. This was exactly what I needed. I didn't wait for my tank to stop bouncing from its sharp stop, I aimed at the German tank and fired. No effect! Petr swiftly drove the tank backwards, and I shouted to Fetisov to load a fragmentation round. Then I saw that the German infantry in the field had stopped. I fired the last fragmentation round at them at point-blank range and saw them flee. We emerged again from behind the hut and were dumbfounded by the view. Flame was slowly enveloping the Tiger. One crewman was hanging dead from the turret. An explosion sounded in the air. The Nazi tank ceased to exist. We'd won again.

I forgot that I had only one shaped round left, ordered Fetisov to load it and decided to kill the assault gun in a one-on-one duel. Instead of calming down, I went looking for trouble! Petr drove the tank in reverse gear to the left of the house and brought me face to face with the assault gun, that was indeed waiting there for me with its gun aimed. He gave me time to get him into my gunsight, but he fired first, hitting the base of my turret with an armour-piercing round. The round destroyed the pig-iron counterbalances of the gun, killed Fetisov, and got stuck in the back wall of the turret. The second round destroyed the gun mantlet, turned the turret to its side and jammed the hatch. I shouted 'Bail out!' and tried to open the jammed hatch with my head. I opened it with great difficulty on the third attempt, pulled myself up, and jumped out of the tank almost at the same moment as the assault gun fired again. My radio operator Elsukov was running some fifteen metres in front of me. I turned back and saw that the Germans, who'd been fleeing a second before, had turned back and renewed their assault. They were just 150 metres from me.

I followed Elsukov towards the nearest buildings, but after running several metres I heard a cry from Petr Doroshenko: 'Lieutenant, help!' I turned around and I saw that he was hanging out of the driver's hatch, caught beneath its lid. I came back to him under fire, pulled the lid upwards, helped him out, and then carried him on my shoulders. Seven quickly spreading bloodstains could be distinctly seen on his padded jacket. There was a ditch in front of the houses that was under German fire from the other side of the ravine. I was about to jump across it, but when I was two metres away the enemy suddenly ceased fire. Apparently they were changing an ammo belt, and I just stepped over the ditch, still carrying Petr Doroshenko.

I was twenty metres from the last huts of the village when I saw the artillery crews of our motorised rifle battalion rolling two guns into position, preparing for battle, and our men with SMGs forming an assault line. My strength left me and I almost collapsed. The orderly of battalion commander Captain Zinoviev and a female medic ran up to me and took Petr Doroshenko. They took us to the village from which I'd started this battle the day before.

The brigade commander came out to meet me. He hugged and kissed me and said: 'Thank you, son.' After that he took me into the hut, where I reported the completion of my mission. After listening to my report, he told me that he was recommending me for the Golden Star of Hero of the Soviet Union; driver Petr Doroshenko for the Order of Lenin; loader Sergeant Fetisov for the Order of the Great Patriotic War 1st Class (posthumously); and radio operator Sergeant Elsukov also for the Order of the Great Patriotic War 1st Class. I should add that this was my second recommendation for the Golden Star, but I only actually received it in 1992!

After taking care of Petr Doroshenko, the medics started to take care of me. The female medic took a small splinter out of my neck. Then she asked me to stand up, but I couldn't. A sharp pain in my right knee forced me to sit down. They started to take off my long boot but couldn't because of the pain in my leg. Brigade commander Fedor Andreevich Zhilin said sharply: 'What are you waiting for? Cut the boot.' I was wearing the long boots that Petr Tyurin had got for me from the destroyed German column, so I begged them not to destroy such good boots. 'Just cut them open,' said Zhilin, 'I'll give you my tailor-made officers' boots that I just received this morning.' After saying this, he put a pair of excellent leather boots alongside my chair. Then they cut off the boot and my right trouser leg, and saw that my knee was swollen to almost twice its normal size. Apparently, it had been hit with several splinters. I couldn't calm down and was shivering with shock. The brigade commander ordered them to give me a vodka shot. I drank half a glass like water and fell asleep soon afterwards.

At nightfall we were sent to the rear. Petr was taken to a hospital for the heavily wounded, while I travelled through several field hospitals and ended up in Tarasha town in a hospital for the lightly wounded. This hospital was set up in great haste; it was poorly equipped and dirty. Wounded were lying on a dirty floor in the reception room and no one took care of them. I decided to get out of there right away. I got a stick and with its help I made it to the house of one of the girls that I'd met in the suburbs of Lysaya Gora in January, when our tank was knocked out. They looked after me very well, and healed my knee in one week. I completed my treatment at home in Arzamas, as I received a leave from the brigade commander.

In April I came back to the brigade, when its HQ was stationed in Boksha village on the border with Romania. However, the brigade commander was no longer Zhilin but Lieutenant-Colonel Pavlovski, who, it seemed to me, was more interested in arranging concerts than training the men for upcoming battles. The day after my arrival he ordered me to report to him, and after a brief interview, in the presence of his field wife and political officer of the brigade Lieutenant-Colonel Molokanov, he announced: 'I appoint you commander of my tank and my adjutant officer.' He'd just arrived at the front, and my Order of the Battle Red Banner (that I received instead of the Golden Star for capturing Kiev) apparently made him very jealous and uneasy. I replied that there was no such office as adjutant of brigade commander and that I'd already been tank commander. If the brigade didn't need me after a year of service at the front, I continued, and he didn't consider me deserving of an office of at least platoon leader, I would prefer to ask for a transfer to the reserve. 'Oh, so you say!' he exclaimed. 'Then you can go!' Jumping forward a bit in time, I can add that this 'general' was discharged from his office after his very first battles, but by then he'd managed to get almost the entire brigade destroyed. However, I was no longer in the brigade at that time.

In the morning I was informed that I was to go back to my former 207th Guards Tank Battalion as a tank platoon commander. But when I reached the battalion, I wasn't happy at all. It turned out that the battalion commander was a Major, a small, old man wearing spectacles, who'd arrived in the battalion from the rear and had no battle experience. This was it, I thought. I was very worried about the future of the brigade. But I suddenly learnt that the brigade was forming a third battalion under Dmitry Aleksandrovich Puzyrev, an experienced tank officer. I asked for a transfer, and thank God, they let me go.

For the whole summer of 1944 we were preparing for the offensive. We received new tanks, but we didn't get a single T-34/85: all our tanks were the 76.2 mm version.

One day we were standing in the tank trenches that were dug at the edge of a vineyard. There was a monastery one kilometre in front of us. All of a sudden a Tiger emerged from behind the monastery. It stopped. Then another Tiger drove up, and then another. There were a total of ten Tigers in front of us. We thought that this was the end, that they'd kill us all: eyes of fear see danger everywhere. But all of a sudden two Russian JS-2 tanks appeared on the battlefield. It was the first time I saw these tanks. They drove up to us and stopped. Two Tigers departed from the main group and advanced a bit, sort of inviting our heavy tanks for a duel. Our tanks managed to fire first, and blew the turrets off both Tigers. The other Tigers decided to leave the battlefield at that and again hid behind the monastery wall. At that moment I heard over the radio: 'Fadin, Fadin, report to the battalion CP.' They sent me to the Brigade CP and then the Corps CP, where the Order of Aleksandr Nevsky and a commission to train at Leningrad Higher Armour Academy, which was training heavy JS tank company commanders, were waiting for me.

The war ended for me in Vienna, when I was deputy company commander in the 20th Guards Tank Brigade. We didn't have any tanks at that time and we were in reserve. Deputy company commander Viktor Chebudalidze, who'd fought his war all the way from Stalingrad, said to me one day: 'Lieutenant, I found an amphibious car with an air radiator. It can drive as fast as 200 kilometres per hour. Let's go to Paris, check out the girls and the city!' So we left the brigade, as we didn't have any tanks anyway. Seeing Paris had been my dream since childhood, but we didn't get to see the city properly – there was a crazy party there, French girls were all over us, hugging and kissing us. It was complete mayhem! The Brits and Americans – everyone partied together. We spent one day there, and then came back to the brigade and received a scolding from our superiors for absence without leave.

CHAPTER 7

'A shell hit the turret, and the tank filled with smoke.'

Petr Ilyich Kirichenko

I was born in Taganrog in an educated family. My father had graduated from the Petersburg Institute of Mines and worked as a mining engineer. My mother was a teacher of German. In 1936 we moved to Moscow, where I finished at German school. All subjects in my school were taught in German, so I could speak the language quite well, and it helped me later at the front.

I had no intention to become a military man, especially a tankman. However, when the war broke out I was drafted, the same as many others. At first I was sent to the Chelyabinsk Military Flying School that prepared navigators for SB planes. But those aircraft had already been taken out of production, and after a few months of studying the school was closed and the students were distributed among other institutions. That's how I got into the training tank regiment in Nizhniy Tagil.

This regiment was preparing radio operators and gunners for T-34 tanks. To be honest, studying the tank's radio system seemed elementary to us after the complicated systems of aircraft. The DT machine-gun was also simple compared to rapid-fire aircraft guns. So after just a month of studying we were conferred the rank of senior sergeants and sent to a march company at the tank plant in Nizhniy Tagil. That's where the tank crews were formed from the former students of different specialist academies.

My crew consisted of four men. The twenty-five-year-old driver Nurdinov Kutduz, a Tartar, was the only one who'd served in the army before the war. The loader Tyutryumov Anatoli Fedorovich was eighteen, like me. The tank commander Gavrilko, a Ukrainian, seemed like an old man to me – he must have been twenty-two or twenty-three at the time. In the spring of 1942 we were sent to the front.

My role in the crew was as radio operator. The communication range of the radio on the move was about six kilometres, so communication between the tanks was rather poor, especially if one takes into consideration uneven ground surfaces and forests. On the other hand, it could pick up the news, both from Moscow and from abroad. That was something I didn't look forward to, because as soon as there was any break in the fighting the commanders and political officers would gather to listen to the *Sovinformbyuro* news summaries. The radio was powered by the tank's generator, if the engine was running, or by the accumulators, but since the noise of the engine interfered with the signal the commanders preferred to use the accumulators. So usually by the end of a broadcast the accumulators were running down, and I had to carry them on my back for recharging.

To be quite honest, I don't think that there was any need for a radio operator in a T-34. The communication system was so simple that any member of the crew could handle it. A radio operator was of little use even as a gunner, because he had a very limited view, and an even more limited field of fire for his MG. On the move I could see nothing but the sky or the ground. So my basic duty in the crew was casual work. I helped to clean the gun, fixed the caterpillars, supplied the ammunition, and refuelled the tank. My physical strength was in great demand. They usually dropped the ammunition packed in boxes near the tank, and I had to wipe the lubrication off the shells and separate the armour-piercing ones from the fragmentation shells.

In winter I had to boil water. We had no antifreeze, so at night I had to empty the cooling system, and in the morning I had to make a fire, warm up the water, and fill up the cooling system again. I also had to clean the tank all the time, especially in winter. It was constantly splashed with mud, and if I hadn't cleaned it the mud would have frozen and the tank would have broken down. Inside the tank I had to wipe oil and fuel stains.

I must say, there was no harassment or humiliating treatment of juniors among the crew. The tank driver, who was the eldest and the most experienced among us, had incontestable authority. He'd served in the army before the war and knew its peculiarities. He never sent us on errands, but always championed us and tried to help. Even the commander listened to his advice. Of course there was still a hierarchy in the crew. The commander was the senior. He got the information, gave the orders, and was aware of the situation. The tank driver was the second most important person, and the loader and I helped him in everything. For example, I helped him change gears on the move. The T-34/76 was equipped with a four-speed transmission, and it took enormous effort to change gears. The driver would set the lever in the right position and start to pull it, and I had to grasp the lever and pull it as well. It used to take several seconds. We had to perform this operation all the time during a march, and it was exhausting. During a prolonged march the driver usually lost two or three kilos. Another duty of mine was to roll a cigarette, make it draw, and put it in the driver's mouth, because his hands were always busy.

In case of emergency I could replace the driver. The T-34 was a rather simple vehicle, and I mastered the driving and firing pretty well. They didn't teach us that in the military school, but the tank driver taught me himself. We could replace each other in the crew, but this was our own achievement, not something required by the Regulations.

We moved from Nizhniy Tagil to Moscow, and joined the 116th Tank Brigade. In the summer of 1942 this was transferred to the vicinity of Voronezh. We unloaded at Otrozhka station and got the order to move to Kastornaya and repel the attacks by enemy tanks and infantry. Unfortunately, we were attacked by enemy aircraft first, and in a few days there was almost nothing left of the brigade. The toll was enormous. The enemy aircraft operated accurately and effectively: they formed a circle, and dive-bombed one by one. By the time the enemy infantry and tank units arrived, we had just a few tanks left. We tried to defend, of course, but my tank was put out of action in the very first battle. Before the battle the commander hugged the tank driver and patted us, the youngsters, on the heads. He had a premonition. He became very pale and sombre. We felt he wasn't himself . . .

A shell hit the turret, and the tank filled with smoke. One of the commander's arms was torn off and his side was shredded. He screamed with pain. It was terrible. We tried to bandage the wound, but we were unable to help him. He'd lost too much blood, and died inside the tank. We'd lost our commander, and there were no officers nearby. The turret wasn't operating, but we still could move. Another tank was standing close to us. Its running gear was broken, but the crew was still shooting. I was also firing from the machine-gun, trying to keep the Germans aside, but I could see nothing because we were standing in a field of ripe cereal, which blocked my view.

It grew dark. There was nobody around, and we could hear that the shooting was already behind us: the German columns had outflanked us from the right. We decided to get out. We took the neighbouring tank in tow and hauled it back to our lines. The Germans were everywhere around us. Somehow we managed to get to Kastornaya and found an officer from our brigade. He ordered us to move to Voronezh. We were terribly hungry. I remember we entered a deserted shop in Kastornaya, found a box of raw eggs, and ate several dozen of them. And there were no consequences! On 11 or 12 July we got to Voronezh. We felt rather uneasy, as we'd deserted the battle and were afraid we might even be executed. On the other hand, we didn't desert the tanks and did everything we could. Thank God, it turned out all right. Together with our damaged tank we were sent to a repair plant in Moscow. My second battle didn't take place until winter. It was the Rzhev-Sychovskaya offensive operation, where our 240th Brigade fought within the 30th Army.

As we were getting ready for the offensive we got our winter outfits of quilted jackets and *valenki* boots. Unfortunately inside the tank any clothes were worn out very quickly, and there were no replacements. Nor was there any escape from lice. We even brought them to Moscow, and only got rid of them there. Where did we sleep? While getting ready for an offensive we lived in dugouts, and during an operation we slept inside the tank. Though I was tall and skinny I got used to sleeping in my seat. I even liked it! After a march the best place to sleep was on the warm transmission, wrapped in a tarpaulin. The tarpaulin was the most important part of a tank! In winter you couldn't do without it. As for food, it was really good at that time: we always had full pots of soup, porridge with meat, and spirit before an offensive.

In the Rzhev-Sychovskaya offensive our brigade made a forced crossing of the Volga and established a bridgehead on the right bank. For two weeks we fought to expand it. Once my tank got stuck in a stream. The stream was covered with snow but the water was running. Its right bank was covered with ice and rather steep. All our attempts to get out failed – the tank got stuck with its stern in the water, the engine and transmission below water level. The Germans were shooting at us. My machine-gun could only shoot in the air, but the commander still managed to hold the Germans off with the main gun. Our tank was the only one left in no-man's land. When it grew dark the commander ordered me to get to our unit and explain our situation. That's where my knowledge of German helped me. I was moving along the German trenches and could hear the enemy soldiers discussing their current state and their plans for tomorrow. When I got to our positions I reported the situation to the battalion commander. In the morning our infantry units went into battle, the Germans were thrown back, and the motorised infantry dragged my tank out. I was awarded a 'For Bravery' medal and soon I was sent to the Chelyabinsk Tank Engineering School.

We studied the equipment and maintenance of the KV tank under field conditions. We were also taught firing. We carefully studied the engine, the transmission, and the running gear, and mastered the driving. Our instructors were very experienced, and had our practice at the plant. I studied for about a year and was conferred the rank of junior lieutenant technician.

In the spring of 1944 I was sent to the tank maintenance company of the 159th Brigade of the 1st Tank Corps. Four repairmen and a driver of the mobile maintenance unit were subordinate to me. At first I had at my disposal an A-type mobile station, based on a GAZ-AA vehicle. Inside was a workbench with vice, tool kits, and a chain hoist. We received spare parts from the depots or dismantled damaged tanks. Later I picked up a captured German Klekner-Deuts car with a diesel engine and a large wooden body and complicated electrical equipment inside. In winter all this stuff broke down. I found a German mechanic and brought him to repair the equipment, but all he could do was shrug his shoulders: 'Elektrik kaput.' He knew nothing.

Our task was to repair everything inside a damaged tank except for the guns. Sometimes my knowledge of German helped me here too. As repairmen we were also obliged to remove the remains of our tankmen from damaged vehicles. I often took some German prisoners to help me drag out the mutilated bodies and clean the interiors of the tanks.

Our brigade took part in the assault on Kenigsberg. Before the assault the people of Estonia presented us with a body of tanks named the 'Lembitu' column. Lembitu was an Estonian national hero who had fought against the Teutonic Knights in the 12th century, and later entered into an alliance with Novgorod. Thus he symbolised both the struggle of the Estonians against the Germans and the friendship between Estonians and Russians.

Our brigade didn't operate by itself in that battle, but formed part of assault groups consisting of infantry, artillery and self-propelled guns. On 6 April 1944 those groups began their assault on the city. The fight was heavy and the toll was great. Many people were killed and many tanks destroyed. The Germans offered fanatical resistance. They fought for each house, each cellar, each stone. However, after four days of fighting we managed to break their resistance and on 9 April they surrendered. Our maintenance company rushed about the city during the battle looking for damaged tanks in need of repair. The situation was rather tense, as the Germans were close. By the end of the operation we'd managed to rebuild almost all the damaged tanks, except for those that were burnt. I was awarded the Order of the Red Star.

Did I see any cases of a tank being deliberately damaged? No. Only once a tank driver forgot to change the water to antifreeze and the engine was broken. It was quickly replaced, but the negligence of the driver was considered cowardice and he risked being sent to a penal company. His good reputation and experience saved him, but he didn't receive any awards after the battle.

Towards the end of the war we had almost no tanks left in our brigade, so they were sent to join another. The rest of us were left in reserve. Then on 9 May we celebrated victory. The war was over.

How did we treat the Germans? That's a difficult question for me. My contemporaries only saw Germans for the first time at the front, when they attacked us with guns, aircraft and bombs. For them it was a simple matter of destroying the enemy as soon as they saw him. Remember Simonov's poem: 'As many times as you see him – as many times you kill him!' But for me it was more complicated, as I'd studied at a German school where the majority of the pupils and teachers were political refugees who'd fled from the fascists in Germany. They were real anti-fascists, and we treated them as very close friends.

As regards the Germans at the front, there could be no doubts. They killed and destroyed us, so how could we possibly treat them any differently? But our attitude towards them gradually altered as the situation at the front changed. At the beginning of the war the Germans we fought were young, healthy and insolent. Even in captivity they kept up their arrogance: 'You've captured me today, but you'll lick my boots tomorrow! You're *untermensch*!' But once we started to beat the Germans, they weren't so self-assured. By the end of the war the Germans we captured were mostly elderly men or youngsters. They didn't care about world domination any longer. They all looked a bit confused – though they fought hard until the end. Of course, they weren't fighting to retain their eastern conquests any more, they just thought that if 'barbarians' like us got into Germany we'd deport everyone to Siberia, rape the German women, set up the *kolkhoz* system and impose Communism on them. They fought to the bitter end, but if they were taken prisoner I saw a kind of relief on their faces: 'Thank God, the war is over for me.'

Our attitude towards the German civilian population was also different. Soldiers whose relatives had been killed or driven out by the Germans, and whose homes had been destroyed, initially considered that they should treat the Germans in the same way. But our people aren't really vengeful, and soon many began to feel pity for the Germans.

I remember one incident in a Prussian town. I drove up to a house to get some water for the engine. A sentry was standing by the entrance to the cellar, and I could hear voices coming up from below. I asked the sentry who was there.

'The Fritzes. They didn't have time to run away. Men, women, children – families. We locked them up here.'

'Why are you keeping them here?'

'Who knows what they are? We won't find them again if we let them out. You may have a look.'

I went down to the cellar. At first I could see nothing in the dark, but then I saw the Germans. It was rather noisy, as the children were crying. Then they noticed me and everything went silent. They looked at me in horror, obviously expecting me to start raping, shooting and killing. When I addressed them unexpectedly in German they were so glad that they tried to give me presents and stuff. I thought: 'So that's what you've come to, miserable people. The proud German nation that considered itself superior to everyone has been reduced to fawning for mercy.' I felt both pity and distaste.

So the attitude gradually changed, from pre-war feelings of friendship, through the savage hatred of the early part of the war, to pity.

CHAPTER 8

'Our tanks were the best.'

Aleksandr Sergeevich Burtsev

I was born on 15 September 1925 in the town of Uryupinsk, Stalingradskaya (now Volgogradskaya) Province. On 22 June 1941 I was going to go fishing with friends, but one said to me: 'Listen, at twelve o'clock Molotov is giving a speech.' 'What about?' 'They've declared war.'

I studied in ninth grade through the whole 1941–42 school year. In the summer of 1942, when the Germans came close to Stalingrad, all my schoolmates who were older than me volunteered for the front and nearly all of them died. We younger guys enlisted in an *istrebitelniy* battalion. Its duty was to catch spies and saboteurs, to guard military installations, and to maintain the blackout regime. There was a shortage of men and the local authorities asked the Union of Young Communists for help. We were issued with rifles and ammunition and we patrolled the town, guarded the District Communist Party building and the City Council building, and helped to guard the butter works and the Leninski plant, which produced mortars for the army. We never caught a saboteur, but we sometimes caught thieves and profiteers.

In the autumn I joined an Agricultural College. In November, when the Stalingrad offensive was being prepared, lots of troops arrived in the town, and some tankmen were billeted in houses neighbouring ours. I got into the habit of visiting them and, as the saying goes, fell in love with the T-34. The tankmen showed it to me and told me about its characteristics. Their commander was

Lieutenant Serguey Antonovich Otroshenko. Believe it or not, in 1944 I arrived in Subbotitsa at the 3rd Ukrainian Front and found myself in a battalion commanded by him – by then a Major.

I spent a year-and-a-half at the Agricultural College and in 1943, being $17\frac{1}{2}$ years old, I was drafted into the army. At first we weren't accepted, but we begged so strongly that the local Military Commissar took pity on us and directed us to the 1st Saratov Tank Military Academy. Even back at school I'd learned to shoot well and to handle firearms, and I knew the layout of tractors well, so the studying came easily for me. That's why just two months after taking the oath I was promoted to the rank of junior sergeant and designated a section commander and then a deputy platoon commander. The cadets wore boots and leg-wrappings, but we commanders were issued with patched up jackboots. But how were we going to clean them? There was no blacking. So we took sugar, moistened it to a porridge consistency and polished the jackboots with that – they shone like patent leather!

There were eight men at a table in the mess. We were given a can of food for breakfast along with white or rye bread and twenty grams of butter. For lunch there was a first and second course and a fruit compote. Vermicelli and stewed meat – I'd never had anything like that at home! That was how they fed us. We all put weight on but nevertheless stayed hungry, for there was a heavy workload. We'd get out of bed at six o'clock. Regardless of the weather we'd go for an exercise run in undershirts, breeches and jackboots. Then came eight hours of study, a couple of hours of leisure time, and lights out at 2300 hours. When we were going to lunch the company commander would watch us from around a corner as we marched up. When we got near the mess he'd leap out and shout: 'Company, about turn! You don't march well, you don't sing well,' and we'd do another circuit. After eating we'd come out kind of relaxed, and he'd be standing on the front steps: 'Fifteen minutes of marching!' That's how we got used to order and discipline.

We spent a long time at the school – eighteen months. For about a year we learned on Matilda and Valentine tanks, then on T-34s. We were taught well. We studied theory in classes and practised on an artillery range, where we were trained for weeks – we drove, fired, analysed tactics for individual tanks and for tank units. At the same time we also learned infantry tactics, for we were required to be able to interact with motorised troops. Our drill battalion was commanded by an old cavalryman named Bourlachenko who'd fought in the Civil War, the Finnish War of 1939–40, and the early part of the Great Patriotic War, but our company commander Draveretski had not been at the front. I could drive and shoot pretty well by the end of my training.

We studied driving practice and tactics on T-26 and BT-7 tanks and fired from the tanks we were trained for. As I said, at first these were Matildas and Valentines, then T-34s. To tell the truth, we were afraid of being posted to fight in foreign-made tanks: the Matildas, Valentines and Shermans were coffins. True, their armour was ductile and didn't produce splinters, but the driver sat separately and if you'd turned the turret and the tank was knocked out of action like that the driver could never bail out. Our tanks were the best. The T-34 was a superb tank.

We were commissioned in August 1944 as junior lieutenants, after which we were taken to the Nizhniy Tagil tank production plant, where we were distributed into marching companies. For about a month we were busy with tactical, firing and driving practice. Then we were given our crews, taken to the plant and shown some tank hulls: 'Here is your tank.' We put the rollers on alongside the factory workers, and helped as much as we could. High-class specialists worked in tank assembly, and there were some really young guys – drivers 13–14 years old were there. Imagine a huge workshop, and tank assembly lines to left and right of you, and a tank rushes in between at a speed of thirty kilometres per hour with a kid like that at the levers! You just couldn't see him! The tank was about three metres wide and the gate a few centimetres wider, and the tank dashes through the gate at that speed, flies onto a platform, and stops dead. Top stuff!

Once we'd assembled a tank for ourselves we took it for a fifty-kilometre drive, and practised firing at an artillery range. Here I have to say a couple of words about my crew. The driver had served a ten-year prison sentence and after a short training session could barely handle the machine. The gunlayer was a portly chap who could barely squeeze into the tank, having been a former restaurant director on a Saratov motorship. The loader was a man born in 1917 with a bit of mental deficiency. There was no fifth member. What a crew – and none of them had combat experience.

After we'd done the fifty-kilometre drive we went out to the range for some shooting. At the command 'Forward!' we moved to the firing line. I ordered: 'Fragmentation shell!' The loader grabbed one and loaded. A short pause. Then the gunlayer fired – into the blue. I yelled at him: 'Shorten the distance!' But the loader was gone, spooked by the recoil. I caught him by the collar and pulled him back: 'Just you load!' Our shooting test didn't go well.

We drove back and loaded ourselves onto a special train and rode via Moscow, Ukraine and Moldavia to Romania. Before we loaded the tank onto the train we'd been issued with a huge tarpaulin measuring about ten by ten metres. I left the loader to guard the tank: 'Watch out, don't let them pinch the tarpaulin.' But when we woke up in the morning – no tarpaulin. I roused everybody: 'Where's the tarpaulin? Do whatever you want, but I need the tarpaulin back by departure time.' I don't know where they found it, but it was brought back.

On the way our loader was left in a hospital with dysentery. By the time we reached Romania the gunlayer had got an infected finger and had been hospitalised too. Thus in September 1944 I arrived at the 170th Tank Brigade with just my driver. When we arrived the company commander, V. P. Bryukhov, summoned all the tank and platoon commanders: 'Look, we've got three good tankmen in reserve willing to go into combat. If someone reckons that some of his crew do not come up to scratch we can replace them.' I requested a replacement driver and was given a new gunlayer and a loader.

I have to say that Vasili Pavolovich Bryukhov was an officer's officer. A brave, talented man, a real commander. He always fought in the vanguard. Who's on patrol? Always Bryukhov! He accomplished tasks by manoeuvre and wasn't given to frontal attacks. It was no accident that he'd become a battalion commander at the age of twenty. He always looked after the youngsters and would send into combat those men who'd had experience, and the youngsters went in second or third until they got used to everything. We got a lot of help from such experienced tankmen. They taught us the skills and tricks of tank combat. They explained to us how to move, how to manoeuvre so as not to catch a shell. They made us get rid of the springs from the latches of the commander's double-flap hatch: even a pretty strong man had a lot of trouble opening that, and a wounded one wouldn't manage it at all. They explained that it would be better to keep the hatches open, making it easier to jump out. They adjusted the guns for us. They did everything to make us battle-ready.

And then came our first attack. The commanders were summoned: 'Do you see the grove? The enemy is there. Your task is to get around the grove and reach the operational open space.' We got into our tanks. The 'Forward!' command came, and off we went. I moved, fired, saw tanks blazing right and left of me. I couldn't see if the crews had managed to bail out or not. The gunlayer fired. I ordered: 'Right thirty, a gun. Left twenty, a machine-gun. Shoot fragmentation.'

I had only one desire – to close in so that the enemy couldn't shoot, to destroy them as fast as possible. I shot one shell after another in the direction from which they were firing. We approached the German positions. There were overturned guns, corpses scattered all over, burning armoured vehicles. We captured the grove, went around it, and entered the open space beyond. The Germans were running away a kilometre ahead of us, towing their guns. When they began to turn some of the guns around we stopped and began to shoot. Then they abandoned the guns and fled. 'Forward!' I was gloating over the scene when suddenly my tank dived into a wide ditch and stuck its gun into the sand. We had to stop and clean out the barrel before catching up with our company, which by then had advanced a kilometre. That was my first fight.

Especially heavy fighting occurred near Szekesfehervar, where I destroyed my first enemy tank. It was afternoon. We were on the attack when suddenly a tank crawled out from a small wood about 600–700 metres ahead with its right side facing us. We learned later the Germans had prepared caponiers and this tank was apparently moving to one of them to take up a defensive position. I told my loader: 'Armour-piercing.' To the gunlayer: 'Right of the grove. A tank.' And he smashed a shell into its side – it burst into flame!

Once in December, as we were surrounding a German force, we stopped to rest after a night march. We disguised our tanks a bit and went to sleep. When we woke up in the morning, what did we see 300 metres from us? German Tiger tanks on a rise, disguised as haystacks. We took to our heels. We started our engines and drove into a hollow. Following the hollow, we took the Tigers in flank and began to shell them, burning a couple. Three of our tanks went up the left slope of the hollow but were quickly set ablaze by tanks which stood somewhere on the right, invisible to us. Then the Germans pulled out and only then did we manage to get moving.

We were on the advance day and night. On the night of 26 December 1944 we captured the town of Esterhom on the Danube. Then we saw a column of about twenty vehicles approaching from the west. We dispersed and lined up our tanks across the road. The foremost vehicle stopped against a tank. Someone shouted to the driver 'Hands up!' but he bailed out and was mown down by a sub-machine gun. The rest of them were either shot or taken prisoner, and their vehicles were full of cheese and sausages. We stocked up with tucker, stayed overnight on the western side of the town, and in the morning continued our advance. Three tanks – the advanced patrol – went ahead. As soon as we'd left the town the advanced tanks came under fire from a grove near the road and all three were destroyed. We rolled back to the town, outflanked the grove, and came to a railway station. We captured an echelon of light tanks there and left them for the trophy-collecting unit that followed us. Entering the mountains we came to the town of Kamarom, on the approaches to which I was wounded on 30 December when a German tank fired at us from ambush. His shell hit the turret. I was shell-shocked and my left arm was broken, and on top of that I was slightly wounded by splinters of armour. The second shell hit our transmission and the tank caught fire, but we managed to bail out.

I lolled about in a hospital until almost the middle of February 1945, and after I'd been discharged I found myself in another battalion, by now as a platoon commander. We were in the second line of defence between Lake Keletz and Lake Balaton. We dug our tank in, dug a hole for the crew underneath it, and covered the tank with a tarpaulin. One crewman was in the tank on watch, while the rest relaxed. We were about three kilometres from the front line. Our breakfasts were delivered at midnight; supper, dinner and 100 grams of vodka at four o'clock in the morning. Once we were having supper underneath our tank when the position was shelled by *Vanyushas*. The tank wasn't hit, but we got quite a fright.

I remember that a battery of self-propelled SU-100 guns was on our right flank. They advanced for about a kilometre and stopped on the outskirts of a settlement. At daybreak one went up like a torch, then a second, third, fourth, fifth, sixth. All the self-propelled guns were destroyed by the Germans.

Soon we began to advance again, and our air force pounded the German front line – it was totally flattened. We saw our aircraft burn and explode in the air, but when we went forward it was a pleasure to see the results of their work – Tigers with their turrets awry.

We were advancing towards the town of Shefron. On 14 or 15 March I destroyed a German self-propelled gun. It was shelling our neighbours from a caponier and didn't see us as my tank closed from the rear. When it tried to leave its caponier to change position we shoved a tungsten-cored shell into it from almost point-blank range. It flared up instantly! Soon after that we smashed a 37 mm gun battery. It was a lucky break: we closed from their rear, rushed in and ran over them. I was recommended for the Red Banner Order but was given an Order of the Great Patriotic War 1st Class. And then I got a Red Star Order. All up I'd destroyed a tank, a self-propelled gun, and I don't know how many small tanks and armoured vehicles, and I'd mown down perhaps about 200–300 infantrymen.

On 30 March 1945 we captured a village and a mechanised column inside it: there were prisoners, vehicles, armoured vehicles, guns, but no tanks. We stopped, replenished our stock of ammo and refuelled. The enemy retreated by about three kilometres. Everything was ready to continue our advance. The battalion commander said: 'You'll be in the advanced patrol.' I ordered my tank forward. I sat on the machine-gun ball joint to the right of the driver, while my gun-layer and wireless operator sat on the turret, with their feet hanging down into the hatches, and about ten assault troops were mounted on the back of the hull. The first tank took off, ours followed, but the road was slushy and the first tank was leaving a deep rut. My driver moved slightly left so as not to get bogged down, and then suddenly – an explosion! The tank had been blown up by a ground bomb (Fougasse). The turret flew away twenty metres, along with the gunlayer and wireless operator. Both remained alive, but their legs were crippled. I was thrown up onto the roof of a house, from which I rolled down into the yard. I landed well – I didn't break anything. I threw the gates open and leaped out into the street. The tank was ablaze, its shells and ammo were exploding. I saw the battalion Communist Party Leader on the ground four metres from the tank. Fuel had spilled all over him and he was burning. I threw myself on him, put the fire out, and dragged him away to the other side of the house gates. My driver and loader who'd been inside the tank were killed, and nearly all the assault troops died. Only I was little the worse for it – just my eardrums burst.

For a week I stayed in the battalion reserve and when I recovered a bit the battalion commander assigned me to the Chief-of-Staff position, since both the Chief and his aide had been wounded.

Once we were taking a settlement. It was situated very inconveniently – in a hollow between two hillocks – and the Germans had entrenched on the slopes. Our first five tanks moved down the road towards its eastern outskirt. As soon as they approached the houses – bang-bang-bang, all five tanks were set afire. But we needed to dash through this village and move on. Three more tanks were sent ahead and burned out. No more tanks were sent, as we found a kind of pass across the hills and entered the village from the rear. We knocked the Germans off one of the hillocks but they kept firing from the other one. The battalion commander's tank was standing behind a house and the wireless operator and I were sitting in a neighbouring one talking when suddenly a shell flew through the window and blew off his head. His brains were blown out, his eyes stared blankly ... I'd seen death face to face before, but I was scared. I left the radio behind, ran out down the front steps, and then to the battalion commander. There were about thirty metres between the two houses and this space was raked by machine-gun fire. I ran about ten metres and a German sent a burst ahead of me. I stopped. When he stopped firing I ran again, and there was a burst behind me, but I managed to run to the commander and somehow we got out of all that.

My most fearful moment came when my crew had become the crew of the company commander. In one fight we were involved in a sporadic exchange of fire with German tanks. Our infantry was ahead of us in trenches. The company commander took the tank commander's seat and told me to lie down for a sleep nearby. Suddenly a drunken infantry captain crawled out of his trench with a pistol, and went along the trench amidst machine-gun fire yelling: 'I'll shoot you all!' Then he came up to our tank and saw me sleeping. He gave me a sharp kick: 'I'm gonna shoot you, you bastard!' 'What are you up to?' 'Why are you stretched out here,' he yelled, 'go and fight!' I went numb. He was just about to pull the trigger when my gunlayer, a well-built bloke, who'd heard the yelling, crawled out and jumped on him from the turret. He snatched the pistol from his hands and punched him hard on the nose! The guy came to his senses a bit, stood up, and went back to his trench without a single word. That was really scary. Had there been no gunlayer around I would've died for nothing.

In May 1945 we handed our remaining tanks over to another battalion. The brigade kept fighting up till the 8th but we were put in reserve. On 7 May the battalion commander was called away.

Although I was only a junior lieutenant I was still the acting Chief-of-Staff, and he said to me: 'Make the arrangements for a celebration. They say the war is coming to an end.' We were billeted in a manor house – there was everything in there, livestock, wine. When the commander returned on the 8th around midnight he said: 'Guys, the war is over.' What followed is impossible to describe – we fired in the air with sub-machine guns, pistols, signal pistols. Then all of us sat at a table and drank for joy.

T-34 produced in 1941.

Battle near Workers Village No. 5, Leningrad Front, 1943. Note that both driver's and commander's hatches are open to increase visibility. Only two out of five road wheels have rubber tyres, the rest have internal shock absorption.

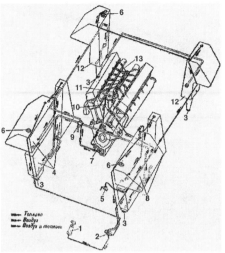

Tank fuel feeding chart: 1- air pump; 2 - air distribution tap; 3 - relief fitting; 4 - right side tanks; 5 - drain valve; 6 - filler plug; 7 - fuel-feeding pump; 8 - left side tanks; 9 - fuel distributing valve; 10 - fuel filter; 11 - fuel pump; 12 - poop tanks; 13 - high pressure fuel pipe. (*T-34 Tank Handbook. Voenizdat NKOM. M. 1944*)

Four-stage (above) and five-stage (below) transmissions.

Guards Colonel V.V. Sytin outlines a combat mission, 1943. A T-34 with hexagonal turret and two hatches is in the background, with behind it a model with a single large turret hatch produced by Factory No. 2112.

T-34/85 on a German road. Note the tankman sitting on the lug of the trunnion ball of the bow machine-gun. Judging from the presence of binoculars he's the commander. Many of the veteran commanders interviewed preferred to sit in this spot when moving through rear areas.

Tankmen with a woman friend. Photo taken in late 1930s.

Working on a T-34/76.

A train with units of the 10th Ural Volunteers Corps about to depart to the front line.

Distribution of valenki felt boots, 1941.

Crewmen tidy themselves up near their tank, Second Baltic Front, 1944.

Tankmen of the 1st Guards Tank Brigade relaxing between battles.

12. Aleksandr Vasilievich Bodnar when a cadet at Ulianovsk Armour Academy in 1940.

Semen Lvovich Aria, 1947.

KV and T-34 lying in ambush in the forest.

A formal portrait of Yuri Polyanovski.

Aleksandr Mikhailovich Fadin when a cadet of Gorki Motorcycle Academy, 1941.

T-34 tanks entering Izyum, January 1942.

Repairing a T-34/85 tank under field conditions, Budapest offensive, 1944.

Petr Ilyich Kirichenko (on the right) with his father, 1941.

Aleksandr Mikhailovich Fadin, 1945.

Driver-mechanic Petr Tyurin, 1945.

Certificate issued to Petr Kirichenko on 16 July 1941, confirming that he was drafted into the Red Army.

СПРАВКА

Выдана настоящая справка призывнику *Кириченко*

Петр   Ильич

в том, что он призван в Красную Армию и подлежит

отправке „____" *16 июля* 194*1*/г.

Выдана для представления по месту работы на предмет

оформления расчета.

Начальник 2-й части
интендант 3 ранга   (САМАРЦЕВ)

„_____" _____194   г.

Л116530   Тип. Ленрайпромтреста. 641

Aleksandr Sergeevich Burtsev, 1945.

Vasili Pavolovich Bryukhov, 1945.

T-34s under construction.

Standing by the tank are: (left to right) A.S. Burtsev, platoon commander Victor Bezrukov, deputy battalion drilling commander Vasadze, and crew members. Picture taken 14 July 1945.

Battle at Workers Village No. 5, Leningrad Front, 1943.

Steam bath and laundry unit.

Battalion commander Vasili Pavolovich Bryukhov (sitting on the driver's hatch) and his deputies, Hungary, 1945.

Crossing the River Svir, 1944.

Refuelling a T-34.

The 'Lembitu' column, 1945.

Arkadi Vasilievich
Maryevski, 2004.

A T-34 in the forest.

Wristwatch taken from the German officer at Lvov by Nikolai Zheleznov.

Nikolai Yakovlevich Zheleznov, 1943.

Georgi Nikolaevich Krivov, 1945.

Tankmen (and women) of the 4th Tank Army.

CHAPTER 9

'Only the luckier, smarter, sharper crews made it out alive.'

Vasili Pavolovich Bryukhov

I was born in the Ural Mountains, in Osa town in the Perm region, in 1924. I was graduating from high school in 1941. My favourite subjects in school were military science and physical education. Although back in 1941 I was only 162 centimetres tall and weighed fifty-two kilos I was considered an excellent athlete. I loved military science and wanted to enter a naval academy after school. It was my dream. They had such a fancy uniform!

We knew that war was about to break out. In February and March 1941, when they started recruiting reservists for the formation of new units, a lot of young teachers left our school. We were stupid enough to refuse to study German! When a teacher told us that we'd need this language in the upcoming war, we said with bravado: 'It's OK, when the war starts we'll speak to the Germans in the language of cannons and machine-guns. We won't speak any other language to them.' At the end of the war, by when I was a battalion commander, I used to take a lot of prisoners, and I couldn't interrogate them, as the only things I could say in German were *Hände Hoch* ('Hands up') and *Weg* ('Move!'). Of course, then I missed the language ...

We had our graduation ceremony on 20 June, and on the 21st our entire class went on a picnic in the countryside. Everyone took whatever they could bring – potatoes, sausages and lard. On Sunday,

22 June we came back into town at lunchtime and heard someone weeping out loud. There were small boys running around, playing horses, with one stick between the legs and another in the air, like cavalrymen with a sabre, shouting: 'War! War!' We all ran home. After some forty minutes I and all my classmates were in the military commissariat. I was so afraid that I'd miss the war! We thought it would last a month or two, not longer.

Batches of recruits were sent away all the time, and by September the city was empty. All men under forty had left, and only women, we teenagers under seventeen and old men were left. I should add that deep in the heartland of Russia we didn't feel the tragedy of the retreats and defeats of 1941. We were quite far from the front. But of course we started to realise that the enemy was strong and that the war would last for a long time. For the whole of that summer I applied and reapplied at the military commissariat, until on 15 September they sent me to the newly formed 1st Ski Ranger Battalion, as I was the local youth skiing champion.

They trained us there for a month, but what could they teach me? I could train them myself. So I mostly assisted the commanders who had trouble with their own skiing. Then they loaded us on a train and sent us to Kalinin. We were caught in a German air raid at the station as we were unloading, so I ended up in a hospital with an arm wound and shell-shock. I learnt later that out of 366 men of the ski battalion only about forty had survived.

Next they sent me to Perm Air Force Technical Academy. I protested wildly – I didn't want to be a technician, I wanted to be a commanding officer! After some attempts to talk me out of it they finally sent me to Stalingrad Armour Academy in the summer of 1942. When the Germans reached the city, those cadets who'd studied for at least three months were sent to the front, while we newcomers were evacuated to Kurgan. Our train was the last one to leave Stalingrad in early September 1942, under awful air raids.

The academy was formed again in Kurgan and our training recommenced. We studied the T-37, T-28, T-26, BT-7, BT-5 and T-34 tanks. I should mention that our base and training range were quite poorly equipped. I saw a German tank training centre in Austria after the war, and of course it was much better equipped. For example, we only had immobile targets for the main gun and stand-up targets for MG practice. A soldier would sit in a trench with the target and received orders over a phone: 'Lift the target! Put the target down!' But the Germans had a system of blocks connected to one large wheel that put in motion both the main gun and MG targets. The wheel was rotated manually, and the interval between targets emerging depended on the speed of rotation. German tank crews were better trained, and it was very dangerous to encounter them in action. At the time of my graduation from the academy I'd fired three rounds from the main gun and one MG ammo drum. What sort of training was that? They taught us a little bit about driving a BT-5, but they only taught us the basics – starting the engine and driving straight. We had tactical training, but it was mostly walking about on foot imitating the manoeuvring of tanks. We had a demonstration class, 'Tank platoon in assault', only at the very end of our training. And that was it! Our training level was very poor, although we studied the T-34 tank quite well.

We had twelve hours of classes in the academy per day, and I studied there for four months. The training programme was actually six months, but the twenty-eight best cadets, including me, graduated early. After graduation in April 1943 I was commissioned as a lieutenant and immediately appointed tank platoon leader. We were loaded on a train and sent to Chelyabinsk, to the 6th Reserve Tank Regiment, in order to receive our tanks. These were not ready yet, and as the factory was short of workers I went to work there together with a friend. I quickly learnt to operate a semi-automatic lathe, and worked for two weeks boring cylinder blocks. We worked for free; in fact, we only received a lunch card. When the factory had produced twenty or thirty tanks it was possible to form a trainload from them. The crews were also ready. We received a tank, drove it fifty kilometres to a firing range and fired three rounds from the main gun and one MG ammo drum, after which the tank was considered officially ready for shipment to the front. We came back to the factory, washed the tanks, and loaded them on a train.

We arrived at Kursk in June 1943 and were incorporated into the 2nd Tank Corps, which was in the second echelon of defence. The battle of Kursk started several days after our arrival. That was my baptism of fire, but as this was a defensive action, not an assault, I don't remember it very well. We repelled the German assaults in some places, in other places we withdrew and then counter-attacked together with infantry. Some veterans can tell you the names of the villages and towns that they fought in so well that I'm amazed. How on earth can they remember the names of all those places? Only now, after visiting the area several times since the war and describing the battles in interviews, can I remember that we fought in Mayachki and Sovkhoz Voroshilova villages.

If you were a commander of a T-34/76, you had to do everything yourself – fire the main gun, lead the platoon over the radio, everything. You realised that you were hit only when an armour-piercing round came through your tank's armour. Was I ever afraid? Not in my tank. Of course, I was anxious when I was given a mission: I knew that I would have to attack and that I could die. Even when I jumped into the tank and took my seat, I was still stressed, but once the fighting started I forgot about it: I just drove around and fired.

When a crew was well trained, it could fire quite rapidly. I'd get a target in the gunsight – a short stop, one shot, another one. I'd traverse the gun from left to right and shout: 'Armour-piercing! Fragmentation!' The engine would be roaring so one couldn't hear the explosions outside, and when I opened fire myself I didn't hear anything that was happening outside the tank. Only when the tank was hit by an armour-piercing round, or a fragmentation round exploded against the armour, would I recall that there were also some guys firing at me. Besides that, exhaust gas from the main gun accumulated inside the turret during rapid fire. In wintertime the ventilation system coped with the gas well, but not in summertime. Sometimes I'd yell 'Load fragmentation round!' to the loader. He was supposed to shout 'Roger, fragmentation,' and after the gun was loaded 'Fragmentation ready!' But sometimes he wouldn't respond. He'd be lying unconscious on the ammo storage, poisoned by the exhaust gases. Few loaders could last out a heavy fight to the end. They had to work harder than the others, and an 85 mm round weighed about thirty kilos, so the physical stress was very high. The radio operator, commander, and mechanic never collapsed in battle. So I wasn't at all afraid inside the tank. When my tank was knocked out and I had to bail out – that was a bit scary. But when I was inside the tank I had no time to be afraid, as I was very busy.

Our corps was in the second echelon in the battle of Prokhorovka. The distance between the tanks there was below 100 metres – it was impossible to manoeuvre a tank, one could just jerk it back and forth a bit. It wasn't a battle, it was a slaughterhouse of tanks. We crawled back and forth and fired. Everything was burning. An indescribable stench hung in the air over the battlefield. Everything was enveloped in smoke, dust and fire, so it looked as if was twilight. The air force bombed everyone. Tanks were burning, trucks were burning. All the communication lines were down – the phone cables were wrapped round our tracks. Our radio was jammed: I was trying to transmit a message, when all of a sudden the message was killed and the frequency was jammed. I needed to switch to the secondary frequency, but who could remember that amid such a battle?

We'd started our assault at eight o'clock in the morning and almost immediately engaged the German Panzers. My tank was hit about an hour later. A round flew in from nowhere and hit the driving sprocket and the first road wheel. The tank stopped, turning to the side a bit. We immediately bailed out and sneaked into a shell crater. The situation didn't favour repair of the tank. That was Prokhorovka! If a tank stopped in that battle, you had to bail out immediately. If you weren't killed by the first round, another tank would drive up and finish you off. We destroyed each other at point-blank range. I got into another tank, but that was also destroyed after a while. The round hit the engine, the tank caught fire, and we all bailed out. We hid in a shell crater and fired at German infantry and the crews of their knocked out tanks.

When I'd still been in the tank, I hadn't lost any time – with my first round I destroyed a German AT gun that was being prepared for action, and I also burnt a Panzer III. The battle lasted till seven in the evening and we had high losses – the brigade had about twenty-five tanks left from its original strength of sixty-five – but on the first day I had the impression that the losses on both sides were equal. The main difference was that the Germans still had reserves, while all our reserves had already been spent. In the evening of 12 July we received an order to hold our ground, and for three more days we repelled German counter-attacks. At first I didn't have a tank and I stayed in the officer reserve of the brigade. Platoon leaders and tank commanders without vehicles were all in reserve. If the brigade needed a commander, they would order you to take over a tank. Company and battalion commanders fought to the last tank of their unit.

Was it scary to get into the next tank after your previous one was knocked out? Pilots who'd been shot down would sometimes become cowards and avoid going back to the front, but not us. They were in a privileged position, unlike tank crews and infantrymen. In the air force a waitress would serve you dinner in a canteen and you'd go to sleep in a clean bed with linen sheets while the mechanics prepared your plane for the next mission. We didn't see bed linen for the whole war: we were always in a dugout or just under our tank in the open. We also had to maintain our own tank – we refuelled it, loaded ammunition and repaired it. Even when I became battalion commander, I would still work alongside the rest of the crew. We didn't have refuelling trucks till the end of the war. They just brought us barrels of fuel on a truck, rolled them off close to the tank, and the whole crew had to refuel the tank with two buckets. Two crew members poured fuel into the buckets, the third one brought them to the tank, and the fourth poured the fuel into the fuel tanks. Everyone took part. When I became a company commander, I felt it was below my dignity to bring buckets, so I only poured them into the tank. It was fifty buckets of ten litres each! We also had to pour in a bucket or two of oil. It was the same story with loading ammunition. They unloaded the ammo boxes next to the tank. First we had to remove the preserving grease from the rounds: this was normally done by the radio operator. When the grease was removed, we had to load the ammo into the turret. One man would lift the rounds from the ground, the second would be standing on the mudguard, the third would pass the rounds on to the fourth man, the loader, who'd place them inside the turret. In the winter we were all filthy, covered with oil and grease, our entire bodies covered with boils as we all had flu.

When we dug a trench, we drove our tank over it, covered the bottom of the trench with a tarpaulin and hung a stove from the bottom of the tank with the chimney outside – that was our accommodation. When the stove was hot, we were sweating, as we were dressed in sheepskin coats, padded jackets and padded trousers. When we went to sleep, we'd leave one man on duty to take care of the stove. If he also fell asleep the warmth quickly dispersed and everyone slowly froze. But if the man on duty didn't fall asleep and continued to stoke the stove, it was possible to sleep.

They gave us food just once a day – they'd bring breakfast, lunch and dinner in the evening. We always had US-made lard. In the autumn we'd dig up potatoes and fry them with lard – great food. This was my favourite dish at the front and I still love it. We always had vodka, because by the time it reached the front line half the men were no longer there. However, when I first came to the front I didn't drink at all. They'd bring a litre of vodka for the four of us, and I'd give my share to the crew. I only started drinking vodka at the end of the war when I became battalion commander. Once we were in enemy territory we took a lot of war booty – mostly wine and canned fruits.

We had tons of lice. In wintertime a tank turned into a real refrigerator, so we were very warmly dressed. When we took off our uniforms and shook them over a fire, lice popped in the fire like the rattle of a machine-gun. When there was a pause in operations we immediately fried all our uniforms and underwear: we removed the bottom from a barrel, inserted iron bars into it criss-cross fashion, and hung our uniforms inside. Then we turned the barrel upside down, replaced the bottom, poured some water into the barrel and set the entire structure on top of a campfire. The important thing was to make sure the uniforms didn't touch the sides of the barrel, otherwise they'd burn. Only young people could stand all this hardship. I believe that young people won the war.

After Prokhorovka we were transferred to the 1st Tank Corps under General Budkov and transferred to the Central Front, where we were supposed to attack towards Orel. There I performed a reconnaissance in force, after which I stopped playing at war.

It happened like this. The brigade commander came and we all fell in. He said: 'Volunteers for reconnaissance in force, one step forward.' I stepped forward without thinking for a second. At that moment, for the first time in my life, some sixth sense in my guts sensed a hateful gaze from the crew behind me. My heart fell, but there was no way back.

We drove through a forest to a grove on a hill, to the CP of a rifle regiment that was assaulting the German defences with no success. Our infantry were a bit below the hill; the German defences were a kilometre from them at the edge of a village. The 159th Tank Brigade of our 1st Tank Corps was supposed to break through these defences, but first we had to pinpoint the Germans' weapon emplacements.

They guided three of my tanks towards the front line and gave me a company of infantrymen, who dug in a little ahead of us, forming three platoon lines. They showed us the direction of our assault and gave us our mission: drive through the German defences at maximum speed and force them to engage all their weapons against us and thereby betray their positions. We were also told not to spare ammo.

We rushed forward. At first the infantry advanced well, but then they were pinned down by fire. My tank just flew forward. I saw my other tanks on the left and right start to fall back, and the tank on the right caught fire. But I rushed forward. The Germans concentrated all their fire on me. All of a sudden there was a hit and the flash of sparks. It got light inside the tank – I thought the loader's hatch had been opened and shouted: 'Akulshin, close the hatch!' 'There is no hatch, it was blown away.' It was amazing: the armour-piercing round had hit the hatch hinge and blown it off.

We were about 200 metres from the enemy when the Germans hit my tank head-on with an armour-piercing round. The tank stopped but didn't catch fire. After the battle I saw that the round had penetrated our front armour by the radio operator's seat, killing him with splinters, and continued on through the tank to the driver's hatch, tearing it off. I was shell-shocked and I fell on top of the ammo storage. At that moment another round penetrated the turret and killed the loader. It was lucky that I'd fallen from the turret with shell-shock, otherwise I'd have been killed too. We'd all have been killed together. When I regained my senses, I saw my driver lying in front of the tank with his head split open. I still don't know what happened to him – had he bailed out and been killed by a mine, or was he mortally wounded inside the tank before somehow managing to bail out and die outside? The dead radio operator was still in his seat, the loader was lying dead on the ammo storage. I looked around: a rocker arm had been torn off and buried in debris and splinters. The Germans had ceased fire, apparently thinking that they'd destroyed my tank. I looked around and saw both the other tanks of my platoon burning. I started the engine, turned on the reverse gear and started moving backwards. The Germans opened fire again at that and I stopped the tank.

Our artillery opened fire shortly after this, and our tanks attacked the village supported by infantry and threw the Germans out of their positions. When it became quiet again I got out of the tank, and loader Leonenko from one of my other tanks walked up to me – we were the only survivors of the whole platoon. He shouted the worst obscenities at me: 'Lieutenant, I won't fight the war with you! Fuck you and your tanks! I have only one request: tell the staff that I'm missing in action. I have a driving licence. I'm off to some other unit; I'll serve as a truck driver.' I said: 'OK.' When they came and asked about him, I said: 'His tank burnt. I don't know if he's dead or alive.' I started to fight the war for real after this battle.

I had to spend about twelve days in the care of the medical platoon, as I had shell-shock and my nose bled. Then I went into battle again.

What can I say about all those battles? It was just war. One day we'd have a successful battle, the next day we were defeated. We'd withdraw, stop, and dig in. The brigade commander brought up new tanks, moved us from one direction to another, and we attacked again. Your tank is knocked out again. You're in the officer reserve again. Then you get another tank. And your life goes on like that in circles until you get wounded or burnt alive in your tank.

One time I almost burnt alive for real. When does a tank catch fire? When a fuel tank is hit. But a tank only catches fire if there's plenty of fuel in it. At the end of a battle, when the fuel tank is almost empty, a tank barely burns. If a tank does catch fire and is enveloped in flames, staying calm demands a lot of bravery. The temperature increases right away, and if flames envelop you, you completely lose control. It was hard for a driver to bail out. He had to take off the hooks, open his hatch, and if he panicked or became enveloped by flames – that was it, he'd never be able to bail out. Of course, radio operators burnt the most. They were in the worst spot, with the driver on the left and the loader behind. They couldn't bail out before these two, and it was all a matter of seconds. It was easy for a tank commander and loader to bail out, but for the others it all depended on their luck.

My tank caught fire when it was knocked out somewhere between Orel and Bryansk. I yelled: 'Bail out!' and started to get out at the very first sign of flames. However, my TPU's jack plug was sitting tightly in its socket, and when I pushed myself up and tried to jump out through my hatch the cable yanked me back into my seat. The loader bailed out through my hatch, and I followed him. My *tankoshlem* rescued me – it barely burns, which is why only my face and hands were burnt, albeit to such an extent that they were covered with blisters. They sent me to a medical unit, where they put some ointment on my burns and put wire cases on my hands, so that I couldn't scratch my skin. After this, whenever a green crew arrived in the brigade I ordered them to clean the sockets and jack plugs of their TPUs so that they'd disconnect easily.

We fought a heavy battle for Bryansk cargo railway station. It was raining heavily. We crossed some small river and rushed into the station, which was full of German trains. It was an awful night battle. The Germans fled in all directions, but we managed to kill quite a few of them. We captured the station, destroyed the trains, and drove further into the streets of the town, finishing off the retreating enemy.

Did we often engage Germans at night? Yes we did. We didn't care if it were day or night. We had orders not to cease offensive operations. The Germans tried to avoid night battles and would rarely engage us in the dark, but did so sometimes. It's hard to fight at night. You have the impression that all the bullets and rounds are flying at you. You see a tracer flying past you some 20–30 metres away, but it still seems that it's heading for you.

It was also hard to find one's way at night – we were often lost. Some crews fell behind on purpose during the night, but it was impossible to prove! At Tata in Hungary we had such a case. It took place on the evening of 29 December 1944. The brigade with its forty remaining tanks formed a battle line in order to attack the town. We had to drive only about 800 metres, or a maximum one kilometre, in the open. But as soon as the Germans opened fire, every battalion started to fall behind. Only my company charged forward. After the battle we investigated this and everyone who fell behind had a reason. One crew's radio failed. Another crew lost the frequency and couldn't hear us. A third crew had its gear jammed and the driver couldn't go any faster ...

When our company charged forward alone, the Germans concentrated all their fire on us. We danced around, trying to dodge their rounds. A lot depended on the driver in such a situation. An experienced driver is a salvation for the crew. He would put the tank into a good spot for a shot; find cover; hide and manoeuvre. Some drivers even said: 'I'll never get killed. I'll place the tank in such a way that a round won't hit it in the place where I'm sitting.' I believed them.

Were there cases of cowardice? Of course. But it wasn't as if the crew bailed out before the beginning of the attack and the tank drove forward empty, though sometimes it happened that a tank took a hit from a mortar or a high-explosive round and the crew bailed out in panic. We had one such case in our battalion. A mortar round hit the front armour of a tank, and the crew bailed out and fled. When the Germans counter-attacked the tank was left in no-man's land, but battalion commander Mukhin took the driver with him and quietly sneaked back to the tank during the night. They started the engine and brought the tank back. The brigade commander did a great job by not court-martialling the crew. He just told them that such a thing should not be repeated. They continued to fight in the same tank.

We had one other case. We were moving to the front at night in order to attack at dawn. One tank commander stopped his tank, saying he didn't like how the engine sounded, and was ordered to wait for the battalion's technical officer. A tank was driving by, and the commander stopped it: 'Is the technical officer with you?' 'No, he's not. Why are you standing here?' 'The engine isn't working well.' 'Oh, really? What about the starter?' 'The starter is OK.' 'Give it to me then.' 'No problem.' So they gave away a working starter and installed a non-functioning one in its place. The next tank drove by: 'What's wrong with your tank?' 'The starter is out of order.' 'Hey, what about the batteries? Are they good?' In this way the commander let his tank be cannibalised for spare parts during the night. When the technical officer arrived, of course the tank was out of order, and it had to be sent for repairs. The crew didn't say a word, but someone informed the battalion's NKVD officer. They wanted to court-martial this commander, but we'd lost so many tanks that morning that the remains of the battalion were transferred to another unit. In this new unit they put him into another tank and didn't court-martial him – they pardoned him.

In late 1943 our corps was transferred to the 2nd Baltic Front. We fought there throughout November and December. It was extremely hard because of the swampy terrain. If you turned your tank off the road it stuck so badly that it couldn't be pulled out. We could only drive on roads, along which the Germans placed ambushes, and we could only attack on a narrow front, employing platoons and companies. During the two months of fighting I never saw the entire battalion form a battle line, let alone the brigade!

We lost a lot of men in those ambushes. It went like this: the first tank was knocked out; the second passed it and was also knocked out. All you could do was wait for your turn. Only the luckier, smarter, sharper crews made it out alive.

At Nevel they ordered us into a swamp, or we got into it by mistake – I still don't know what happened there. We had just seven tanks left in the battalion. We drove along a road and reached a clearing, and then wherever we tried to drive it was a quagmire, and the Germans blocked the road behind us. We formed a defensive perimeter in the clearing and repelled the Germans all night long. I was a company commander. One platoon leader and another company commander were killed during the night, while the third company commander and the battalion commander, Captain

Kozhanov, fled from the battlefield. However, in the morning these two apparently regained their senses and came back. I'd already taken command of the battalion by then, and I'd decided to break out of this trap the same way that we'd entered it. All of a sudden Kozhanov arrived, and yelled: 'Forward! Your brothers are bleeding and you're just sitting here!' Only four tanks made it out.

By ill luck we drove straight into the CP of the rifle division our brigade was attached to. The regiments of this division were assaulting Vasilki village to the west of Pustoshko railway station, on hills to the right of our tank trap. The Germans had built good defences there, with AT guns and tanks. I think we were trying to bypass Vasilki village when we got stuck in the bog. The division commander stopped us and ordered us to support his infantry. I said: 'Comrade Colonel, we have no fuel, no ammo, and we haven't eaten anything for twenty-four hours.' 'You'll get everything now.' They gave us food, and brought in ammo and fuel. Kozhanov said to me: 'My tank is out of order. Take three tanks and drive forward.' We put together the crews for the three tanks – quite a lot of men had been wounded. Then we walked to the front line to reconnoitre. I immediately said to the division commander: 'Comrade Colonel, I can see your tanks burning.' I could see several tanks burning like campfires in front of the village. 'Your tanks are burning. What can we do with three tanks? We'll die for nothing!' 'Shut up or I'll execute you! Fulfil the order!' I led the platoon to the assault. We passed the infantry, pinned down in a valley under a hurricane of fire, and rushed into the village, where the Germans burnt us all one by one. My tank was hit first on its side and then on its road wheels, and caught fire. I bailed out but the others didn't. That was it – the whole crew was killed. The infantry covered me with their fire, and I crawled back to our lines. The driver from another tank also survived.

We came back to our initial position and more tanks drove up, so I volunteered to lead them as a tank rider. That was my first and last battle as a tank rider. After that I swore that I'd never do it again. When we reached the front line, the other tank riders were off the tank in the twinkle of an eye, and I was left alone behind the turret. I thought all the bullets were flying at me – the whistling and shrieking of bullets and shrapnel ricocheting from the tank's armour was all around me. It was a nightmare! I've no idea how I survived. We captured the village, and then the brigade sent a car to pick us up.

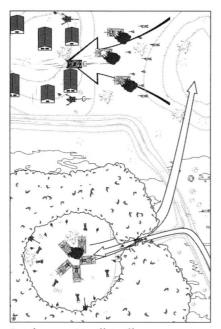

Battle near Vasilki village.

Then we were transferred back to Ukraine as part of the 170th Tank Brigade, in which I fought until the end of the war. When we arrived the Korsun-Shevchenko operation was already over, but battles with the German forces at Kirovograd continued. Our sister battalion under Captain Rodin lost almost all its tanks in one day at Plavni village: its first company was all hit by mines or got stuck in a river, and the second company was also completely destroyed when it tried to bypass the minefield, so out of twenty-one tanks they had only five left. On 8 January 1944 Captain Rodin was himself killed in action. He had only four tanks left by that time and they were attacking some village ten kilometres north-west of Kirovograd, but failed to capture it. The brigade commander Colonel Nikolai Petrovich Chunikhin, and the political officer Georgi Ivanovich Negrul, drove up to the battalion. Chunikhin calmly said that the village had to be captured and the encirclement thereby sealed. But Negrul started to curse Rodin: 'You this and that! You can't capture some shitty village? Coward!' Rodin was a talented commander, always calm, but at that point he lost his temper: 'I'm a coward? I will capture it!' Chunikhin tried to stop him: 'Don't rush, calm down. Look around and plan your action carefully.' But it was too late. Rodin gathered his surviving officers: 'Perevozchikov, go on the right. I'll be in the middle, Arakcheev on the left. We capture this village or we all die. Chashegorov, go to the Brigade HQ and report it when I've captured this village. If I get killed, I want no political officer making any speeches at my funeral!' They were all killed, except for one tank crew. It was Chashegorov who told me this story.

In the summer of 1944 they took us to the rear for rest and replacements and our new offensive started on 20 August. Our artillery had pounded the German defences to such an extent that we could barely drive over the ground – the former front line was like a moonscape, there were so many shell craters. So for the first fifteen kilometres there was no opposition from the Germans at all. We only encountered organised resistance at their second line of defence along the Valuislui River. But by the end of the first day we were already behind the German lines. There was no longer a recognisable front line, just pockets of resistance.

How did we fight? We'd approach a village and scouts would report that it was occupied by Germans with artillery and tanks. We'd bring up an artillery regiment attached to our brigade. The brigade would also deploy. Depending on the mission and terrain we'd deploy one or two battalions in line. The rest would stay in reserve. Then we'd engage the enemy. If he put up stronger resistance in the centre, we'd envelop his flanks. Two adjacent companies of the two battalions would tie down the Germans' centre in a firefight, while the other two companies outflanked them. We'd defeat the Germans and drive on. It is hard to describe a battle: you have to see it. All commanders up to company level would go into battle with their tanks. A battalion commander would be with the reserve, and led the battalion from there. He'd see who fell behind and who didn't. As soon as the Germans put up strong resistance and burnt a couple of our tanks, the rest would start slowing down – no one wanted to die! When he saw that the battalion commander would immediately get on the radio: 'Bryukhov, step on the gas!' I'd pass the order on to my company, but still they'd drive at tortoise speed. I had to rush forward and lead them by example. I made a calculation that our company lost eighteen company commanders killed during the entire war. I only counted the killed ones, not the wounded. Statistics for battalion commanders would be roughly the same. A company commander would fight till the last tank in his company, a battalion commander till only two or three tanks were left. You bailed out from one burning tank, and you had to drive another one. Sooner or later you'd get wounded or killed.

Of course, experienced tankmen lived longer. A simple example. A replacement company of ten tanks would arrive, but we might have four experienced tank commanders in the battalion reserve. So we'd take away the four weakest tank commanders from the ten that had arrived and either send them back to a factory to bring more tanks or put them in the battalion reserve. We'd then replace them with the four experienced commanders. Drivers and other crewmen might also be replaced. After a couple of weeks of fighting only one or two young commanders would be left out of the six, while probably only one 'old pal' would be killed during the same period. Experienced crewmen were killed 30 per cent less than green replacements. Battle experience is an important thing! Even one battle could teach you more than your entire armour academy course.

I personally knocked out nine tanks in my T-34/85 during the Yassy-Kishinev operation. I can remember one of the battles very well. We had passed through Kushi and were approaching Leovo in order to join the 3rd Ukrainian front. We were driving through a cornfield, with corn as high as our tanks. Nothing could be seen, but the sort of trails made by tanks were heading across the field in all directions. At a junction I saw a German tank drive quickly along a trail parallel to ours and disappear into the corn again (after the battle we found out it was a Panther). I ordered: 'Stop. Sight thirty to the right, tank at 400 metres.' Judging by the direction of his movement, we expected to see him again at the next crossing. The gun-layer traversed the gun to the right and we moved to the next trail. The German, in turn, had spotted us, and tried to bypass me through the cornfield. I looked into the panoramic sight at the place where he should emerge from the corn – and he did! We had to kill him instantly: if you let a German tank fire first and he missed with his first round, you had to bail out right away, as he'd always get you with the second one. German tank crews were like that. I shouted to my gun-layer 'Tank!' but he didn't see it. Half of the Panther's hull had already emerged from the corn. So I grabbed the gun-layer by his collar (he was sitting in front of me), threw him down onto the ammo storage, and took his seat myself. I aimed, and hit the Panther in the side. It caught fire like a petrol barrel and none of its crew bailed out. Of course, when the German tank caught fire my prestige as a commander skyrocketed among my crew. But for me, that tank would have hit us and we'd all have been killed. Gun-layer Nikolai Blinov felt very humiliated and was very much ashamed.

I destroyed a lot of tanks in Romania and Hungary. The nights were short and light. We drove up to a channel and stopped. There was a road on the other side and a German column was withdrawing along it. I managed to spot the silhouette of a tank against the sky and fired at it. It caught fire. The next tank stopped and jerked around, trying to pass the burning one, then tried to turn around, but didn't

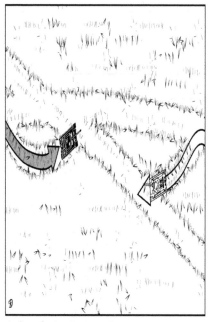

A battle in Romania.

make it – I destroyed it with my second shot. A pursuit is an easy type of battle.

In October 1944 I led the forward task force of the brigade and was the first to cross the border between Romania and Hungary, at Battonya. I captured a crossing on the Tisa River and held it for twenty-four hours till our main forces arrived. The battle was extremely hard, as the Germans tried to break out of our encirclement with all their strength. I was recommended for the Golden Star of Hero of the Soviet Union for this battle, but I only received the decoration in 1995.

After this operation I received a bonus for destroyed enemy's tanks for the first time. Nick Maksimov and I went to Timisoara and partied for three days. We ordered ourselves *kubanka* hats, fine uniforms and long leather boots. All of these fine items were tailor-made in twenty-four hours. But in order to get these bonuses you had to prove that it was you that knocked out a tank: eyewitnesses were necessary. We had a special commission that would drive around and check the results, if they weren't too lazy.

When the war was over, an order came to summarise all the operations of the brigade. They drew a map and the brigade commander held a meeting, which included a report by the chief of staff about the enemy's losses and our own. It was really hard to count our losses – we didn't always accurately record how many tanks were destroyed. But we could easily calculate the enemy's losses from our daily reports. All of a sudden the chief of staff said: 'If I believed all the reports of battalion commanders Bryukhov, Sarkesyan, Otroshenkov and Moskovchenko, we should have finished the war six months earlier, as we'd have destroyed the entire German army. So I always divided by two all the numbers in your reports and only then sent them off to Corps HQ.' I think that Corps HQ also divided the reports by two before forwarding them to the Army HQ, and so on. I guess that after all this dividing the reports ended up some-what more reliable. Our daily reports were written in the following fashion: 'We attacked the enemy here and here. During the day we advanced so and so many kilometres on so and so wide a front. We reached the line at so and so. Enemy's losses: so and so many tanks.' We counted them accurately, as we were paid bonuses for them, but mortars, artillery pieces and personnel – who bothered to count them? No one. We'd just write down 'about fifty infantrymen'. When we were in defence, and were just firing at the German positions, we'd write down 'two guns and one mortar destroyed by our fire'.

In general, it was hard to fight the Germans. I didn't have any hatred towards them; they were just an enemy that had to be destroyed. I didn't harass the POWs; I just gathered them and took them to the rear. There was one incident in Hungary, at Budapest, on 25 or 26 December 1944. My battalion (I was battalion commander from late 1944) was about twenty kilometres ahead of the main forces of the brigade and reached Vertesboglar, cutting the road to Budapest. We stopped in a grove on a hill. About one kilometre from us there was a small village in a valley with a road through it, and a large German armoured column was driving along it. I counted sixty-three tanks. It would have been insanity to engage them with my fifteen tanks, so I reported the news to the brigade commander. He ordered me to continue observation and called in the air force. They smashed the German column at Bichke.

We stayed in the grove. While we were standing there, three German phone operators who were laying a cable bumped into us. We grabbed them and tied them up. We tried to talk to them, but none of us could speak German. We put them into a shell crater and set a guard over them so that they wouldn't run away. Then we saw an Opel-Admiral car driving in the opposite direction to the column. It was a high-class car, and we thought it was some top brass. They turned off the road and drove to the left of our grove along a field road. I jumped onto my tank, grabbed an SMG, and shouted to the driver: 'Cut them off!' He rushed forward and intercepted the car. I jumped out and fired a burst into the car's engine. It stopped. The officers and driver inside the car were dumbfounded. I pointed my gun at them and ordered: '*Weg!*' They got out, three officers and the driver. I continued: '*Hände Hoch!*' They raised their hands. Then one of them suddenly ran off in the same direction as the car had been driving. I chased him, as I thought my crew could deal with the other ones, but those Germans didn't move an inch.

All of a sudden the fleeing German stopped, ran back to the car, grabbed his briefcase, and ran off in another direction, towards the armoured column on the road. I chased him again. I fired two bursts at him on the move, and missed both times. At the third burst my gun jammed. I started to jerk the bolt, and the German, realising something was wrong, turned around, pulled out his Parabellum pistol and fired. He missed, but it was my turn to flee. I ran towards the tank while he chased me. Then I had a bit of luck – I jerked the bolt again and my PPSh worked. I turned around – he was still running at me – and fired a long burst. It looked like the German hit an invisible wall and fell down. I walked a bit closer and fired another burst at him just to be safe. I picked up his briefcase, wristwatch, and the Parabellum. I already had two handguns on me – one on my belt and one in my breast pocket, but for some reason I forgot about them when my PPSh jammed. I looked into the briefcase and saw some maps in it. I thought the maps must be important for him to run back to the car to get them. We towed the car back to Brigade HQ with the prisoners. It turned out that the maps were a plan for a counter-attack at Sekeshfehevar. I was awarded the Order of Suvorov for this episode.

So I killed that German and I didn't feel sorry for it at all. I didn't touch the ones who didn't resist; I just sent them to the rear. The enemy is always the enemy, but I never executed them for no good reason. In the winter of 1945 we captured five Germans in a battle. The fighting died out in the evening and we stopped to get some rest. The battalion political officer and supply officer Vasili Selivanov came along and brought fuel and ammo. They said: 'Commander, let's have dinner together.' They readied a table and put a bottle of wine on it. Vasili said: 'I'll go make sure that your men are getting everything they want.' 'OK. Make sure that everything is in order.' He came back shortly: 'Everything's fine. The men are fed, the tanks are refuelled and reloaded with ammo.' I said to him: 'There are five Germans sitting in a hole. Take them away when you go.' He looked confused. 'What's wrong with you?' No answer. I realised something was wrong and went to see the Germans, taking Vasili with me. I'd put them into a hole and set a guard. It turned out that Vasili had come to the hole and asked: 'Who are these?' 'Germans.' 'Nazis!' he cried, and he shot them all. When I saw this, I was furious. 'You son of a bitch, what have you done? If you want to shoot Germans, come into battle with us tomorrow. Just get on my tank and kill as many as you please!' I gave him a proper scolding. The political officer walked up. We sat down and discussed the situation with him: 'You should be court-martialled for this,' he told Vasili. 'Take a shovel and bury them, so that they're not seen.' So Vasili buried the Germans in front of the entire battalion. He was never in real combat. A supply officer is always a supply officer. I think that men who'd been in real combat would never shoot a prisoner. Maybe there were such people, but I didn't have them in my battalion.

But there was an incident at Krajovo in Romania, where we stopped for three days to repair our tanks and await the supply units. One of the tank commanders in our battalion was Lieutenant Ivanov, from the Belgorod area. He was thirty-five years old, a Communist who'd been chairman of a *kolkhoz* before the war. His village was occupied by Romanian troops while he was at the front, and during their retreat they took away all the young villagers and put the Communist party members and their families into a barn and burnt them alive. It was only when our brigade passed near his home village, and he requested permission to visit it, that Ivanov learnt of this. His neighbours told him how the poor people had yelled and cried as the barn was drenched with petrol, and how the Romanians had fired through the barn walls to finish them off. This is how Ivanov's family died – his wife and two children.

When Ivanov rejoined the brigade he was a different man. He started to seek revenge. He fought very hard – sometimes it seemed as if he was seeking death – and he didn't take any prisoners: if someone tried to surrender to him, he killed them immediately.

But in Krajovo it happened like this. He and his driver got drunk and went into town to look for female company. It was September, a nice autumn evening. They walked into a house where an older man and a young woman of about twenty-five were drinking tea. The woman had an eighteen-month-old baby with her. Ivanov took the baby and gave it to the young girl's parents, and told the girl to go into another room. Then he said to his driver: 'You go fuck her first, I'll go second.' So the driver went into the room. But he was only eighteen years old and most likely he'd never been with a woman before. Sensing his inexperience as he started to undress her, the girl managed to jump out of the window and ran away. Ivanov, hearing the noise, rushed into the room: 'Where is she? You son of a bitch, you let her get away!' Then he fired one burst through the window with his SMG and the girl fell down. The two of them gave the matter no further thought and left. If Ivanov had wanted to deliberately kill her he'd have definitely missed, as he was drunk, but he'd fired without taking aim. Only one bullet hit her, but it went straight into her heart.

The next day her parents and the local mayor came to the brigade headquarters, and the day after that *Smersh* discovered the criminals and arrested them. Ivanov confessed right away that he'd shot at the girl, but he hadn't realised that he'd killed her.

The court-martial took place on the third day after the tragedy. The entire brigade stood in formation in a field, and the mayor and the girl's parents were also present. The driver was crying like a baby. Ivanov said to him: 'Be a man! They won't execute you, so stop sobbing. They'll just send you to a penal company and you'll redeem your honour with your blood.' And that's how it turned out. The driver was sentenced to twenty-five years' imprisonment, commuted to service in a penal company.

When Lieutenant Ivanov was asked if he had anything to add, he stood up and said: 'Comrade judges, I committed a crime and I ask you not to show me any mercy.' Just like that, simply and firmly. Then he sat down and calmly picked his teeth with a grass stem.

Then they announced his sentence: execution in front of the entire brigade, the sentence to be carried out immediately.

It took us some fifteen minutes to fall in. They stood Ivanov in front of a grave that had been dug beforehand. The lieutenant-colonel who was the brigade *osobist* told our battalion *osobist*, who was standing with the rest of us: 'Comrade Morozov, execute the sentence.' The latter didn't move. 'I'm ordering you!' Still Morozov didn't move an inch. Then the lieutenant-colonel grabbed him by the arm and pulled him out of the ranks, calling him the worst obscenities: 'I'm ordering you!' Only then did Morozov walk over to Ivanov.

Lieutenant Ivanov took off his side-cap, bowed to us and said: 'Forgive me, brothers.' That was it. Morozov said to him: 'On your knees.' He said it very quietly, but everyone heard – there was an awful silence in the air. Ivanov knelt down, putting his cap under his belt. 'Bend your head forward,' said Morozov. When he bent forward our *osobist* shot him in the back of the head, and Ivanov fell to the ground and jerked in agony. It was a horrible sight.

Morozov turned and walked away with the smoking gun in his hand, swaying from side to side as if he was drunk. The lieutenant-colonel shouted: 'A control shot! A control shot!' But Morozov walked on without hearing. Then the lieutenant-colonel himself ran to Ivanov and fired one, two, three rounds at his head. I remember that although Ivanov was already dead, his body still jerked at every shot.

The lieutenant-colonel pushed the body into the grave with his foot: 'Bury him.' So it was done. 'Dismissed!' But everyone stood frozen in formation for fifteen minutes. There was a dead silence. Ivanov had always fought well, and was a respected officer, and everyone knew that the Romanians had burnt his family alive. He could have asked for mercy, and he could have said that the girl's death was an accident, but he didn't. After this we had no more incidents with the local population in our brigade.

However, we had a lot of venereal disease, but in most cases the men got this from our own women. Did people date at the front? Of course! Girls were coming to us because they wanted to get married, and quite a few got married at the front. Even decent girls tried to date officers, preferably senior officers. Guys who were good troopers were also popular – those who were always in battles, getting lots of decorations. I was still just a company commander when they started to talk about me at Brigade HQ – Bryukhov did this, and Bryukhov did that – but I was very rarely there: they'd never seen me and only knew of me by my last name. One time the brigade commander said: 'Report to my HQ, I'll brief you.' As I heard later, all the HQ female personnel got excited: 'Bryukov is coming!' Then I drove up in my tank, a tiny, skinny guy in dirty overalls, and the girls all heaved a sigh of disappointment.

Quite a lot of girls left our brigade pregnant. Field wives were common among senior officers, from brigade commander upwards. Our brigade commander lived with a female doctor from our medical platoon. Our political officer lived with his female accountant. Other girls dated officers who they liked, or officers whose privileges they liked, but it was all voluntary: there were no rapes. The girls at the front had a hundred times more difficult time than we men. I felt especially sorry for the female combat medics. They drove on tanks, evacuated the wounded from the battlefield, and as a rule would only get the Medal for Combat Service – soldiers mocked them that it was a Medal for Sexual Service. Very few girls received the Order of the Red Star. Most of those who did dated their commanders.

There were 1,200 men in the brigade, all young men, but only sixteen girls, and all the men tried to court them. A girl would find a man that she liked and they'd start dating and then living together. The rest were jealous: 'What a slut, a field wife.' That's how many good girls received bad reputations – just because of slander and jealousy.

I finished the war in Austria. My personal score in the fighting? I lost nine tanks and burnt twenty-eight German tanks. I only received a salary bonus for nine of them, but that wasn't the point.

CHAPTER 10

'If you don't go, you'll be executed.'

Arkadi Vasilievich Maryevski

Just before the war started I graduated from high school and got a job as clerk in a police station. Then from August 1941 I served at the military registration and enlistment office and took care of call-up papers. I was seventeen years old at the time, which is too young for service in the Red Army. In the late autumn that year I received a new list of about fifty recruits' names. As I read through them I recognised nearly all of them as my ex-classmates, fellows with whom I'd grown up. How could this be? All my classmates going to the army, while I stayed behind to shuffle papers? No way! I took a blank call-up sheet, filled in my name, and took it to Major Degtiariev to sign. He asked: 'What's wrong with you? We'll give you a military title and you can work in my department.' I argued: 'Sir, I wish to serve with my classmates, my comrades.' He replied: 'Well, go then.'

That's how I was recruited into the army. I wrapped my belongings in a piece of cloth – bags weren't used back then – and went to the station, where we recruits were given a passenger carriage to take us to the assembly point in Gorky. The assembly point was packed. The first night I was there someone snatched my pack with all my possessions, including my food. I woke up hungry, and food wasn't provided. It's a good thing my companions helped out with what little they could.

I passed the medical examination: 'Limbs intact, eyesight normal – valid.' We were sent to the Kasan region to form an infantry battalion. We were accommodated in long earth-houses, and received a warm welcome from our officers. All of them were good guys from regular regiments. I remember our platoon commander, Lieutenant Illarionov, a very tall fellow. About twenty days later we pledged our oath.

I was assigned to guard an area near the storehouse. The storehouse itself was a long wooden hangar, one half of it filled with general goods and the other half with food. It was winter, and snow covered the ground. I heard someone coming, so I called 'Stop! Identify yourself!' 'Patrol commander, Senior Sergeant Naumkin.' 'Password?' He had the right password. He came up with a sledge and two horses. He asked: 'Haven't frozen over yet?' 'Yes, it's cold.' I had only an overcoat and a pair of felt boots, which I had to pass on to the next man when we changed guard shifts.

Senior Sergeant Naumkin took my rifle and used the bayonet to break the lock. In accordance with military regulations I shouldn't have let him do it, but I was only seventeen and, after all, he was a patrol commander. He loaded the sledge with food and fur coats and left. I stood there for another four hours until the change of the guard. The next day Naumkin came up to me and said: 'Come into my office.' After I came in he offered me some food – all of it stolen from the warehouse.

The storekeepers reported the missing food and the investigators found us out quite quickly. I didn't deny anything and was sentenced to death without a tribunal. The whole episode happened a couple days before the departure of our regiment to the front line, and the chief commander of the regiment, Colonel Bubnov, must have asked the NKVD to commute the death sentence. So I was sent to serve in the penal battalion instead.

How did I get out? All I remember is that I was given ten bullets for my rifle. Then there's a gap in my consciousness. I can remember trying to shoot, clicking the trigger, but I'd run out of bullets. Then someone shook my shoulder and said: 'Enough, the Germans have fled.' All around me lay the bodies of penal battalion soldiers, but I was alive. After writing a report of the attack I was released and even awarded with a medal, 'For Courage'. I was sent back to my previous regiment. I've no knowledge of where Naumkin ended up.

For a while I fought in the 322nd Division. For the most part we prepared for offensive operations. I recall how one night we did a sixty-kilometre march. The officers went on horseback and the rest of us on foot, in the falling snow. We knew that the assault would begin only after the artillery was in place. It took us a whole week, if not more, to haul everything into position. We didn't have anywhere to sleep, so we made little huts out of branches – during the whole war I didn't sleep under a roof even once! We also brought portable furnaces with us. Scarcely any rest was given to us: there were tactical exercises, shooting practice, and so on, in preparation for battle.

One day we were lined up. An officer from the tank division called 'Car drivers and mechanics – one step forward!' Before the war my uncle worked as a chauffeur, and he'd given me a few driving lessons in a truck. The officer asked me: 'Have you ever driven a car?' I replied: 'About five kilometres or so.' 'Step up.' That's how I became a tank driver and mechanic! Experienced tank drivers taught us everything from scratch. The famous T-34 model wasn't yet available, so we started on T-60, T-70 and BT-7 tanks.

Our instructors explained why we should never wear our whole combat suit: the less bulky we were, the more chance we had of getting out alive if the tank was hit. With petrol engines these iron coffins burnt as easy as matches. Getting out of a tank in time was one of the most important skills to learn.

Then came the real fights. Four of my tanks were burnt, but I wasn't injured. The first time I got out just in time as the petrol tanks were about to blow. Of the people killed, most were commanders, who sat in the turrets. Later on, after getting promoted to a T-34 company commander, I never sat in the turret and usually drove the tank. Turrets were hit more often, giving those inside them little chance. Maybe that's the reason I made it.

Later we got a few repaired T-34 tanks, and I became a tank commander because I was a sergeant and had graduated from high school. In the new tank I felt more than comfortable, though unfortunately the field of view was limited to short glimpses of the sky and ground, but the gun was powerful. We managed to communicate with each other inside the tank: the gunner pushed me when he was ready, I immediately made a short stop and he opened fire. We did our job well.

In the summer of 1942 I became a junior lieutenant and was sent to the armour academy at Omsk with others like me who'd received field promotions. We had the ranks but no knowledge of how to actually command a tank. For about three months we learnt battle tactics, had shooting practice, and went to factory No. 174, where we participated in assembling tanks. The factory had no conveyor assembly: everything was put together by hand.

At the end of 1942 we got new tanks and were sent to the Stalingrad front. My crew's driver was Misha Mironov, born in 1922. Before the war he'd worked as a tractor operator. As I mentioned before, I commanded my crew from the driver's seat, so Misha was our radio operator. Kolya Jibreiev, born in 1924, was the loader, and the gunner was Ivan Pechorsky, a Siberian hunter and an excellent shot: I could never be as precise. He hit targets if not with his first shot, then definitely with his second. The crew was fully interchangeable. All of us could drive and fire.

Michael Fedorovich Pankov was in charge of the tank corps. The 17th Tank Brigade in which I served was under Lieutenant-Colonel Shulgin. He never sat in his tank. During the assault he drove a jeep, weaving his way between the tanks with a stick in his hand. God help you if you stopped your machine during battle: you'd hear a knock on the driver's hatch: 'Open the hatch!' And as soon as your head was out a swift blow from Shulgin's stick would follow. It happened to me once. My tank engine stalled, and sure enough I heard knocking outside. But I took off my helmet and put it on my knee, and so put my knee up through the hatch when I opened it. And he hit my knee a couple of times without noticing! Then I managed to restart the engine and resumed my advance. Some time later, after I'd forgotten the whole incident, Colonel Shulgin called me in and asked: 'Where did you learn to deceive your commanders? Why did you trick me?' 'When, Comrade Colonel?' 'I was told you put your helmet on your knee. Why didn't you put out your head with the helmet on?' 'Comrade Colonel, I think a good commander should never jeopardise his head!' 'Son of a ... Good! Dismissed!'

By the Orlov offensive operation I was already in command of a tank company, and when battalion commander Pochinka got injured I was temporarily assigned his post. The headquarters' chief was Captain Nikolai Petrov. Like me, he had once served in a penal battalion. He'd fought as a pilot, and after serving in the penal battalion was reassigned to the tank forces. 'I'll never go back to the air force, I'd rather burn on the ground,' he used to say.

Shortly before one offensive operation we were given a map. We discussed the operation with Petrov, and I concluded: 'Look, Nikolai, it's going to be our grave there.' He replied: 'You're right.' One of the gun loaders, who went by the nickname Spirka, was a foolhardy man who'd got into trouble with the law back in his hometown. He was well known in the battalion for taking a few other people like him over to the enemy's lines in search of food and drink. So I said to Petrov: 'Listen, Spirka has probably been over to the German lines. Let's ask him about it.' We sent for Spirka. I asked him: 'Have you been over to the German side?' Spirka lisped (he had gold false teeth): 'Yesh, maybe. Why?' 'Where exactly did you cross?' Spirka replied: 'We croshed by the swamp. No Germans there.' 'How deep is it?' 'About waist high.' 'What's the bottom like?' 'We didn't get stuck, commander. I can show you.'

So Captain Petrov and I armed ourselves and went. We walked around the swamp, feeling the bottom. There weren't any Germans. After getting back we changed clothes and went to the Brigade HQ to report. We were received by Colonel Shulgin, and General Pankov was also there. The room was quite bright and had a table with a map and orders on it. Colonel Shulgin addressed me: 'Well, Crow-head!' he said (my hair was jet black). 'What did you and Petrov come up with?' At that very moment Commander-in-Chief Rokossovsky came in: we had our backs to the door so we didn't see him. I answered: 'Comrade Colonel, may I address Major-General Pankov? We won't take the assigned path.' Then I heard a voice behind my back. It was Rokossovsky: 'Why won't you go?' We jumped. 'Commander-in-Chief, it's certain death, we'll lose men and tanks.' He calmly replied: 'If you don't go, you'll be executed.' 'Commander-in-Chief, our reconnaissance tells us that we can cross the swamp.' General Pankov said: 'You'll sink all your machinery.' 'We won't. The bottom is hard. We'll also pile up logs, and cross the swamp one by one so the Germans won't know.' Rokossovsky said: 'Do it.'

We took the whole tank battalion across the swamp. As a result the tanks took the first defence line without any losses. Later on the Germans recovered, so that by the time we captured Orel city only four tanks remained out of thirty-three. For this operation I was awarded the Aleksandr Nevsky order.

CHAPTER 11

'If your unit still existed, you had to be with it!'

Nikolai Yakovlevich Zheleznov

I was $17\frac{1}{2}$ years old when the war started. I'd just graduated from school. Of course, we all hoped that the war would last only two or three months, that the enemy would be routed, and that victory would be ours. But the enemy turned out to be far stronger and more perfidious than we'd expected. So when, at the beginning of July, the Germans captured Minsk, my father told me: 'Son, it's time for you to find a job.' I went to work as an apprentice metalworker at the 205th Factory, which manufactured devices used to direct anti-aircraft fire. In three months, after passing an examination, I became a fourth grade metalworker. Then at the beginning of August our family received news that my older brother Mikhail had perished in the fighting at Smolensk. It was such a loss for our family – you can't imagine it!

In October, when the Germans were approaching Moscow, the decision was made to have our factory evacuated to Saratov, and so I started packing for the journey. My family sewed a clothes sack for me out of tarpaulin – there were few rucksacks back then, they were expensive, and we didn't earn much. The departure date of our train was set for 22 October, but on the 15th, when the evacuation of the national government started, panic gripped Moscow. I saw the workers of the Hammer and Sickle Factory come out into Ilyich Square when their management tried to flee with their families and possessions loaded onto company trucks. There was no limit to the workers' indignation. They began stopping the trucks, throwing the bureaucrats, their squealing families and their possessions out on the street. All their things were immediately looted. These disturbances quickly spread through the city. People began looting stores. I saw an out-of-control mob loot a three-storey department store and carry everything off to their homes.

After arriving at Saratov, we quickly rebuilt our 205th Factory, setting it up in the building of the Agricultural Institute. By the fifth day after our arrival we'd recommenced assembly of our devices! We worked 14–16 hours per day without any days off. In February 1942 we moved our beds right into the workshops. You'd sleep for about five hours, then they'd wake you up and you'd go back to work. We lived and worked with one purpose: to give the troops at the front everything necessary and as soon as possible. This isn't a slogan, nor propaganda! We really lived that way.

In May I said to the guys with whom I worked: 'Let's all go to the front. Enough feeding lice here!' So we all went to the military commissariat. The military commissar, Colonel Smirnov, heard us out and said: 'You're workers in a defence factory, and aren't eligible for conscription. If your factory management allows it, then you may come.' We managed to convince our factory director to let us go to the front, and soon we were drafted.

At first I found myself in the accelerated training course for infantry sergeants. This training lasted for a month-and-a-half, after which they gave us the rank of sergeant. On graduation day they formed us up on the parade ground and the school chief read out our new ranks. Then he came down from his podium and announced: 'Atten-hut! Listen to my order! Anyone who has higher or incomplete higher education – ten steps forward! Anyone who has technical or incomplete technical education – five steps forward! Anyone who has finished ten grades of school – three steps forward! March!'

Everyone moved. Some took three steps, some five, and some, like me, ten. But there weren't many of us: back then an education of ten grades was considered to be a lot – most guys had only four to seven grades of schooling. So they formed us up in columns and led us to the military commissariat. Our 'buyers' waited there: a tank officer, an officer from the Military Political Academy (VPU), and an air force officer. Every one of them had four 'ties' on their collar tabs – colonels. At first they picked us according to our wishes. One of my friends said: 'Guys, let's all become tankmen! It's very distinguished! You ride, and the whole country lies before you! You're on an iron horse!' It was really tempting. But as soon as we went to the tank officer, I heard the officer from the VPU call to me. He said: 'Do you want to get into the Military Political Academy?' 'No, I don't,' I replied. 'I've already decided to become a tankman.' He said: 'You might be sorry. You'll have a hard time there. Tank service is difficult. Why don't you become a political worker? You'll graduate from the academy, become a company political officer, and if you prove yourself capable you might even become a battalion commissar!' But I didn't yield to his enticements, and on 25 June 1942 I was accepted into the 1st Saratov Tank Academy.

For about a month we trained on British Matildas and Canadian Valentines. I have to say that the Valentine was a very successful tank, low to the ground, with a powerful gun and a quiet engine. I'll tell you later about how two Valentines burned three Tigers in one battle. But the Matilda – that was simply a huge target! It had thick armour, but the gun was only 42 mm, with a prehistoric sight. It was clumsy, had poor manoeuvring capabilities. Its two weak 90 hp Leyland engines could barely make it go 25 kph on a road, and on an unpaved road even less! But at the end of July our academy received T-34 tanks, and our training programme was changed to studying the T-34.

We were trained as tank and tank platoon commanders at the academy. First of all, we learned about the equipment – the main gun, the machine gun, the radio, the gearbox, the chassis, and the engine. While we already had some idea about the turret and the chassis, we knew nothing of the diesel engine, for example. Besides that, we studied various regulations: the guard service regulations, the field regulations, and so on. At the range we practised various tank battle tactics as part of a platoon or a company, and learned about mutual support between tanks. Of course, they taught us to drive a tank, and to fire the gun and machine-guns. There was no time allocated to the study of German tanks, but in the hallways all over the academy there were large posters depicting German tanks with their tactical and technical characteristics, their vulnerabilities, and we absorbed that knowledge.

The daily schedule was as follows: from 0900 until 1400 we had classes, then dinner and personal time until 1600. From 1600 until 2100 there were more classes. We walked around the academy in military uniform, and were punished with extra duty for untidy appearance. The under-collar had to be white at all times, all the buttons had to be sewn in place – no allowances were made for wartime. The discipline was strict, and despite the equality in military ranks no fraternisation with your squad commander was allowed.

Everyone who graduated from the academy with excellent marks, including myself, was offered the chance to stay for another three months to go through political training, after which you could take the position of a deputy battalion commander for political work at the front. I didn't refuse. I was appointed a platoon commander in the 7th Cadet Company of the 2nd Tank Battalion. I was nineteen at the time, a mere boy!

After the end of our studies they sent us to Gorky to receive our tanks from the Krasnoe Sormovo Factory. We were quartered at Bolokhna, with the 3rd Reserve Training Tank Regiment. That's where we received our personnel and started combat training, as well as undergoing exercises for entire platoons and companies. The manoeuvres took place at the range, where crews worked on tasks such as attacking, defending, or marching as part of a platoon or a company. After the completion of manoeuvres we practised firing from our tanks. As a platoon commander I had to make sure that all the crew members could replace one another. I tried to ensure that every crew member was capable of driving the vehicle and firing the main gun and the machine-guns if the need arose.

Such exercises allowed us to instil in every crew member clear knowledge of his duties, and in tank and platoon commanders the knowledge of their place on the battlefield and the ability to control a battle. After all, control of operations was an integral part of a battle. The platoon commander observed the battlefield and gave orders to the tank commanders of his platoon, to open fire on a target or to move. But more often there was no time to give an order, because if you spent too much time commanding others you could let your own death in. Everything depended on the tank crews of a platoon being able to act independently.

Our exercises were carried out in training vehicles, but when they sent us to the front they gave us brand new tanks. Though they all looked just the same, that was only at first glance. Each tank, each tank gun, each engine had its unique peculiarities. It was impossible to know them in advance and they could only be uncovered in the course of daily service. In the end we turned up at the front in unfamiliar vehicles. The commander didn't know the accuracy of his gun. The driver didn't know what his diesel could do and what it couldn't do. Sure, they'd adjust the guns at the production plants and make fifty-kilometre test-runs, but that wasn't enough at all. Obviously, we tried hard to learn more about our machines before combat and took every opportunity to do so.

In the spring of 1943 we loaded onto a train that took us to a place near Moscow. The 4th Tank Army was being formed there, and our 30th Urals Volunteer Tank Corps, in whose ranks I spent the entire war, was a part of it. In the summer the army deployed to the south-west of Sukhinichi, and that's where I had my first battle. The first battle is the scariest one. I'm asked sometimes: 'Were you afraid?' I'll admit it – I was. Fear came on you before an attack, when you turned on your communications unit and waited for the order: 'Advance!' God alone knew what awaited you five or ten minutes later. Would your tank be hit or not? You were young, healthy, and wanted to live, but in several minutes you could cease to exist! Of course, none of us yielded to our fears, but every one of us was afraid. But during an attack some kind of additional, imperceptible power would turn on and guide you. You weren't human any more, you could neither reason nor think in a human way. Maybe that saved us.

On the evening of 25 July we deployed to our jumping-off positions. The mission given to us by the brigade commander was to force the River Ors. The 63rd Brigade, of which I was a part, was deployed in the second line, the first line being composed of the 62nd Tank Brigade and the 30th Motorised Rifle Brigade. After forcing the Ors, they ran into German defences on, I believe, Hill 212, which they couldn't break through. Then the corps commander ordered our brigade to force its way through the enemy and advance towards the south, to capture Borilovo, then Masal'skoe. However, the brigade's engineering reconnaissance had been conducted poorly, and our tanks got stuck in the mud while crossing the Nugr' River – its basin was swampy, and the opposite bank was a vertical wall. So our first battle wasn't successful: our attack literally bogged down.

Then we were transferred to a different sector of the front, where we enjoyed greater success. The Germans were defending the edge of a village, where they had both anti-tank guns and dug-in tanks. In that battle I destroyed two guns and a dug-in Panzer III. I fired my gun at it twice and it went silent. The two guns that we crushed weren't to my credit, but my driver's. I only managed to give the order: 'Misha, left! Gun!' And when we drove over it we saw another one nearby, about ten metres away: 'Smash the other one, or it'll turn and fire into our backside!' We killed lots of infantrymen. When we reached the other end of the village I saw a large group of Germans – about 150 men – fleeing away from us through a field. I rushed after them and started firing the machine-gun. One fell, another, a third, fourth, fifth, tenth. Of course, I wasn't the only one shooting – our company broke through, and our infantry were also firing. Who knows if it was me who killed them, or someone else? But I think I killed maybe twenty-five men in that battle. I was awarded the Order of the Red Star for it. Of course, we also suffered losses. Our battalion, which was supposed to have twenty-one tanks, lost five to seven in that battle.

You ask how we received our offensive missions? The company commander gave platoon commanders orders to move from one reference point to another in the direction in which the company was supposed to advance. My task was to drive that distance and stay alive. The company commander's orders came in on the radio throughout the battle: '21st, 21st, change your direction! Left, 200 degrees, German gun.' That meant you had to turn, otherwise it could fire into your side.

We continued our advance and reached L'gov Station after a number of battles. In reality we were incapable of advancing further. We'd lost tanks, infantry. Our losses were significant. Only one or two tanks remained in each company. The brigade, which was supposed to have sixty-five tanks, consisted of no more than twelve at the end of the operation. Those tanks and their crews were then taken away from us and given to the 197th Tank Brigade. It was common practice during the war to take all the surviving tanks in a corps and reform them into one brigade, which would continue fighting, while the other two brigades were withdrawn for reorganisation.

After the Orel offensive was over we were pulled back for reorganisation. We received new equipment and crews, and in February–March 1944 our army took part in the Proskurov-Chernovitsy offensive operation. That's where the battle I want to tell you about happened. I didn't participate in it, since we were in the second line, but I observed it. It happened on 23 or 24 March near the town of Skalat. We were driving on a road towards Kamenets-Podol'sk when the forward detachment, consisting of three T-34 tanks, was destroyed by the fire of three Tigers deployed in a village on a small hill. Due to the fact that we only had 76 mm guns, which could penetrate a Tiger's front armour only from a distance of 500 metres, the German tanks were deployed in the open. But just try to approach them and they'd burn your tank from 1,200–1,500 metres! They were cocky! In essence, until we got the 85 mm gun we had to run from Tigers like rabbits, and look for an opportunity to turn back and get at their flanks. It was difficult. If you saw a Tiger 800–1,000 metres away and it started 'crossing' you, while it moved its gun horizontally you could stay in your tank, but once it started moving it vertically you'd better jump out, or you could get burned! It never happened to me, but other guys bailed out. But when the T-34/85 entered service, we could stand up against enemy tanks one on one.

There were bushes to the right of the road, but they weren't tall enough to conceal a T-34. Then the brigade commander, Colonel Fomichev, made the right decision. He was a very capable officer: it was no accident the men called him 'Dad'. He sent two of the low-profile Valentine tanks from our 7th Motorcycle Battalion, and they, using the bushes as cover, approached the Tigers to within 300–400 metres. By firing at their sides they destroyed two tanks, and then the third one. A fourth Tiger was on the slope of the hill and didn't see what was happening to his left. Then it crawled away somewhere. In this way the left flank of the German defence became exposed and we rushed into the breach through the brush. We were met by anti-tank artillery, but it was only 100–200 metres from the brush to their positions, and a tank could cover that distance in 25–30 seconds. After all, a tank attacks at high speed, continually changing direction – if you drove straight you could consider yourself going right into the netherworld. The artillery managed to fire several shots, after which the guns were crushed and the German infantry fled. It's only in movies that the infantry lets the enemy tanks through. In reality, as soon as tanks appeared and were about to break through the defences, the infantry ran away through the trenches.

We got held up for two-and-a-half to three hours at that village, but entered Kamenets-Podol'sk in the evening. We lost two tanks on the outskirts, destroyed by a battery of anti-aircraft guns. Their crews burned. I saw them when they were buried – grown men reduced to mummies the size of a twelve-year-old child. The skin on their faces was reddish-bluish-brown. It was scary to see then and it's very disturbing to recall now.

Our reconnaissance team reported German trucks on the outskirts of the town. We went to have a look. There were so many trucks there! Probably around 3,000, if not more! Apparently, these were the supply columns of the enemy's Proskurov group of forces. The trucks were stuffed with sausage, ham, various cans of food, chocolate, cheese. There was also plenty of alcohol – French cognac, Italian wine. I especially remember Amaretto. I remember the taste of that liqueur as one of the pleasures of the war. Besides that we also captured several German tanks in working order, but we didn't use them – too dangerous. Russians are half Asian, and you have to take into account that among them were Kazakhs, Tajiks, Uzbeks, Tartars, and Mordvins: you could climb into a captured tank, and they'd open fire on you with all their guns, and you'd burn for nothing. I, for one, kept myself as far as possible from German vehicles.

The town of Kamenets-Podol'sk was deep in the German rear, about 100–150 kilometres behind the front line. The German Proskurov group was breaking out towards the Dniester, and the town, occupied by our brigade, was in its way. We didn't expect a blow as powerful as the one dealt to us on 29 or 30 March. On that day we were ordered to advance to a suburb, the village of Dolzhok. After reaching the last houses, I saw about forty enemy tanks and SPGs moving right at us. I started pulling back without firing a shot. I had no chance against so many – one shot and I was a corpse. We retreated in reverse gear practically to the banks of the River Smotrich, where I placed my tank behind some bushes so that only its turret was visible. Infantry deployed in defence nearby. One of our tanks was to the left. An approaching German SPG fired at it and the round ricocheted off its armour and flew into the town. I couldn't see the SPG itself, so I fired at the flash of its muzzle. The SPG burst into flames. It was on fire, thank God! No other tanks appeared, but the German infantry continued their offensive. They marched in two lines of 50–60 men each, firing their SMGs on the move. I started spraying them with my machine-gun and they dropped to the ground. Then I fired 10–12 rounds from my gun: 15–20 men jumped up and fled, the rest remained lying there. At that point everything quietened down. I made the infantry who were with my tank, a squad of seven men, dig in around us, fearing that during the night the Germans might throw grenades at the tank. But all went well and the night was calm. The Germans didn't attack any more, having apparently bypassed the town. Soon we were pulled back for rest and replacements.

You ask how we interacted with the infantry? They rode on top of our tanks, and we communicated with their platoon commander. I was a platoon commander and he was a platoon commander, but I was in charge! I was carrying him, not the other way around. I would order him: 'Deploy the outposts there and over there, so the enemy won't sneak up on us and fire a Panzerfaust. If they burn the tank, I'm finished and you're finished.' Infantry protected the tanks: after all, life would've been really difficult for them without us! If we came under fire, or when we were breaking through enemy defences, the infantry would usually dismount, although some of them remained on the tank. They would hide behind the turret. I've already mentioned that a tank attack was at high speed. You'd zigzag through the field like a hare so you wouldn't be hit, and God forbid if an infantryman got under your tracks and you ran him over! That would've been a disaster! Of course, tanks could push far ahead of the infantry. It's only in the movies that they show you tanks attacking in a line with infantry behind them – in real life it was the way I've described it. That's the only way you could survive.

The next operation in which I participated was the Lvov-Sandomierz offensive. I fought in a T-34/85 there. There were still only few of them at that time – my platoon had just one. Our corps was sent to exploit a breakthrough. We marched towards Lvov, not encountering any resistance. When we liberated the town of Zolochev, the corps commander replaced the 61st Brigade, marching in the vanguard, with our 63rd Brigade. The brigade commander assembled us and said: 'Lieutenant Kriukov's platoon will form the forward detachment, Lieutenant Poligenki's platoon will be on the right flank, and Zheleznov's on the left.' My platoon was reinforced with an SMG platoon and two ZIS-3 guns, which we were to tow behind our tanks. I put the sub-machine gunners and artillerymen onto the tanks, and sent the motorcyclists forward; the platoon and trucks with ammo were somewhat behind them. We advanced in this way on an unpaved road about three kilometres from and parallel to the main forces of the brigade, using our radio to communicate with the battalion commander.

When we were approaching a small village about twelve kilometres from Zolochev, I saw clouds of dust about 1.5 kilometres ahead of us. I immediately gave the order to stop and deploy in defence on the

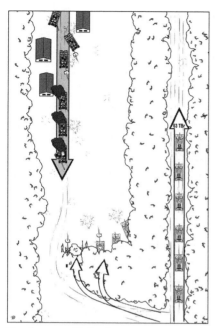

Battle near Zolochev.

edge of a forest about 400 metres from the village. The motorcycle scouts returned and reported that it was an enemy column approaching. I thought that maybe they had two or three tanks, and the rest were infantry. We could take care of them like a cook takes care of potatoes. There were motorcycles and three Panthers in the forward detachment of the column. I said on the radio: 'The first one's mine. Kozlov, yours is the second one. Tikhonov, take the third one.' After letting them close to about 600 metres, we fired on my command. The tanks burst into flames and our infantry and artillery eliminated the motor-cyclists. Then the German column deployed, and it turned out that it had no less than twenty tanks! They pulled back to the village and started shooting at us and I ordered a retreat. I said to my driver, Petukhov: 'Kolia, let's go right.' He turned, and then an armour-piercing round slammed into the gearbox. It got jammed, and our fuel tank broke open. The tank started burning. I managed to yell: 'Guys, bail out!' Thank God, everyone got out. I shouldn't have turned: we should've just driven back to the forest in reverse, and then turned. But I started turning in the open and received a round for my labours. My other two tanks retreated successfully, the artillery-men and infantrymen rolled the guns into the forest, and we reached the road and went on to catch up with the brigade. As I remember, the Germans didn't press on further, but turned back. Since I was the platoon commander, I simply got into another tank. If your unit still existed, you had to be with it!

When our brigade entered Lvov my replacement tank was also destroyed after a hit in the engine. It started burning, but once again we managed to jump out. When I was running, a mortar shell exploded nearby, and I was slightly wounded by its fragments. Guys quickly dressed my wounds and we started advancing behind our tanks on foot. We reached a building where the Gestapo had been located. I opened the door. There were carpeted marble stairs in front of me, leading to the second floor. I went upstairs and stopped at an oak door with massive shiny bronze knobs. I opened it and found myself in a room that I took to be the reception area of the chief of Gestapo. There was a large desk with massive filing cabinets in the room. I thought it was suspicious that all the drawers had been pulled out of the left-hand cabinet, but I didn't pay any attention to it and went on to the door leading to the next room. Suddenly I felt that someone was hiding in the filing cabinet, and turned to see a hand holding a Parabellum being raised above the surface of the desk. I immediately pulled the room door open and tumbled through it. The German fired, but missed. I fell to the floor, turned around. My wound opened from such sharp movements, and blood started flowing again. I crawled to the door and looked through the crack. I saw a German officer, an *oberleutnant*, climbing out of the cabinet. I put my own Parabellum against the crack and fired. I hit his right shoulder and he dropped the gun. Sub-machine gunners and my tankmen, who'd been looking around on the first floor, heard the gunfire and ran inside. This *oberleutnant* was standing there with his hands up, and he had a watch on his left wrist. My driver said: 'Comrade Lieutenant, he has a good watch.' He took it off him and said to me: 'Take it as a keepsake, to remember how you miraculously survived.' So I took the watch. And the officer? I ordered him taken out and shot. If he hadn't fired, I would've spared him. But since he'd tried to kill me – a dog deserved a dog's death.

In general, I must say we hated Germans with a passion, though when we reached Germany there was an order to treat the local population well, so we didn't touch civilians. Sometimes we even fed the children. Every tank had a case, or even two, of looted chocolate, and we treated them to this chocolate. Loot! That deserves a special mention. In an offensive the support services would fall far behind us, and we ate from the battalion field kitchen only when we were resting! But after a battle, there was always something available, because the German soldiers weren't as poor as us. They had everything. We also had everything, but somewhere far back in the rear, so little of it reached us. Otherwise, everything we had was from loot: sausage, cheese, tinned meat. But their bread was terrible, not only tasteless but it didn't even look like bread. It was same as chewing sawdust. I also recall the 1.5 kilo cans of smoked pork fat we received via Lend-Lease. It was cut into ten-centimetre long and one-centimetre wide strips, with paper in between. You'd take two or three slices, put them on a piece of bread, drink half a cup of alcohol, chase it with that sandwich, and life was beautiful! Here's how we drank: we poured 100 grams of pure alcohol into an aluminium cup and placed a mess tin with water next to it. We'd gulp down the alcohol, then follow it up with water, and no problems! You know, the 100 grams we were supposed to receive were drunk by the guys in the rear. We drank looted alcohol – although, I never drank before battle, no way. To drink meant to burn. After the battle, if you survived, then you drank!

When we reached the Vistula and crossed to the Sandomierz bridgehead, only five tanks remained in the battalion. The first company had three tanks, and the second two. And we, the officers of the battalion, were all in these five tanks. Where else would we go? We had no reserves. So, willy-nilly, you became an extra crew member. With these forces and the 6th Mechanised Corps, which had also suffered losses, we were defending ten kilometres of the front. Infantry was deployed in a thin line ahead of us, and we were 200–250 metres behind them. The defence was such that if you spat on it, it would've fallen apart. But the Germans didn't go for us. Either they were incapacitated, or there was another reason.

One time our battalion commander led the tank commanders out to reconnoitre. We came to the infantry. Their company commander met us, and we crawled into no-man's land, looked around, allocated the sectors of fire, and returned to the trenches. It was time to go back to our tank positions. The infantry lieutenant warned us: 'Don't go through that clearing, it's been sighted by the Germans.' But our battalion commander said: 'No big deal, we'll manage to get through it.' The Germans fired three rounds, and seven men were killed, four of them platoon commanders and three tank commanders. I received a concussion. My Parabellum saved me. It was a wonderful weapon, superior to our TT in every way. One of the German shells exploded nearby – about three to four metres away – and a fragment meant for me hit my sidearm and twisted it. I was thrown headlong by the explosion, and blood was coming out of my mouth, ears, and nose. As they told me later, at first they thought I was dead, but as they were wrapping me in a groundsheet to bury me I moved. I got lucky: they could've buried me. I had a most severe concussion, but the medical platoon sorted me out, and in about fifteen days I began hearing and speaking normally.

While we were deployed at the Sandomierz bridgehead, I destroyed a Panzer IV. Here's how it happened. I was an excellent shot with a tank gun. I even participated in the best gunner competition that Leliushenko, the 4th Tank Army commander, organised during a lull in the fighting. So, one time the battalion commander said to me: 'Look over there, there's a German tank.' I said: 'I see it.' The German tank was crawling along parallel to our defences minding its own business, about 1,200–1,300 metres distant. 'You can shoot well. Go ahead, kill it.' I got into a tank, looked through the sight, aimed, and fired. The round went to the left and above the German tank's turret. I fired again – the same thing happened. The German had already turned towards us – he'd noticed we were shooting at him, and was trying to find out where we were. I got out of the tank – why would I want to get burned in it? – and said: 'You know, the sight is either off or has been intentionally put out of commission.' The battalion commander said: 'Yes, bad business. Go find another tank to shoot from.' I went to another tank that was behind a shed. I said to its commander: 'Come on, drive it out, I'm about to burn a German.' 'Where is the tank?' he said. 'I can't see it.' 'Well,' I said, 'let's go take a look.' We walked out from behind the shed: 'See it?' 'OK,' he said, 'let me do it myself.' 'Hold it, he's mine.' He drove the tank out, I got into the gunner's seat, and with my very first round I hit the enemy tank on the front. It burst into flames! I got it right between the hull and the turret. Two men jumped out, but the other two apparently remained there. They awarded me an Order of the Red Star for that, and also gave me a bonus of 500 roubles. It was common practice to specifically award the tank commander for a knocked-out enemy tank. After all, the crew's purpose was to provide support for the commander. However, generally all the survivors were decorated after an operation.

In late autumn we were pulled back to the village of Zimnovody, which was located about twenty kilometres from the front line. We received replacements and started crew training and manoeuvres. We organised a practice range there with a specially equipped training platoon – three tanks whose guns had built-in rifles. You would aim it as a gun, but the shot would come from the rifle inside it. We practised firing at a moving target, at an immobile target, and even at a moving target 500–1,000 metres away while you were moving

Action at the Sandomierz bridgehead.

yourself. But I must tell you, in battle I always fired from a stop. After all, when you're driving, all you can see is earth-sky-earth-sky flashing in front of you, and you can't hit anything while on the move.

When the Vistula-Oder operation began in January 1945 we marched about fifty kilometres in the second line. Then our battalion was pushed ahead to act as a forward detachment. In the evening of 12 January we approached the village of Peshkhnitsa in the dark. It was on the approaches to the town of Kel'tse. It was a large village with houses standing in two or three rows. The brigade commander deployed our battalion into a combat formation, and we commenced the attack. I'd transferred to the 3rd Battalion prior to this operation. Here's why: in Zimnovody we lived with Poles in their houses, and we went with Polish girls. We were young, after all. I was only twenty. I usually visited them with my company commander, Leshka Kudinov. We rode in the same tank with him. I was the 1st Platoon commander and had four tanks – my three, and the tank of the company commander. So one time we went there was a gypsy woman with her children there. She told us: 'Here, let me read your fortune.' We declined, but then the Polish girls jumped in: 'Yes, what're you afraid of? Let her do it.' Leshka agreed. She took his left hand, looked at it, then looked at him, and said in broken Russian: 'I hate to tell you this, but you'll get killed! This line here – it ends.' 'Well, fine,' he replied, and pushed me forward. 'Go ahead, tell his fortune.' She took my hand: 'You,' she said, 'will live long, but will suffer. You'll be seriously wounded.' 'Well, I'll probably lose my arm or leg,' I thought. Our mood immediately soured – we didn't feel like talking, and dancing didn't make us happy. When we returned, Leshka said: 'Nikolai, let's change your fate. As a company commander, I can't get transferred to a different battalion. But since you're a platoon commander, you can do it easily. Especially since there's a shortage of platoon commanders in the 3rd Tank Battalion.' I said: 'Very well.' And so I participated in this operation as part of the 3rd Tank Battalion.

As we entered the village, the Germans opened fire on us. One tank started burning, another, a third one . . . They were firing from close range. My tank drove into an intersection. A corner house was on fire, and I could clearly see a Tiger silhouetted against it. The distance was no more than 120 metres. I pushed the gunner's head, he slid down onto the ammo, and I got into his seat. I looked through the sight but couldn't see where to shoot. So I opened the breach and aimed the gun through the barrel. My round hit the enemy tank's side, and it burst into flames. I returned to my seat, took off my glove, and was about to switch the radio to internal communications, when at that moment I lost consciousness. As I figured it out later, a German tank parked about fifty metres in front of us saw the flash from my shot and put a round right into the front of our vehicle. I came to lying on top of the ammo, at the bottom of the tank. The tank was on fire, I couldn't breathe. I saw the broken head of the driver: the round had gone through him and between my legs, but apparently a fragment had gone through my boot, and my left leg was twisted at the knee. The loader was lying dead next to me with his arm torn off. The gunner was also dead – practically all the shell fragments had gone into him: he basically protected me with his body. I pulled myself up to the commander's hatch, but couldn't climb out – my left leg, broken at the knee, wouldn't bend. I remained hanging there. My legs and butt inside the tank were already burning. A blood-filled shroud covered my eyes – my eyes got burned on top of everything else. Then I saw two men walking by, I said: 'Guys, help me climb out.' 'Zheleznov?' 'That's me!' They ran up to me and pulled me out by my arms: my boots remained inside the tank. As soon as they dragged me away, the tank exploded. My clothes were on fire, but they threw snow on me and managed to put it out.

When they took me to the medical platoon, even Ania Sel'tseva, a senior lieutenant, started crying: 'Kolia, how did you manage to get so badly burned?' Thirty-five per cent of my skin was burned! Did it hurt? What do you think! The skin was hanging down even on my face! I said to her: 'Give me some water, I'm thirsty.' She poured me not water, but alcohol, and said: 'Drink!' I cursed her: 'Why did you give me alcohol instead of water?' 'It'll help you. It will dull the pain.'

They took me to the army hospital. They put a cast on my leg. The biggest problem was that I couldn't see anything, my entire face got swollen. My eyelids grew together and they had to cut them open. I'm not going to talk about it or I might start crying. It was Ivan Sergeevich Liubivets and his orderly who saved my life.

We failed to take that village and retreated into the forest. The next day, before the attack, Leshka Kudinov got out of his tank and stood at the side of the road smoking. And then he collapsed. An armour piercing shell had torn his leg off, and he died from blood loss. The gypsy had been right. But it would've been better if we hadn't known about it.

I spent two months in the hospital. They discharged me when the army was fighting for Berlin. My face became pink, all covered with scars, and my leg didn't bend properly. But they told me I would work it out in my unit. It was true, the leg got better. The shell fragment had hit the meniscus, and at first it didn't bother me. I lived almost fifty years with it. Recently I had a knee prosthesis installed, the meniscus having worn out, and the fragment was removed. Doctors looked at it: 'How did you manage to walk?' 'Normally.' 'What do you mean, normally? The fragment was inside the joint, and you walked normally?' 'Well, I limped slightly.' That's why I was transferred to duty in the rear. I wanted to serve in the HQ, but that didn't work out.

And that's how my war ended. I'm even with Germans. I lost three tanks and burned three of theirs, plus an APC. And how many men I killed – I'm not counting that.

CHAPTER 12

'Once you stop, your time is up!'

Georgi Nikolaevich Krivov

Before the war we lived not far from Tashkent. At noon on 22 July the radio announced that war had broken out. Together with my friends I rushed into the enlistment office, but we were under the call-up age, so we were not allowed to go. I spent late 1941 and the beginning of 1942 working at an aircraft construction plant as a turner apprentice and later as a turner. The plant had been evacuated from Moscow.

In the summer of 1942 I entered the Kharkov Tank School, which had been evacuated to Cherchik. I was $17\frac{1}{2}$ at the time. First of all I had to face a credentials committee and a medical board. 'Do you want to be a tankman?' the doctor asked me. 'I do.' 'Then go.' Next I had to pass some exams that were also rather a formality. Some entrants made up to forty mistakes in the dictation, but still they were admitted.

At first the studying was difficult for me. We had almost no time to sleep. It felt like you had to get up just a few seconds after you went to bed. We felt terribly tired, but I managed to hold on. After seven months of studying I was conferred the rank of lieutenant and sent to Nizhniy Novgorod with my company. That's where we starved! There'd been no problems with food at the Tank School, but now we had nothing but the scanty rations of the home front. Sometimes we managed to buy some stuff at the market, but still it wasn't enough.

I was really amazed by the speed of tank construction. When my crew was given our first tank, it was actually nothing but an armoured box. We watched the assembly process for some time and then went to have our dinner. In an hour we were back, but our tank was missing. We located it after a while, and found that the assembly process had already gone as far as mounting the turret. Each day the plant assembled twenty-five tanks! Soon our tank was ready. As the commander I got a watch, a penknife, and a silk kerchief to filter the fuel. And so we went to the front.

My crew consisted of four men. The driver, Grigori Ivanovich Kryukov, was ten years older than me. Before the war he'd worked as a driver. He'd already taken part in the fights for Leningrad, and he mastered the tank marvellously. I think that it was due to him that we survived our first fights. The radio operator, Nickolai Nickolaevich Tikhomirov, was also older than me. He was a taciturn fellow who felt cold constantly. He never took off his coat. To me it looked strange, for I always went into battle wearing nothing but trousers and a shirt. Even the waist-belt made me feel uncomfortable. The poor guy was killed still wearing his coat. I liked these two guys from the very beginning, especially after we split a bottle of vodka on my nineteenth birthday in the train.

My relations with the fourth member of the crew, the loader Bodyagin, were not so good. I rebuked him for something on the train, but he didn't pay attention. I repeated my words, but instead of obeying he started saying something about stupid commanders being thrown off the train. I tried not to pay attention to this bullshit, and Kryukov told him to shut up. Bodyagin was an unpleasant fellow. He felt pessimistic about everything, because he thought that we'd burn soon. I never thought like this, though I knew it could happen. I didn't want to think about death, and so I didn't. As for Bodyagin, he did, and there were plenty like him. They felt uneasy, they suffered, and they were actually the first to be killed. They were slow, and that was crucial. It was very important to move quickly at the front. I was able to get in and out of the tank in a second, and so was the driver. That's how we survived.

We arrived at the front in October 1943 and joined the 362nd Tank Battalion of the 25th Tank Brigade of the 29th Tank Corps of the 5th Guards Tank Army.

On the night of 16 October we made a forced crossing of the Dnepr over a pontoon bridge not far from Mishurin Rog. An infantry battalion had crossed the river ahead of us and captured a bridgehead. They managed to push on three or four kilometres but met resistance, so we were sent to back them up. It rained all day long, but in the evening the rain stopped and that's when we got the order to advance. We moved slowly towards the forest. Twice we had to stop when German aircraft bombed our infantry units. The planes were levelling out just above us, but fortunately they didn't notice the tanks. We crossed the trenches, and for the first time I saw dead soldiers, lying in unnatural poses. The orderlies were bandaging the wounded and carrying away the dead. Several soldiers peeped out from the trenches, smiling: the tanks had arrived! It was a pleasant feeling.

We reached the western part of the forest when it was already getting dark. Our orders were to get ready for the offensive. We hoped that we wouldn't attack in the evening, but I still ordered Bodyagin to watch out for the company commander giving the signal. We prepared the tank for battle, checking the engine and the running gear and wiping the grease off the shells. Soon I saw Bodyagin waving his hands: 'Start the engine!'

That was my first battle, without any preliminary reconnaissance. There was rising ground ahead of us, and we couldn't see what was behind it. The right thing would have been to check first where the German defence line was situated, but probably our command wanted to attack unexpectedly. They even forbade us to communicate by the radio. We crawled slowly along the soggy ground. There was nothing in the periscope except the ground and the sky. When we got to the top of the rise my first impression was: 'How damn beautiful!' The huge circle of the sun seemed to be sitting on the horizon. I looked down and saw a forest belt about 800 metres away. Everything looked quiet. I remembered the words of more experienced tankmen: 'As soon as you see the enemy, fire'. I was sure there'd be no effect from such aimless firing, but I felt it was better to follow the advice. Suddenly several anti-tank guns fired at us simultaneously. I was trying to adjust the sights to target one of them, but in vain. It was impossible to aim at anything on the move, we needed a stop, but I remembered the words of my friends: 'Once you stop, your time is up!' We were firing non-stop. Our compartment filled with smoke, my eyes ached, and I had a tickle in my throat. Fortunately the hatches of the turret were slightly open, and Bodyagin was continuously throwing out the spent shell cases, otherwise we'd have suffocated. The strain was rising to the limit, but I was repeating to myself that it would not last long, there would be a break.

A tank caught fire to the left of us. Two tanks blew up to the right. Bodyagin was shouting something waving his hands. It appeared that one of the shell cases had ricochetted from the catcher, and its front edge had caught on the gun retainer. Bodyagin couldn't remove it, because his hands were burnt all over from throwing the cases out of the compartment while I was firing. I remembered our commander telling us to bring the cases back after the fight and wished he was with us and experienced all that hell himself! I grasped the case and pulled it out. The German lines were drawing closer. I looked out and saw a gun. The tank driver shouted: 'Hold tight!' We crushed the gun, and for some time I kept firing, but it was dark now and we couldn't see anything. We'd passed through the German defence lines, but we didn't know where to go. I asked the radio operator if there'd been any orders. 'I think they ordered us to pass the forest to the right, and then the communication was broken.' I told the driver to turn right and we crawled forward slowly. On the way we passed a haystack and I fired at it, in case someone was hiding inside. Of course, there wasn't a soul. Soon I saw a village ahead of us. We stopped and I asked the crew what we should do in their opinion. They kept silent. So I said: 'Turn round and go back along our own tracks.' Our orders hadn't said anything about a village. We drove back till we reached the stack, and stopped the engine. I could hear somebody talking, but I couldn't make out the words. Suddenly someone spoke in Russian, so we headed that way. Three soldiers jumped up as if out of nowhere, with clumps of grenades. I jumped down from the tank immediately. 'Who're you?' they asked. 'We're returning from the battle,' I said. 'So why're you coming from the German side? We were going to treat you with the grenades!' These soldiers turned out to be scouts. They were going to the village to see if there were any Germans inside. So we had a smoke and went on our way. That was my first battle. When we got back to the battalion I found out that almost all my friends had been killed in the fight. Several more experienced tankmen survived, but the youngsters were annihilated.

After our attack the Germans retreated, and then we started driving them out. I remember the fights for Pyatihatka, especially the loot. During the fight we advanced to the station and found two trains. One train carried the wounded. They tried to offer some resistance, but all of them were killed. The guys rushed in to look for loot. Our battalion commander advised us to take warm clothes and socks, but we were young, and all we could think of was vodka, pistols and field glasses. For example, all the commanders were supposed to have a revolver, but I wasn't given one. Only at the end of the war did I acquire an automatic pistol.

I remember a funny incident. We found a burning German car. Bodyagin ran to have a look and brought back two or three tins with canned food. They were warm, so we expected to have a warm dinner. The loader and the radio operator opened their tins and found canned meat, but the tank driver and I found only canned vegetables. We threw our tins away in disappointment. But when the loader and radio operator ate the meat they found vegetables at the bottom. It appeared that they'd opened their tin from the 'meat side' and we'd opened ours from the side with the vegetables. It was such a pity!

After the Pyatihatka operation I met the corps commander, General Kirichenko. We were approaching some settlement, when someone in the outskirts opened fire. A tank commander was killed. We retreated into the forest to bury our killed friend and to decide what to do next. Suddenly we noticed a Willys Jeep coming up from the village. At first we thought they were Germans, but then somebody recognised a staff officer and General Kirichenko. It appeared that he was following the tanks along another road, and had dropped into the village. The Germans who'd fired at us had already retreated by that time. Kirichenko greeted us and said humorously: 'Well, guys, I've liberated the village, now you can resume the offensive.' He seemed to be a nice fellow, friendly and sociable, and not at all arrogant. He stopped to have a snack, and shared his sandwiches with us.

In the evening of 24 October we got the order to leave Nedayvody village and move towards Krivoy Rog. Supplies of shells and fuel were brought by a type of tank without a turret, which somebody named a *Zhuchka*. We hardly had time to refuel. We advanced for about fifteen kilometres and camouflaged in a village. We left the tanks in house gardens and covered them with the branches of fruit trees that we'd cut down. I sent Bodyagin to ask our hostess for a hot meal, because we hadn't had one since the beginning of the offensive. Soon he came back and said that the hostess promised to cook hot potatoes in half an hour. A bit later I had to go to the company commander's house. As I approached I saw the battalion commander's tank, which had been left almost uncovered. The thought flashed through my mind: 'They keep telling us to camouflage, but they ignore their own advice. They must be already inside having a dinner.'

As soon as I came up to the house the company commander, Trishin, appeared at the door. 'Get ready. You'll go as a scout!' It was the last thing I wanted to do, but I had no choice. However, I didn't have the chance to carry out the order. About ten minutes later two German aircraft attacked the village and both Trishin and the battalion commander, Major Lekar, were killed. Major Lekar had paid with his life for his careless attitude towards camouflage! A tank commander, Lieutenant Danelian, immediately gave an order to drive our tanks to the other side of the village and thereby saved us from heavy losses, because the German aircraft returned twice more and attacked the same part of the village. A new battalion commander arrived in the evening. This was Senior Lieutenant Golovyashkin, who'd been Major Lekar's deputy. We hardly knew him. I'd only seen him once before.

In the evening we drove further. To be honest, I fell asleep, and I woke up only when somebody knocked sharply on the side of my tank. It was the battalion commander. He ordered me to take a mortar and several infantrymen and start off on the reconnaissance. It appeared that Fomenko and Savin's tanks, which had been sent earlier, hadn't come back. He told me to drive at a low speed, and if something happened I was to launch a red flare.

The infantry with their mortar settled behind the turret, and Bodyagin and I stood on the seats trying to see in the darkness. After about three kilometres I heard the sound of a tank moving in our direction. It sounded like a T-34, but I was on the alert, because I knew it could be Germans in one of our tanks. When I finally saw the outline of the tank and a man standing up from the turret, I felt instinctively that it was Fomenko or Savin. We stopped almost simultaneously. I jumped down and ran to the other tank. It was Fomenko. It turned out that he and Savin had driven up to the railway line and found the Fritzes carrying something along the station platform. Savin stayed there and continued observing them, while Fomenko returned to the battalion. We drove back to our column and ran to the battalion commander's car.

Fomenko suggested that we attack the Germans immediately, while they were not ready, but Golovyashkin decided that we should consult the corps commander. After half an hour he told us that he couldn't make contact, and we should move to Vechernij Kut village, which was situated two or three kilometres away. Danelian was the one to express our collective disappointment: 'We're doing the wrong thing, losing our advantage.' We sent Fomenko to bring Savin back, and drove into the village. When we finished camouflaging it was already morning. Kryukov fell asleep inside the tank, and we went into a house and finally had some hot potatoes.

As we were finishing our meal we heard bursts of sub-machine gun fire at the other side of the village. My radio remained silent, so I decided to run to platoon commander Ermishin, whose tank was standing behind the neighbouring house. I found no one there and had to return to my tank. The shooting stopped. Finally the platoon commander's radio operator ran up to us and explained what had happened: 'Our gunners fired at a German convoy that was heading to the village. They noticed it and opened fire! Fools, they should have waited and taken all the Germans prisoner! Now all they've got is a dozen Fritzes and two or three carts. The rest escaped and hid in the fields. And our positions have been revealed!'

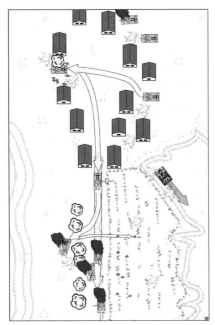

Battle near Vechernij Kut.

At that moment a shell whizzed by and exploded somewhere in the middle of the village. The radio operator ran off, and we felt like hunted wolves, not knowing where the enemy was. The bombardment intensified. The Germans attacked from different sides, and we could already see the black smoke from burning tanks. My nerves were on edge, when finally I saw Ermishin. He grabbed me by the sleeve and made me run for about twenty metres with him. We came to a large square. 'Do you see the tree at the other side? Move your tank there! Find a position to observe the northern side. And prepare the mortar. Go!'

The tree had no leaves, and I couldn't camouflage the tank. We removed the mortar. The commander of the mortar unit told his guys to help us hide the tank. One man was cutting the branches and all the rest were covering the tank with them. After a couple of minutes a shell exploded about twenty-five metres away. I cried to Bodyagin 'Get inside the tank!' and jumped into the hatch. I hadn't yet reached the floor when a second shell exploded nearby. I fell down into my seat and felt my head all over: everything seemed to be there. Then suddenly a terrible thought flashed through my mind: 'A bracket! The third shell will hit us!' Nothing can be compared to the horror of expecting inevitable death! But everything went quiet. All I could hear were moans outside the tank. I opened the hatch and looked out. Two mortar men were lying not far from the mutilated mortar. The commander was lying near the shell-hole. The man who'd been cutting the branches was lying under the tree. Just two had survived by jumping into a ditch. I could see no sign of Bodyagin. Then I heard somebody calling me from the neighbouring house. Tikhomirov and I rushed inside. Bodyagin was standing there trying to bandage himself. He was shaking. His stomach was pierced with holes and blood was running down his neck from a wound in the cheek. I grabbed the bandage and tried to help. We put Bodyagin down on a coat in a corner.

What should we do? I rushed to the tank, but I wasn't sure what I could do without a loader. Meanwhile the commander of the sub-machine gun unit and his adjutant Petr ran up to me: 'Your company commander has left the village and ordered you to follow him. We're retreating.' We got inside the tank. Petr asked about Bodyagin. They'd been friends since the fight for Pyatihatki. I didn't say anything about Bodyagin. I just told him to get in and take the loader's position, and we drove out of the village to catch up with the company commander. There was a belt of forest to my right, and empty fields to my left. About 800 metres behind the forest there was a row of hills, where I could make out the commander's tank and two other tanks close to it. Ermishin was driving to the right of them, parallel to the forest. I told Kryukov to speed up. It seemed to us that we saw flashes in the hills, but at the same moment I heard the voice of the sub-machine gunners' commander: 'Lieutenant, there's a Tiger to the left of us!' He was right – I could see the turret moving in the hollow to our left. I began to turn the turret, ordering Petr to load an armour-piercing shell. But the Tiger disappeared in the hollow behind a tree. I fired a couple of times in its direction. Kryukov cried out to me that Ermishin's tank was burning. I saw two people jump out, and another one, but there was no fourth. In a few seconds the two tanks ahead of Ermishin's also caught fire. Several men jumped out of them and ran into the field. I knew it was the Tiger somewhere nearby who'd probably hit them. I cried to Kryukov: 'Grisha, turn right, behind the forest belt, it'll cover us!' He turned quickly, but within twenty metres we were hit. The Germans were shooting from the hills.

The tank braked sharply and I hit the gun with my face. Blood gushed from my nose. I shouted to Kryukov to start the engine, but he couldn't. We were hit! He turned round and cried something, pointing behind me. I couldn't make out the words, but I turned round and saw tongues of flame in the engine compartment. In an instant I felt the heat and smelt the burning oil. 'Bail out!' I opened the hatch and immediately heard the roar of an engine. Could it be our tank? But the ensuing burst of machine-gun fire explained everything: there was a plane diving at us! I rushed under the tank. Out of the corner of my eye I noticed Tikhomirov's body hanging out from the driver's hatch.

I couldn't stay under the tank, because it could explode any second. Bullets were hitting the armoured body. Kryukov shouted at me: 'Lieutenant, the Germans!' We got out from under the tank and dashed to the field. The shooting increased. Whizzing bullets made me bend down. I was praying that they didn't hit me in the legs – I didn't want to be taken prisoner. Then I realised I could fall down as if I was hit, and I did. I was breathing like an exhausted dog, but the shooting stopped. They believed I was dead. Kryukov toppled over just like me. Thank God, he was alive. We took a few breaths, jumped up simultaneously without any signal and dashed further. The shooting started up again, but soon I noticed that the bullets were racing overhead. Now we were being persecuted by the plane! I fell on the ground face up, so that I could see my death. The plane raced over us, almost hitting the ground with its wheels. I stretched along a plough furrow and started to dig myself into the ground. The plane dived once more, but it couldn't see us so it didn't shoot.

When everything went quiet we stood up and went on. Kryukov was carrying a sub-machine gun that he'd picked up near the tank.

We took turns carrying it, because it seemed very heavy. Suddenly we heard a deafening blow behind us. We turned round and sighed with relief: it was our tank turning into a shapeless mass. We went down to the hollow and found a spring. We washed and had some rest. Then we moved on and soon found the guys from the sub-machine gun unit. There were just three of them, including Petr! One of them had a splinter in his shoulder, so we took him to the spring and bandaged the wound before moving on further. In another depression we found several other men, including Ermishin's radio operator. He knew nothing about the rest of the crew. It seemed to him that Ermishin had escaped from the tank, but then he lost him.

Thus we gathered together thirteen men, including the commander of the sub-machine gun unit. He had no boots on, but what really surprised me was that his rank straps were also gone. Still, he began to give orders immediately, though his rank could no longer be seen. Kryukov and I decided not to pay attention to his orders and tried to keep out of his way. Petr also joined our 'group'. Several of the sub-machine gunners went off in the direction of Nedayvody, but found a large open space in front of them, and returned. We dozed till nightfall, and then moved on to catch up with the rest of the battalion. We reached the village in the early morning, and fell asleep in the very first house we found. The house was already packed with soldiers.

In the evening we all gathered in one of the staff houses of corps commander Kirichenko. They analysed the tragedy and we learned that the person to blame was a communications officer. He'd left the radio transmitter to a sergeant and gone to his date in the neighbouring village. He was killed in the bombardment, and Kirichenko called him a traitor and regretted that we didn't have the chance to execute him publicly. I was surprised that no condemnation was expressed towards Golovyashkin. It looked like the communications officer was the only person to blame. At the end of our meeting the General promised that everybody would be given a decoration. However, I never got that award. Only at the end of the war did I get the Order of the Patriotic War and the Order of the Red Star for the fights for Kenigsberg and the Zemlanski peninsula.

After those fights I was put in the reserve of the 5th Guards Tank Army, and later I was sent home to garner the crops. We lived in a village in the Sarychansk region of the Dnepropetrovsk district. The village abounded in young girls, and most of our guys found temporary wives there. The crops were forgotten. Then we got the order to gather the crops for our army. I was appointed the chief of the mill, so I was giving out the orders wearing my tank helmet! We were supposed to work day and night, but in the evening the mill used to 'break down' and in the morning we used to start the 'repairing'. Thus the year of 1944 passed very smoothly for me. Perhaps it saved my life.

At the end of 1944 I was sent to the front reserve, and at the beginning of 1945 I was posted to the 159th Tank Brigade of the 1st Tank Corps. This corps had undergone many fights, and we had no tanks in our brigade. After a month and a half we got a column of tanks that were presumably assembled from the Estonian people's money. This was the famous 'Lembitu' column.

We didn't take much part in the Kenigsberg assault. The infantry, artillery, and air force did the job all right. Later we were transferred to the Zemlanski peninsula. The tanks of other brigades broke the German defence line, and our brigade was sent through the gap. We found the Germans at night near a place called Germau. Three tanks drove forward as scouts and were lost, and in the morning of 16 April we started the offensive.

Germau lay in a bit of a hollow, and the Germans entrenched on rising ground behind it. By that time only the company commanders' tanks were left of our battalion. I was in charge of one of them, because my company commander had been injured. Two other commanders, Levitski and Shutov, were allowed not to participate in the attack: everybody realised that the end of the war was coming, and nobody wished to be killed in the last few fights.

We drove towards the rising ground. My driver didn't take the tank along the road, but turned to the right. Perhaps he was avoiding some obstacle, or maybe he did it on purpose. Anyway, at that moment we were hit in the left side. I tried to get out, but the hatch wouldn't open, so I jumped out from the loader's hatch. There was a huge shell-hole in the ground just near the right caterpillar. I had no time to think, so I jumped down this hole. It was no less than five metres deep. And I didn't break anything! My driver was already at the bottom. He said he was injured: a splinter had gone into his heel. We bandaged the wound and crawled to the village, where I left my loader to accompany the tank driver while I crawled forward to a trench. When I got there I found my pistol was clogged with soil and unusable, so I had to discard it. I went back to the crew and somehow we crawled to the houses. I found a fur coat in the basement of one of them, laid down on it, and fell asleep.

I woke up in the morning and heard noises outside. I went out, and saw a line of German captives. It appeared that the German defences had been broken when I was sleeping. Then I went to my tank. There were thirty-seven holes in it! The trunks containing my loot were blown to pieces – nothing was left except my photos and some clothes. Well, to hell with the loot! Unfortunately many people were also lost, even some men from the reserve. I remember a young boy who showed us a photo of his girlfriend. He was sent into battle instead of an injured commander, and burned near Pilau. I didn't take part in any more fights, because there were no tanks left. I was placed in the reserve.

How did we treat the German civilians? I'm not an angry man. I remember I asked a German for a light. He gave me a box of matches, I lit a cigarette, and gave the box back to him. Our guys laughed at me, because they thought it strange. As for the others ... there were some incidents. The guys who'd lost their relatives during the German occupation were merciless. Once a boy whose family were killed by the Germans got drunk, took a sub-machine gun, and fired a burst at a column of prisoners. Of course he was punished, but he'd already killed several people. I also saw a dead girl with a torn skirt lying under a broken cart. There were guys who looked for German girls. I only felt disgust. But all sorts of things happened. People are different, and they have different issues. Perhaps if my family had been killed I'd have sought revenge for them.

In May our corps was getting ready to join the war against Japan. The weather was awful. We were sitting at a railway station recalling the few last fights. We talked about an incident when a tank hit a landmine and exploded. The loader was thrown in the air together with the turret. They flew for about twenty metres. All the crew members inside the tank were killed, but the loader survived. After three days he returned from a field hospital with nothing worse than a stutter. Now everybody laughed. Suddenly we heard a gun firing outside. We went quiet in alarm. Was it the Germans? Then somebody said: 'No! The war is over!' We rushed outside. Bullets were racing all over the sky. The war was over! I grabbed somebody's rifle and began to shoot. I can't describe the happiness that I felt. Nobody slept that night.

Glossary

AA	Anti-aircraft artillery.
AT	Anti-tank artillery.
'Bed mesh'	Sprung steel German bed frames taken for use as additional tank protection.
CP	Command post.
DT	*Diagterev tankovyi*, Diagterev light machine-gun adapted for installation in tanks.
'Faustpatron'	Russian nickname for German Panzerfaust and Panzerschreck anti-tank weapons.
Frontovik	Someone who'd served in the frontline.
HE	High explosive.
Istrebitelniy battalion	Literally an extermination battalion, a type of local paramilitary unit formed in the early stages of the war to keep order in rear areas.
JS-2	'Josef Stalin 2' heavy tank.
Katyusha	Russian BM-13 multiple rocket launcher.
Kolkhoz	Collective farm.
Kombat	Battalion commander.
Komsomol	VLKSM, the All-Union Lenin's Communist Union of Youth.
Komsorg	Leader of a unit's *Komsomol* members.
Kubanka	Cossack fur hat.
KV	'Kliment Voroshilov' heavy tank.
MG	Machine-gun.
NKVD	'People's Commissariat of Internal Affairs', secret police predecessor of the KGB.
Osobist	NKVD officer.
Panzerfaust	German self-propelled anti-tank grenade launcher.
Politruk	Political officer. Each commander of a unit from company upwards had a deputy responsible for political work.
PPSh	'Shpagin' sub-machine gun.
PPZh	*Pokhodno polevaia zhena*, 'frontline wife', term used to describe a girl who lived with an officer at the battlefront.
Shtrafnik	Soldier sentenced to serve in a penal company (privates) or battalion (officers).
Smersh	*Smert shpionam*, 'Death to spies', military branch of the NKVD.
SMG	Sub-machine gun.
Sovinformbyuro	Central office responsible for news coverage of the war.
SP or SPG	Self-propelled gun.
Tankoshlem	Hat worn by tankmen.
Tridtsatchetverka	Russian name for the T-34 tank.
TPU	*Tankovoe peregovornoe ustroistvo*, tank intercom unit.
Valenki	Felt boots.
Vanyusha	Russian nickname for German Nebelwerfer six-barrelled rocket mortar.

Index

71-TK-3 39, 40

Abashin, V. 82, 84, 85, 88, 90
Akulshin 134
Aria, S.L. 7, 11, 16, 18, 26, 36, 38, 41
Armies Russian:
  3rd Guards Tank 15
  5th Guards Tank 66, 171, 179
  5th Guards 71
  4th Tank 13, 158, 166
  Armour Academies:
  2nd Gorki Automobile and Motorcycle 75, 76, 77
  1st Kharkov 7, 170
  Stalingrad 7, 128
  1st Saratov 119, 156
  Ulyanovsk 45
Avetisyan 81
Arzamas 75

Balaton Lake 123
Battonya 142
Beredin, A. 67
Berezanka 92
Berlin 21, 44, 169
Bessonov, E.I. 11
Bichke 143
Blinov, N. 141
Bobylskaia 56
Bodnar, A.V. 5, 12, 16, 20, 22, 26, 29, 30, 31, 37, 40–43, 48, 52, 56
Bodyagin 171, 177
Brigades Russian:
  20th Guards Tank 96, 108
  21st Guards Tank 90
  22nd Guards Tank 78, 97
  3rd Mechanised 69
  30th Mechanised 158
  49th Mechanised 35
  3rd Tank 69
  2nd Tank 57
  9th Tank 69
  17th Tank 152
  24th Tank 29
  25th Tank 171
  29th Tank 67

35th Light Tank 45
61st Tank 162
62nd Tank 158
63rd Tank 158, 162
116th Tank 112
159th Tank 114, 133, 180
170th Tank 121, 139
197th Tank 159
Bryansk 135
Bryukhov, V.P. 5, 7–13, 15–17, 19–21, 23, 25, 26, 29, 34, 36–38, 121, 140, 142, 147
Burtsev, A.S. 2, 5, 7, 9, 10, 12, 16, 17, 20, 23, 29, 41
BT-5 128, 129
BT-7 28, 120, 128, 151
Budapest 143

Cheliabinsk 66, 129
ChTZ 28
Chumachenko, D.A. 81, 83, 85, 91, 96
Chunikhin, N.P. 139
Corps Russian:
  1st Guards Mechanised 69, 72
  5th Guards Tank 78
  6th Guards Tank 13
  12th Guards Tank 11, 24
  5th Mechanised 21, 97
  6th Mechanised 165
  8th Mechanised 43
  16th Mechanised 4
  1st Tank 114, 133, 180
  2nd Tank 129
  29th Tank 171
Cyclone 42

Dashukovka 98, 99
Dedov 72
Defence Fund 21
Division 88th Infantry 92
Divisions Russian:
  322nd 150
  1st Guards 66
  15th Tank 3
  32nd Tank 4
Dolgushin 51
Dolzhok 161

Donbass 68
Doroshenko, P. 96, 97, 99, 101, 102, 104–106
DT 7, 35, 40, 73, 103, 110
Dubovitsky, V. 78

Elsukov 97
Esterhom 122
Erenburg Ilya 18

Fadin, A. 5, 8, 9, 10, 12, 13, 15, 17, 18, 20, 78, 90, 108
Fetisov 96, 106
Fronts:
  Kalinin 49
  Volkhov 65
  3rd Ukranian 119, 141
  2nd Baltic 137
FW-189 71

Gavrilko 111
Glukhov, N.E. 11, 26, 29
Golubenko 78, 80, 81, 82

Ivanov 145
IZh-9 76

JS-2 108
JSU-152 17, 84
Ju-87 71

Kamenny Brod 86, 89
Kamenets-Podolsk 15, 159–161
Karabuta, V. 91, 93
Kastornaia 112, 113
Katukov, M.E. 3
Katyusha 52, 54, 63
Keletz Lake 123
Kenigsberg 115, 179, 180
Khalkhin-Gol 5
Kharkov 4, 28, 66, 73
Kiev 79, 86, 99
Kirichenko, P.I. 7, 9, 10, 11, 13, 17, 19, 24–26, 31, 35, 40
Klivcy 50–52
Kleshevoi 92
Komsomol 53, 118
Komsomolskaya Pravda 53, 56

Konstantinov 55
Korotych 66
Korsun-Shevchenko 98, 139
Koshuba, V.N. 45
Krajovo 145
Krapivin 58
Krasnoe Sormovo 28, 32, 157
Krasnovodsk 58
Krivov, G.N. 7, 8, 10, 13, 16, 18, 19, 29, 33, 34
Kivoy Rog 174
Kryuchkov, N. 2
Kryukov, G.I. 29, 171, 176, 178
Kubinka 25, 30
Kuma River 59
Kursk 129
Kushi 141
Kuts 60, 62
Kuzmichev, Nikolai N. 21
KV 30, 45, 47, 48, 49, 114

Leliushenko 166
Leningrad 4, 29
Leonenko 134
Linz 74
Lodz 21
Lvov 4, 163
Lysaya Gora 95

M4A2 Sherman 16, 120
M-17 46
Maryevsky, A.V. 9, 11, 13, 16, 18, 19, 21, 26, 29, 36, 42
Matilda 24, 30, 119, 120, 156
Matveev, S.V. 3
Medvedev 49
Mineralnye Vody 58
Miroshnikov 48, 49
Molotov cocktails 34
Morozov, A.A. 28
Moscow 23, 25, 44, 45, 48, 56, 73, 76, 77, 112, 113, 121, 154, 170
Mozdok 59
Murashko 69, 71

Nevel 137
NII-48 23, 26, 36
NIIBT 25, 30, 31
NKVD 137, 150
Novaia Praga 72
Novomoskovsk 69, 70

Orel 133

Pakhomov, I. 70
PAK-38 23
PAK-43 43
Panzer II 40, 50
Panzer III 22, 23, 30, 40, 50, 95, 131, 158
Panzer IV 22, 30, 32, 40, 79, 87, 95, 103, 166
Panzer V Panther 23, 32, 39, 44, 140, 141
Panzer VI Tiger 23, 32, 38, 44, 67, 88, 89, 104, 105, 108, 122, 123, 156, 159, 160, 168, 177
Panzerfaust 24, 35
Pechersky, I. 21, 152
Peshkhnitsa 167
Peshkova, N. 15
Petrov, N. 152, 153
Petukhov 163
Pogoreloe Gorodische 49, 55
Polotsk 11
Polianovsky, Yu.M. 5, 8, 13, 18, 21
Polianski, N.A. 80
Poltava 66, 72
PPZh 19
PPSh 19, 35, 144
Prokhorovka 130, 131, 133
Pyatihatka 173

Radzechow 3
Regiments Russian:
  19th Training Tank 57
  3rd Reserve Tank 78, 157
  6th Reserve Tank 129
  225th Tank 57
  20th Tank 71
  242nd Rifle 98, 99
  382nd Guards SPA 74
Rodkin, A.K. 9, 20, 26, 32, 33, 35, 42, 43
Rokossovsky 153
RSI-4 40
Russiianov 72
Ruza 47, 48
Ryabyshev, D.I. 43
Rylin, N. 60, 61, 62
Rzhev 49

Skvira 91
S-35 39
Savkin, M.F. 3
Semiletov, V. 80, 82, 84

Shakhovskaia 49, 55
Shishkin, N.K. 17
Shulgin 11
Shvebig, A.P. 11, 24
Simonov, N. 3
Slepov 53, 54
Smersh 11
SPAM 20
Stalin, J.V. 4, 5, 76
Stalingrad 65, 118
STZ 42, 49
SU-76 25
SU-85 90
SU-100 74, 123
Svechin 22
Szekesfehervar 122

T-26 45, 47, 120, 128
T-28 37, 128
T-60 47, 49, 50, 51, 52, 151
T-70 25, 151
Taganrog 62
Tarasov 52
Tarascha 93, 95, 96, 99
Tikhomirov, N.N. 171, 178
Timoshenko, S.K. 30, 35
TPU-3bis 41
TT 35, 165
Tyurin, P. 86, 88, 89, 90, 92, 93, 95, 106
Tyutryumov, A.F. 111

Upper Ufalei 56
UVZ 28, 33, 66
UZTM 28

Valentine 16, 24, 119, 120, 156, 160
Vereschagin 60, 62
Vinogradar 84
Vitebsk 11
Volga 46
Voronezh 65, 112, 113
Voshinski, M.P. 80
Voznyuk 78, 83

Willys jeep 59, 174

Yaroshevski, V.I. 21

Zheleznov, N.I. vii, 2, 10, 13, 14, 16, 18, 21, 32, 37, 41, 162
Zhilin 98, 106, 107
ZIS-3 162
Zolochev 162

Stackpole Military History Series

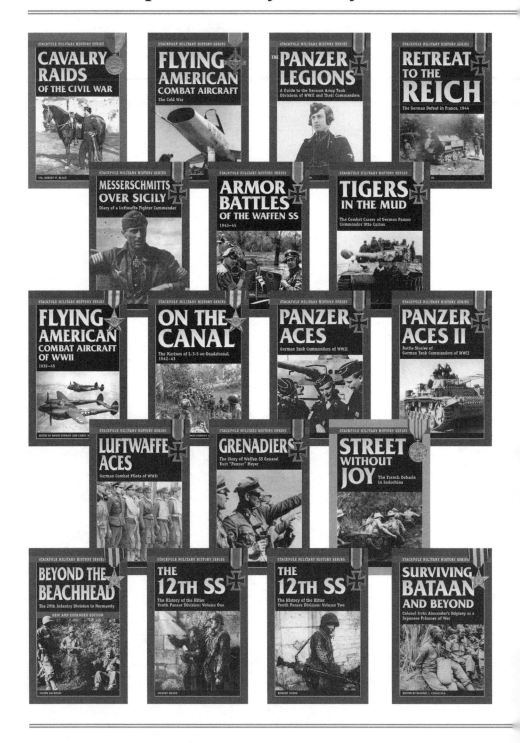

Real battles. Real soldiers. Real stories.

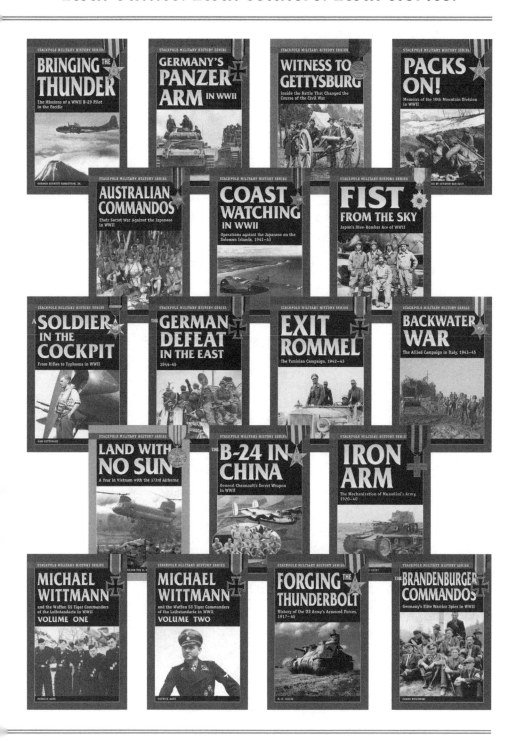

Stackpole Military History Series

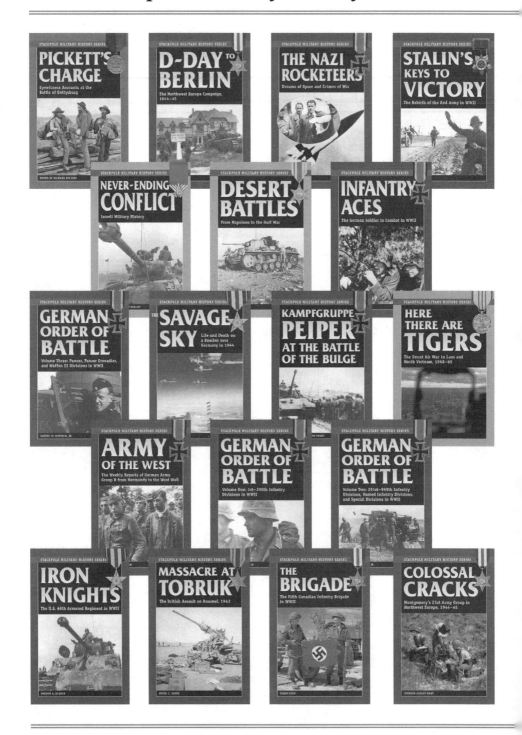

Real battles. Real soldiers. Real stories.

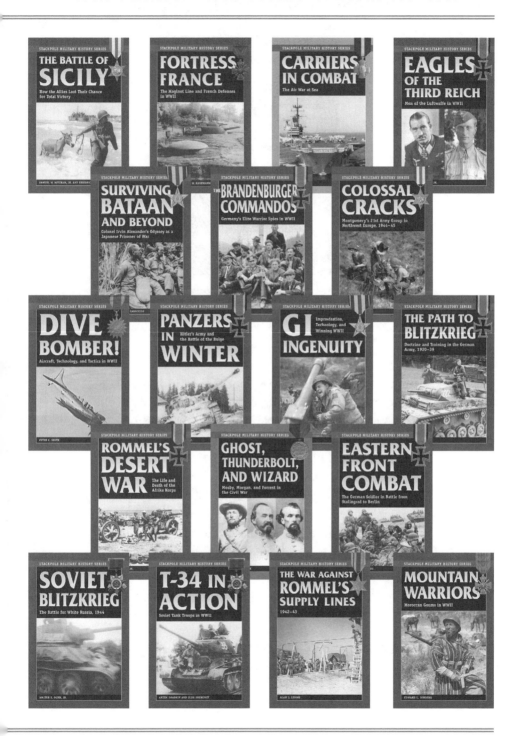

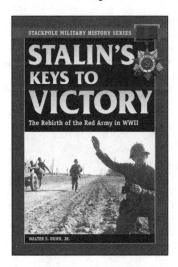

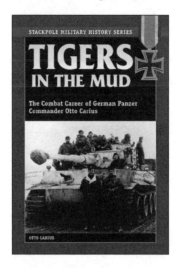

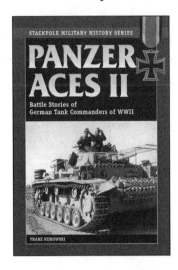

Stackpole Military History Series

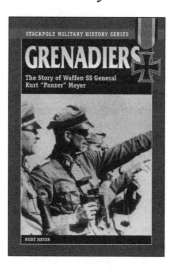

GRENADIERS

THE STORY OF WAFFEN SS GENERAL
KURT "PANZER" MEYER

Kurt Meyer

Known for his bold and aggressive leadership, Kurt
Meyer was one of the most highly decorated German
soldiers of World War II. As commander of various
units, from a motorcycle company to the Hitler Youth
Panzer Division, he saw intense combat across Europe,
from the invasion of Poland in 1939 to the 1944
campaign for Normandy, where he fell into Allied
hands and was charged with war crimes.

$19.95 • Paperback • 6 x 9 • 448 pages • 93 b/w photos

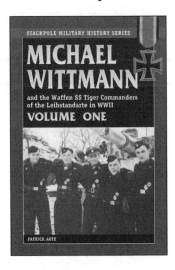

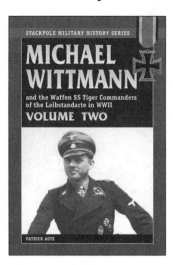

Stackpole Military History Series

ARMOR BATTLES
OF THE WAFFEN-SS
1943–45
Will Fey, translated by Henri Henschler

The Waffen-SS were considered the elite of the
German armed forces in the Second World War and
were involved in almost continuous combat. From
the sweeping tank battle of Kursk on the Russian
front to the bitter fighting among the hedgerows
of Normandy and the offensive in the Ardennes,
these men and their tanks made history.

$19.95 • Paperback • 6 x 9 • 384 pages
32 photos • 15 drawings • 4 maps

Stackpole Military History Series

GERMANY'S PANZER ARM IN WWII
R. L. DiNardo

No twentieth-century military organization has been
as widely studied as the German war machine in
World War II, and few of its components were as
important, influential, or revolutionary as its armored
force. Nevertheless, there are almost no truly
integrated studies of the organizational, economic,
personnel, doctrinal, and tactical factors that affected
the panzer arm's performance. Drawing on military
documents, memoirs, battle reports, and other
original sources, DiNardo fills that gap with this
detailed look at the rise and fall of German armor.

$16.95 • Paperback • 6 x 9 • 224 pages • 27 photos • 17 diagrams

WWW.STACKPOLEBOOKS.COM
1-800-732-3669

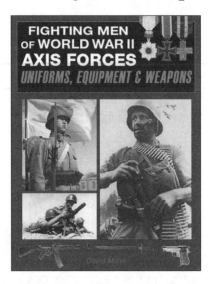